PRAISE FOR SPLIT...

I hope you will find that the book you are about to read engages you and fills you with fascination in equal parts, as it did me. It is also at times, a harrowing read, but then if it was not there would be no inspiration, no 'rising above' – the valuable gift that real-life accounts such as this have to offer us. This is Maggie's story.
Dr. George Blair-West, Psychiatrist,
author *The Girl In the Green Dress*

In her work, Maggie consistently engages with tough, complex themes – childhood abuse, mental illness, adoption, migration – and she does so bravely, unflinchingly, with a deep commitment to making art out of the difficulties she's lived through. I have no doubt readers will benefit from her insight into issues that many people have struggled with but remained silent about. Her writing can do much good in the world.
Lee Kofman, *The Writer Laid Bare*

A rare and fascinating journey into the origin and turmoil of living with Multiple Personality Disorder - a candid, often harrowing account of the enduring power of the human spirit. Sometimes shocking, often enlightening, always compelling.
Michelle Tom, *Ten Thousand Aftershocks*

Illuminating, absorbing, harrowing and hopeful, this beautifully written memoir will keep you reading, feeling, and thinking to the very last page. An exquisitely written memoir of an extraordinary life.
Anna Featherstone, Founder Bold Authors

SPLIT is a book to inspire and inform every trauma survivor who doubted they had a future, every family member or supporter who wondered what they could do to help, and for anyone wanting to understand and reduce the stigma around mental health struggles.
Alan Close, *Before You Met Me*

The voices of Maggie, Annie, and her tribe of girls echo throughout this memoir. SPLIT is confronting, if we close our eyes and block our ears, we learn nothing. If you feel anger, sadness, confusion, and ultimately courage and strength,
then SPLIT has done its job to break the silence.
Sarah Martin, *Dear Psychosis*

SPLIT

A LIFE SHARED: LIVING WITH MULTIPLE PERSONALITY DISORDER

MAGGIE WALTERS

Blue Gum Publishing

First published in Australia in 2024 by Blue Gum Publishing

Blue Gum Publishing acknowledges the Traditional Owners and their custodianship of the lands on which this book was written, the Widjabul Wia-bal people of the Bundjalung Nation, who are the original storytellers of this region. We pay our respects to their Ancestors and their descendants, who continue cultural and spiritual connections to Country.

Copyright © 2024 Margaret Walters

SPLIT A life shared: living with Multiple Personality Disorder
ISBN: 978-0-6486038-0-1

The moral right of Margaret Walters to be identified as the author of his work has been asserted.

This work is copyright. Apart from any use permitted under the *Copyright Act 1968*, no part of this book may be reproduced or transmitted in any form or by any means, electronic or mechanical, including photocopying, recording or by any other information storage or retrieval system, without prior permission in writing from the publisher.

Cover design: Hazel Lam
Cover Image: Stocksy

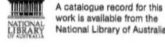
A catalogue record for this work is available from the National Library of Australia

*This book is dedicated to every person struggling
through their own intimate web
of trauma recovery.
Breathe.
One day at a time.
You've got this.*

WARNING:

Readers should be aware that sections of this book describe episodes of explicit sexual violence and trauma. Warnings have been placed at the start of these chapters. Ensure your own emotional safety and have a support network in place before reading.

There is a list of resources available at the end of the book.

CONTENTS

Foreword	XI
Introduction	1
Part One: Annie's Story	7
Part Two: Maggie's Story	149
Part Three: Co-Existence	247
Epilogue	349

FOREWORD

by Dr George Blair-West

[The following is an extract. The full original document can be found at www.maggie-walters.com.]

I hope you will find that the book you are about to read engages you and fills you with fascination in equal parts, as it did me. It is also at times, a harrowing read, but then if it was not there would be no inspiration, no 'rising above' – the valuable gift that real life accounts such as this have to offer us.

Allow me to put Maggie's experiences into some degree of human and medical context. This requires a crash course in the condition of Dissociative Identity Disorder (DID) and its contextual history.

If I was asked to capture DID in one sentence, I would say: it's a testimony to how the human mind really can develop superpowers … and fly away. This is the most important thing to understand about this condition, previously called Multiple Personality Disorder (MPD). It is not a mental illness. This is worth repeating as not only is it not intrinsically a mental illness, it is, perhaps, the most powerful adaptive response that the human mind is capable of when it is faced with the most destructive trauma that humans are capable of.

The capacity to mentally dissociate and create another part, or personality in a child who is being abused serves two key purposes. First, it allows the child to hand off to this newly created part all the horribleness of the rape experiences – becoming, what we call, an exiled part. The exile can then be banished from day-to-day awareness. This allows another, 'executive' part, to present a 'normal' face to the outside world without being overly troubled by the horror of what's happening at home. Then rinse and repeat, creating part after part after part.

The high-level dissociation required to create DID relies on two preconditions.

Firstly, a plasticity of the mind that is typically only found under the age of eight, or thereabouts. As our brains mature past early childhood, we cannot dissociate so pervasively as to create separate personalities.

Secondly, it requires 'betrayal trauma'. This is where the peak perpetrator is a primary caregiver. Typically, this is a parent. Betrayal trauma means the child must do something that literally tears them apart, they need to create a personality that will behave positively towards the abuser. Try to imagine the mental gymnastics involved as a seven-year-old girl, minutes after a violent rape, has to respond warmly to her father to ensure that she continues to be fed, kept warm and housed.

When I started my psychiatry training 40 years ago, MPD, as it was then known, was not even vaguely understood. It was a weird footnote at the very extreme end of 'crazy' in psychiatry. It is only relatively recently, over the last twenty years or less, with the interest in trauma therapy that DID came to be understood as being the result of 'early complex developmental trauma.' Indeed, DID, now rightfully, is finally recognised, at least by those of us who specialise in trauma, as the ultimate form of a post-trauma syndrome.

How common is it? Sadly, much more common than was thought – just over one percent of the population here in the West – giving us at least 250,000 cases in Australia. It's prevalence, predictably tracks extant child abuse. For this reason, the limited data suggests it is most common in less developed countries where children's rights, and the protection of these rights, are not upheld. More concerningly, these survivors are typically diagnosed as 'possessed' and treated with exorcism. There is no worse example of 'blaming the victim'. This 'treatment' also neatly 'solves' the other problem, that for every person with DID there is by definition at least one person who should be in jail for a very long time.

In *'The Girl in The Green Dress'* co-authored with my patient Jeni Haynes, who also has DID, we recount, that for the first time in Australia, and apparently, the world, Jeni and her different personalities were allowed to give testimony on the basis that her condition was evidence in itself that serious crimes had been committed. Her diagnosis was the very basis for the prosecution. In all previous cases, DID was used as a defence, typically against homicide charges.

Tasked as the expert witness to explain DID to the court, I was impressed at how readily the judge recognised that Jeni's condition, in and of itself, was both necessary and sufficient to bring the case. In the end, Jeni's father was jailed for forty-five years, which would well exceed his natural life.

Finally, the world is changing and DID is coming of age both in medical and legal realms.

The reluctance of my colleagues to diagnose this condition is very simple. It's the same reason that has allowed this condition, which has a similar prevalence and disability as schizophrenia, to be overlooked and underfunded for so long. None of us, doctors and the general public equally, want to acknowledge that horrible sexual abuse of the worst kind is being perpetrated on young children. We just don't want to think so little of human beings. It's perfectly understandable – until someone with DID sits down in front of you and *decides* to let you in to the reality of their life.

Indeed, DID is the only psychiatric condition in which, if the patient does not want you to make the correct diagnosis, you can't. They have to let you in to glimpse their system of management. Even then, therapists with their own high expectations of the human race, and with almost no routine formal training, will struggle to make the diagnosis. The clarity of abuse recall, decades later, can also be hard to believe. It makes sense, however, for a therapist who understands dissociation, that a part of a person banished in exile for thirty years, can exist with no intervening memories. They can recall the last thing that happened to them like you and I can recall what we had for breakfast.

Most of what I have learnt in treating trauma and dissociative disorders has been taught to me by my patients. Routine training of young doctors wanting to specialise in psychiatry still largely ignores training in diagnosing and treating DID. I would like to finish with sharing a lesson Jeni taught me as we worked together. I was describing to her the two purposes of creating alternate personalities – exiling the destabilising trauma almost completely from awareness, and being able to appear 'normal' to the world – when Jeni added a third. This was the most important, and to me the most inspiring benefit.

The perpetrator takes pride in dismantling the child, literally breaking the self, so as to have a totally compliant victim, in every sense of this word. DID allows the true, innocent essence of the child to hide, safe from the unknowing abuser. It is a truly glorious 'fuck you' to the abuser who has no idea of the light, self-love and strength that is protected and quietly waiting ...

This essence knows the truth. It knows that this abuse was neither deserved nor just at any level. It waits, with great patience, knowing this truth, until one day the war is over and the quest for healing can begin. From the healing, the 'rising above' happens in which that innocent child finally gets to flourish into the life that it incarnated to fulfil. And in rising above, it carries with it a strength and a resilience that those of us who have had 'normal' lives cannot imagine. This is Maggie's story.

In closing I would like to say: Maggie I am humbled before the courage and vulnerability it took to write this book. Fronting up to your pain and doing the therapy work is equally awe-inspiring. Yet again I find myself asking myself, with some self-doubt, if I had had your experiences, would I be up for these challenges? You have my deepest respect and I'm sure the gratitude of those many others who have had similar but different versions of this powerful narrative you're about to share.

With much admiration,
Dr George Blair-West, Psychiatrist

SPLIT

INTRODUCTION

First Things First

I exist in an unsettled life. Thirty years ago I was diagnosed with Multiple Personality Disorder (MPD). This means I have distinct and different personalities which, depending on the situation, can take over my mind and body, often triggered by situations out of my control. MPD is now called DID or Dissociative Identity Disorder. When I was diagnosed, it was still called MPD, and because this is the term I have always used, I will continue to call it MPD throughout this book.

Externally, I deal daily with ordinary routines. I take kids to soccer, have coffee with friends, iron clothes and cook for my family. All things done deliberately and methodically, to remind me of the normal life I strive for. Internally, I have a tribe, *The Girls*, who talk to me, share their perspectives and pain. They are my personal reminder of the years I survived. These *Girls* are called *alters*, specific individual personalities who lived my childhood and protected me from the abuse in my home. Today, their existence is mostly internal, with subtle influences on my daily routine, arising from triggers and images of my childhood. As a result, my life is often unpredictable and chaotic.

This book is my story of living with MPD. But how do I share that? How do I explain to someone who is neurotypical how my multiple brain works? I have one body but numerous minds, each with their own identity and existence. And yet, they are all still me – we are all parts of a whole.

Imagine you are at an exhibition, standing across the room from a large tapestry. From a distance you appreciate its totality. On closer inspection, you can see how the individual threads have been intricately woven together, their colour and purpose are unique. Pull out any of those threads and the tapestry is incomplete, it would no longer convey the image the weaver intended. This is probably the simplest way I can describe what it's like to be multiple. When you step back and look, you see me. But if you take the time to get to know me, you will begin to see my alters and the way they have each influenced my life.

SPLIT is the story of how we – *The Girls* and I – have survived our life. It is the journey from a childhood of abuse and trauma to my acceptance of this history and its ramifications for me as an adult. For me, this healing has been an exploration into *truth*. I invite you to take this journey with me, into the truth of my past, of who I am now and the nature of MPD as I live it.

But the challenge remains – how can I help you make sense of this kaleidoscope that is me?

Here is a little map, a few guideposts, if you like, to help you find your way through the story you are about to read.

For a start, how and when did I become MPD? When the abuse began, I (Maggie) went away to the deepest darkest part of my mind to protect myself. For the duration of my childhood and young adult life, I (Maggie) did not exist. Instead my mind created *Annie*, my primary alter, to take over the functioning of the mind and body which had been Maggie's. In time, when needed, more alters *became* to live with each variation of new abuse Annie's body was subjected to. Annie, if you like, became the system administrator. As a group, these alters are known to me as *The Girls*.

Our story is written from different points of view. *Annie's Story* is written by Annie, *Maggie's Story*, by Maggie. Same body, different identity, different time. Maggie returned at a point when Annie could no longer cope with the ramifications of decisions she had made. Faced with Annie's need to escape, Maggie *re-emerged* to take control once more of their shared body. *Annie's Story* is told with her permission with me (Maggie) in charge of the keyboard.

The section titled *Co-existence*, told primarily by me (Maggie), is the story of Annie and Maggie learning to live together, but with Maggie in charge of their body. Annie interjects on a few (clearly identified) occasions. At times in *Annie's Story*, in the section called *Family Affair*, Annie allows several of *The Girls* to write their own story. Those voices are clearly identified at the start of those chapters. And when I say they wrote it, I mean just that – it's their story, in their words. Mine may have been the fingers on the keyboard, but mentally I stepped aside and let them write their truth.

I have used pseudonyms throughout the book to protect the privacy of those individuals concerned. For the alters, I have chosen names which I feel reflect their role and place in our system. The only exception to this is me, writing as Maggie, and an alter named *Writer* who specifically requested to keep their identity in this story. If any of this sounds weird, you ought to try living this way!

In the course of my life I developed relationships with a few therapists. I have chosen to identify them by numbers, rather than pseudonyms. This is done firstly to show the linear relationship I had with each of them, and secondly to reinforce their role in my life – to provide me with a safe and secure space to process – a place that was somewhat removed from the reality of my daily struggles.

Memory is elastic, I understand this. It is fluid, it changes, it shape-shifts. I continue to have what I call 'postcard memories' which haunt me, creating triggers for coping mechanisms such as anxiety, hypervigilance and lack of trust (to name a few) which I am constantly learning to manage. These trigger memories are so strong I have almost complete certainty that they are accurate recollections of the life this body has lived, albeit from the perspective of the alter who experienced it. Put simply, this is how living with MPD is for me.

Every person who is *multiple* has a point, a moment when, in order to protect themselves, they split. I suspect it is never a conscious choice, instead it is instinctual, driven by the need to survive. Trapped physically in whatever circumstances we have found ourselves, the only way to endure is to emotionally disappear.

I was three when this happened to me. With the prospect of a new job for my father and new opportunities for us, our family was immigrating to the United States from the United Kingdom. We crossed the Atlantic, not on some fancy cruise liner, but a cargo ship with a small number of berths for paying passengers. Our destination was the Port of Houston, Texas.

I was excited! I remember standing at the railing in a blustering storm, relishing the pelting rain and the salt of the seawater on my face. My brothers were nowhere to be found, hiding in their cabins with Father, unable to handle the wild seas. As for me, Mother tied a long scarf around my waist for safety and I held on tightly as I peered between the bars, wave after wave of white foam roaring into the boat. I hung on to the railing, laughing and giggling as the waves buffeted the hull beneath my feet. I felt utterly safe and secure in my mother's care. I knew she would never let me fall into the ocean. And when she tugged me back in the lee of the cabins, I knew she was protecting me from the dark sea and monsters I imagined lurking beneath the waves.

There were only a few passengers, and the captain took great pleasure in entertaining us. We would sit at his table as he regaled us with tales of his exotic journeys. I don't remember any details but can still feel the wonder when I think of our dinners with him.

He invited my older brothers to the wheelhouse, showing them how the ship navigated the vast ocean. I tried to follow, but at the base of the stairs, the captain turned and smiled at me, 'Not for you, dear. I'm sorry, but you are too little and it wouldn't be safe.' He patted me on the head, and I watched, bereft, as the three of them climbed the stairs without me.

I occupied my days wandering with my mother and family around the ship or sitting in the galley playing games as we edged closer to our new life in America. Everything about this trip was an adventure and delighted my heart.

Then there was a night when storms raged and thunder rattled the ship. I should have been tucked away safely in the crib in my parents' berth. But somehow the locks had come off and the crib rocked back and forth as the wild seas pummelled the ship. I was terrified. I stood up, hanging on to the crib railing, crying out for my parents. I heard grumbles and saw Father get out of bed. I reached out instinctively, seeking shelter in his arms. Instead, the back of his hand struck my face with a force that reverberated through my entire body. I lost my balance and sat down, stunned.

Then – nothing.

I was gone.

This was the moment my protective system of alters began its journey to becoming. I was no longer a three-year-old child crossing the Atlantic, but a wisp of memory, forgotten and hidden away.

Maggie was gone and Annie took her place.

PART ONE:
ANNIE'S STORY

WHERE WE BEGAN

When Maggie sat down in her crib on that boat travelling to America, she left and I took her place. My name is Annie. I was three when I *became*, and while Maggie slept, her mind protected, I became the vessel through which this childhood would be lived.

I remember our house, just outside of Austin, Texas, where I grew up. My parents were proud first-time homeowners. A modest middle-income one-level brick house with turquoise and pink wood trim set on an acre surrounded by Central Texas cedar. It seemed grand to my child's perspective. I had my own room, just down the hall from my parents' large master suite. My brothers, seven and ten years older than me, were not so excited about having to share a room, but at least they were at the other end of the house. We had a well-equipped kitchen, dining room and living area. There was a formal entertainment area, closed off to the rest of the house. Mother kept this immaculate. The living room fireplace burned warm in winter and in summer became a perch to sit with friends, warm breezes streaming through the house, providing respite from the hot, humid Texas weather. The verandah overlooked our overgrown and expansive backyard, where secret trails led down steep hills, shortcuts my brothers would use to get to their friends' homes. At the side of our property was a hill where Father taught me to shoot a 22-calibre rifle at the age of eight. I remember being a better shot than my brothers and how it pissed them off.

We arrived in America with an established network of friends. Father secured employment before we left England through a fellow British immigrant, Stanley Peters. They both worked at the University of Texas, in the Nuclear Engineering Department. The Peters lived near us and were central to our social network. This network provided the cover for the dark and violent secret which would become my life.

Mother and Father changed jobs and took on new opportunities over the years. But it was this house, this home, where my siblings and I grew up. It was the centre of my world and would remain so until I left home at the age of eighteen.

These are the facts of how my life as Annie began. But these facts hide the truth. Beneath this veneer of domestic normalcy I was subjected to a childhood of abuse. And while I was an *alter* myself, I also became the organiser of *The Girls,* the system of *alters* who became, and I had to manage.

In truth, those early years were chaos. I was a child with no ability to comprehend what was going on. I simply existed to survive. Internally, my life resembled an unruly mob. With each new episode of abuse which we – *The Girls* – couldn't understand or manage, POW! a new alter was spun off. It wasn't that each new situation created a new *alter* to live it, rather, each of *The Girls* had a specific role required by the circumstances she faced and for each new variation of pain, a new alter *became.* Sometimes, this pain could be anticipated, and an existing alter was prepared, or expected to take over because that was her role. Other times, it was not so clear, and if an alter did not exist to fit the age and circumstances required, a new *girl* simply came to be. This was how I lived my childhood.

I do wonder how, as a small child, I *did* this. I don't know if there's a clear answer. It seems I had an innate ability to sense new danger, and instinctively adapt to those circumstances, to stay one step ahead of it. I knew fear when Father took me down the hallway to his bedroom, or when his friends would walk through the front door. I knew something was coming. But I never remembered the detail of each event. Instead, I would find myself back in my bed, curled up and sleepy, with pain and bruises, the cause of which I could not recollect or explain.

As we got older, I realised my job was not to protect *The Girls* from each event they had to live through, but to equip them to survive. We would come together, drawing strength from each other and our connectedness. It was this strength which made all the difference to our survival.

I heard somewhere that multiplicity is indicative of a creative, adaptable mind. I'm not sure if I agree. But multiplicity served its purpose well and saved this child's mind and body. But it has also left both Maggie and I with huge gaps in our combined memory. These gaps, of course, were lived by alters. Alters who survive still, trapped by memories of abuse in dark corners of our mind.

Little Soldiers

My little army waits, ready for battle,
anticipating deployment.
Soldiers ready to sacrifice themselves for the greater good.
    No choice, no will.
    A job to do.
    Each with a mission and purpose.

They know the battle that lies ahead,
    some more practised at the routine than others,
    each aware of the hell that awaits.
With determined acquiescence,
    their armour goes on
    for a battle they are doomed to lose.

Their job is to distract, take up space.
    They are no fools,
    fear and trepidation rage through their small bodies,
    repeating again
    the horror they know so well.

Still, they remain steadfast.
    They listen for that order,
    for a moment or unspoken signal,
    when the body they protect
    can take no more.

SPLIT

Who will step into the fray?
    Choices are made.
    With a sigh, and resignation,
    the little soldier stands forward,
    moving into the war zone.
    The goal is simple and singular.

Survive.

FAMILY AFFAIR

CHRISTMAS GIFT

Christmas Day was always glorious in our home; presents, decorations and a wonderful Christmas lunch. But it couldn't hold a candle to the extraordinary experience of a Twelfth Night Party, celebrating the epiphany of the Festive Season. For my parents it meant a grand event, inviting people from near and far to join us.

For one brief moment each year, I watched my mother transform into a glimmering holiday angel. As an eight-year-old child I believed it was the charm of the Christmas season. In truth, Mother was so focused on entertaining and preparing for the delights of the holiday, she didn't have time to bother with me. I was grateful for the respite, my child's mind making it something of a magical fairy tale instead.

For weeks before, I could hear Mother humming and working away in the kitchen, fastidiously making her traditional mince pies and sausage rolls, cheese balls, sherry trifles and other delectable concoctions. I would often watch quietly from the kitchen door, or peek over the counter as the miracle of pastry rolled out before my eyes. 'Oh, it's just an excuse to extend the Christmas Season, such a magical time of year,' Mother would say to me, third glass of wine in hand, smiling, apron white with patches of flour as she floated around the kitchen.

Watching Mother get dressed for these occasions was captivating. She transformed from ordinary working mother to Queen of the Realm. I remember sitting on the end of her bed, watching in awe and adoration. Hot rollers in her short hair became a stunning mass of curls around her face. Her make-up, from the simplest eye shadow to velvety lipstick was perfection. But Mother's dress always took my breath away. Each year she would have a new creation made by her favourite dressmaker, soft layers of fabric swishing and shimmering as she mingled with her guests. In those moments, I was certain I had the most beautiful mother in the Universe.

The cornucopia of food laid out was international – from the traditional British fare, which had to include black pudding, sausage rolls and mince meat pies, to Mexican spicy jalapeño cheese balls and Portuguese custard tarts. I would watch in awe as she put out her whisky-laden Christmas pudding, thick custard trickling down the sticky sweet dome, Mother's particularly special British treat.

There was always more than could be eaten. 'Excess is important,' Mother would say as she placed each overflowing platter on the tables. 'It makes people feel comfortable and welcome.' Then with an uncustomary gentle touch on my back, 'Now scoot. None of these treats are for you, you're already too fat.'

Friends and acquaintances came from near and far. The draw for this event was as much the novelty of a European ritual celebrated in Central Texas, as the vast array of food and drink provided. My mother was a goddess, floating amongst her devotees, laughing and engaging with every guest, making sure each one felt like they were the centre of her world.

I was allowed to linger around the edges of these parties, no rules or bedtime, sneaking treats and relishing each illicit morsel. Adults would talk to me, pat me on the head and then ignore me. Sometimes, Father's friends would smile at me, nauseating, threatening. All I could see were images of these men with *The Girls* and I would slink away in fear and shame, seeking the comfort of food while Mother entertained in all her glory.

For those few weeks during the Christmas Season, I pretended that Mother did actually love me.

PORTRAIT OF A PRINCESS

Mother was a gifted artist. She would copy the masters, from Rembrandt to Botticelli and Raphael, especially portraits and landscapes, her finished canvases hanging throughout the house. She had a studio in one corner of the living room where the sweet smell of oil paint always lingered, seeping down the hallway and into other rooms as she set to work on her latest rendition of some classical work.

There was one portrait Mother was particularly proud of. She did an interpretation of *Portrait of a Girl*, by a Dutch painter named Johannes Verspronck. She was a beautiful girl with blonde hair and big blue eyes, dressed in a matching blue dress with layer upon layer of lace around her neck and on her bodice. Mother's interpretation gave the girl distinct golden ringlets and a bold bright sky-blue dress, rather than the pale eggshell blue of the original. She liked to call this her Portrait of a Princess.

I would sit on a stool in the living room, the portrait sitting on an easel in the corner, while Mother would brush my knotted hair and compare me to this image. I was fat and ugly; this girl was pretty – beautiful even – and certainly not fat. She had a pale white complexion, while I was olive-skinned. This portrait was the complete opposite of who I was, and Mother seemed to relish letting me know I was not the fantasy daughter she craved. Then she would begin to wonder out loud if the girl in this portrait held any resemblance to the two daughters she had miscarried.

The Girls were doomed when Father started to use us. In her own way, Mother groomed me to please him. Encouraging me to spend time behind shut doors with him as a small child, saying I needed to learn how to make Daddy happy. My child's mind believed by doing this, I would earn *her* love.

Of course I was wrong, and her loathing for me intensified. So I did what I knew best. I split. I kept the fat, ugly and disgusting parts close to my heart and created the perfect daughter, an alter who was beautiful and could be the child Mother wanted.

I remember how I did it. I thought about all the things Mother had said about the portrait she had painted and willed *Pretty Girl* into existence. It was that easy. In her beautiful blue dress and delicate lace collar, *Pretty Girl* was the mirror image of Mother's portrait. Her sparkling blue eyes matched her dress, and lovely blond ringlet curls bounced on her shoulders when she turned her head. The daughter I knew Mother really wanted, *Pretty Girl* would wait, untouched by the ugliness of the rest of *The Girls'* lives. This was her job, to wait for Mother. I left her on a park bench, happy and smiling, because this would please Mother.

Then, in my childlike, *everything-has-a-happy-ending* way, I was confident that some of Mother's love for *Pretty Girl* would find its way to me.

WORKING GIRL

[*Trigger Warning. This chapter contains descriptions of sexually explicit violence.*]

Time for Work: *Annie*

There were signs. Mother might be going out for one of her unending cocktail hours with friends, or Father might invite some of his colleagues around, sharing a beer or whisky as they laughed on the back veranda. These were the more recognisable, *get yourself prepared because shit is about to hit the fan* moments. But there were less obvious signs too, when I (or *The Girls*) would feel a change in the energy of the house, subtle, but perhaps because of this, more terrifying indications that it would soon be time to go to work, to be *used*. *The Girls* became attuned to these moments.

    Father enjoyed sitting in his chair in the living room after dinner with no shirt on, especially in the hot Texas summer. He would pore over a science journal, peering at it through his thick, dark-rimmed glasses. In the other hand, he would cradle his precious whisky. From when I was very young, this was his nightly routine.

I remember (I think I was probably ten?) I would walk past him on my way to bed and he would look at me over the top of his glasses with a faint sneer, baring his teeth slightly and licking his lips. He would take his hand with his whisky glass and run it over his exposed torso, resting it for a moment on his bulging breast, the cool touch of the glass making his nipple stand erect. Sometimes I think he did it just to tease me, scare me and keep me on edge. Sometimes, nothing happened. Sometimes it did. Either way, I was afraid. I think this was what he wanted, to toy with my emotions. It was something he was good at.

Then came decision time. When *The Girls* were little, everyone knew whose turn it was to come out. It was instinctual. And when the abuse began, it was their job to deal with it, each one handling the abuse differently. As they got older, and the narrative behind the abuse began to change, they learnt to adapt quickly. They would read the situation and the required *Girl* would step up and take her role.

Learning the Ropes: *Little Girl*

I was almost four when work started. Mommy and Daddy's bedroom was at the far end of the house, down a long hallway. I loved the way they decorated their bedroom, with light blue paint the colour of the sky on the walls and curtains with big beautiful dark blue and gold flowers on them. I liked those curtains. They were bright and happy.

Sometimes, when Mommy was out, Daddy would take me down to their bedroom, holding my hand, telling me what a good girl I was. I would sit on the floor and he would sit on the bed. He would give me books to look at and point to pictures of nearly naked ladies and talk to me about how they looked or what they were doing. Daddy told me how beautiful they were and asked me if I wanted to be beautiful too.

I wanted to be pretty for Daddy. I loved him and wanted to do everything I could to make him happy. He talked to me about how they looked, how this one sat and how it showed off how pretty she was. Or this one, when she does this, she looks happy, what do you think? Why don't you try it? You sit that way and touch yourself the way she touches herself. So, I did. Then he would ask how it felt. I didn't understand. I liked how it made me feel, but I also didn't like it, which made me think I must be a horrible person. Daddy said I should like it. He said it was a good thing and I should enjoy it. Then Daddy would do it to me because he said it was nice to let someone else make you feel nice too. I didn't think it was nice, but wanted to make Daddy happy, so I did it anyway.

Then he said he wanted me to learn how to make him feel good too. He said this was something important, and I would need to know how to do it. Sometimes I thought his eyes were sad when he told me this. When I think about it, maybe this was wishful thinking. He got me to kneel between his legs. He said I should touch and hold his thing. This part of his body made him a man, he said. In the same way, I had the bits inside me making me a woman. I put one hand on the top of his leg and touched his thingy with the other. It was soft and floppy. Then he said to just gently rub back and forth with my hand, and it would change. It did change! It got HUGE!

He put both my hands on his legs and put his hands on top of mine and held them there. Then he looked at me very seriously and said I needed to suck on it like a lollipop, with my mouth. Ewww! Why would Daddy want me to do that? I tell you what, it didn't taste like a lollipop! His hands were pushing down hard on mine. He made some strange noises and then put a hand on my head and said suck harder. I did what he said because I loved Daddy, but I think maybe I was a bit scared too. Then I felt this gooey sticky stuff in my mouth, and I wanted to spit it out. It was all over me. He pulled away and laid back on the bed with his eyes closed. He told me I was a good girl, and I should go and get cleaned up.

    I did the things Daddy told me to because I loved him. He said he loved me too, especially when I made him feel good. Why is it when I made him feel good, it made me feel bad?

Work Conditions: *Mute Girl*

Long tangled brown hair a halo on her pale skin
She is young
Too young
Younger than she should be
Standing in dark hallways
Trembling
I have been here before
Her chubby body stands firm
Toes curling into shag pile carpet
Heart pounding in her chest to the beat of a drum
Rigid and resistant is her posture

Pulling back from the hand that takes hers
With a quiet, sideways glance, she dares to look
Hands that should be gentle and loving
Are wrinkled and gnarled

His skin
the feeling of sandpaper as she pulls back from his touch

One step back – then another
She has to fight, but it will be of no use
Stumble, and again – always again
He extends his arm and drags her down the hallway
She concentrates on her dress, full of holes, old and worn
If I count the holes will that help me not be afraid
Her legs lock
Another stumble – she picks herself up

Always a need to fight
A hope that it might be different
She is dragged
The carpet that was soft under her toes
Now abrasive on her face
Another stumble, pitch forward
The hallway seems so long
Get your act together brat
Do what you are told

Compliance is easier
Maybe that will be enough – this time

She steps in resignation down the hallway
Wondering for a moment if her mommy and daddy
Will ever love and rescue her

Going to Work: *Middle Girl*

I'm a bit more grown up, I'm nine. Things have changed with Daddy, I think. Not sure what though. Daddy made sure I had what he called a proper introduction to being a woman. He said I had learned all the things I really needed to know and it was time to be treated like the woman I was becoming. He said I needed to have a man make love to me. It was his job. This was important, he said, to help me grow and learn about myself. So instead of being on the floor, or between his knees, he told me to get on the bed and spread my legs as far apart as I could, and he would take care of the rest. It was scary because I could barely breathe. I felt squished, and it hurt. He promised me the next time wouldn't hurt so much because now I was a woman. He did it again later, and it didn't hurt – so much. He said I was Daddy's girl now.

The times Daddy's friends came over it really hurt. Some would come and go, but there were regulars; his work friends, or this neighbour who acted like he was in charge. He was a big, tall man and I think he just liked to hurt me.

Daddy would tell me to go and sit on the bed in his and Mommy's bedroom and wait. I could see our back patio through the sliding glass door; there was a table where these men would sit. They talked and drank so much! Some would smoke too. I would get bored waiting, but then one would get up and come into the bedroom through the glass door. Then I was scared, I knew what was gonna happen.

They came in, and told me to lie down on the bed, it was just like Daddy had taught me. They would take turns. I never fought, I kinda guessed it would hurt less.

I don't know why Daddy let it all happen. He would never do it when they were around. At first, he would stand there and look a bit sad (or was I hoping that?). After a few times watching, he just went and sat on the patio with the others.

They would do lots of things to me. Did they do it because they were drunk? They would stumble and laugh, so maybe it was it. Sometimes they would tie me up or put pretty see-through clothes on me. One man said he wanted me to enjoy it as much as possible and it took him forever to be done! He enjoyed it, I guess. I didn't. There was one really big man who especially liked to see how much he could hurt me. I thought him being so fat would hurt the most. But it was worse. He made me turn over and get on my tummy. He pressed his hand really hard on my neck and grunted. Then he got angry and said it wouldn't work and grabbed two pillows from the top of the bed and told me to put them under my stomach. He put his thingy inside me back there. It hurt so much! I cried and begged him to stop, but he didn't listen. He made heaps of huffing and puffing noises, and then he fell flat on top of me. I couldn't breathe and thought I was gonna die! Another man laughed and rolled him off me. Someone said there was blood on the bed and I should go and get cleaned up.

After a while, I learned to close my eyes and think about other things. I would feel it, but in my head I made myself think about chasing birds and butterflies or riding a horse fast across a big field. I would run away in my head as far as I could from them, which helped a little.

I think maybe this was when I realised Daddy didn't love me – that what he wanted from me wasn't love. I think what he wanted was for me to make him feel good. I just know I didn't feel good.

We Want to Quit: *The Girls*

Run away. Fast. Quick.
    Little legs thumping pavement.
    Bang the door.
    Run up the path.
    Scream to get away.
    Fire consumes.
    Hope is suffocated.
    The devil licks us with furious flames.
    Claws ripping our flesh.
    Raw from the fight.
    The heat devours
    All we want is the cool cement on our burnt cheeks
    To ease the pain.
    A voice whispers — *gotcha*.

Employee of the Month: *Slut Girl*

I like sex. No – not true. I *love* sex. I know grown-ups don't think it's right for a kid who's eleven to love sex, but I don't care. I do. I love it 'cause it makes me feel good. Ain't nothin' wrong with that.

Yeah, so it was more like this for me. There were ugly fat men, other guys too. Mostly the same ones, over and over. If I'm honest, they did get a bit boring! Some of the other girls didn't like it. But I figured, they let themselves not like it and they got hurt and were embarrassed. So, I thought, why not make a bad job better? I just decided to do it and enjoy it. Why not?

They liked it too, the men, when I started to really get into it. They would even have bets as to who could get me to enjoy it the most (sometimes I did have to pretend, coz they were stupid and drunk). They got me to dance for them, and just prance around the room. It was like, *touch yourself, sit on my lap...no time like the present! Show us what you have!* I was smart, I picked up on the signs. I liked to slide slowly up onto the bed. I would hike up my dress and spread my legs really wide, exposing my good stuff while they decided who would go first. They wanted me, and I loved it. Yeah, okay, some were a bit rough, I won't deny it. But the best ones? They took all my clothes off and kissed me all over. It wasn't just about donkin' me, they wanted to share it with me, and kissed me absolutely everywhere. Oh my!

The only sorta hard thing about being me? Daddy hates me, thinks I'm trash. I used to do this coz I thought he would love me for it, but he didn't. So I don't really care anymore. I did at first, but not now.

I figure he gets what he deserves. He trained me to be this way and decided to share me around. So, tough, I don't care if he hates me anymore or not. I wanna survive. Ya gotta do what ya gotta do!

Made Redundant: *Runaway Girl*

Yeah, so by the time we were fourteen, surprise, surprise, life got worse. What was worse? Maybe because instead of Dad's friends just wanting sex, they had started doing things just to scare or hurt me more. They would tie me up so I couldn't move my arms or legs; stretch me out with my arms above my head and my legs spread wide. Sometimes the ropes were so tight they left marks on me. Did they think I could escape? Good grief, they were morons. Scary morons, but still morons.

Maybe the scariest part was waiting. They would tie me up and just leave me. They'd go out and have a drink and smoke their gross cigars then come back and talk about me like I wasn't there, like I was some sort of piece of meat. I lost weight, they liked me getting curvy and having big tits.

On the inside, I was scared. And pissed off. I knew I had to be careful. If I pretended to be scared, it would make them happy. And if they were happy, it didn't hurt so much. It was the trade-off. Making sure they saw me as scared kept me safe. Not sure I can explain it very well. I was pissed off too. Being pissed off made me feel like I had some control, I guess. But I had to hide my feelings, because if I showed them, they would hurt me more. I put up with their shit so I could be in control of me.

There was this guy called Richard. I reckon he knew I was pissed by the way he looked at me. I think his goal was to scare me more than I had ever been scared before. They had gone off and left me on the bed. Kinda thought they'd forgotten about me. I closed my eyes and thought about what my life would be like when I left this crappy house forever. I think I fell asleep because I woke up when they grabbed me.

One guy held my arms tight and the other my waist. This was different – they'd not done this before, so I was legit scared. They laughed the whole time and I couldn't move at all. And then Richard, he was big and fat, he stood next to the bed and started talking to the other guys and said he wondered if he could make me really hurt – get me to scream, he said. The whole time he just stared at me and chugged on his cigar. Then he waved it under my nose and blew smoke in my face. I choked and gagged. The other guys laughed. Richard put the hot end of his cigar just under my right boob. There was a nasty burning smell – pretty sure it was my skin. I wanted to scream so bad, but I kept my mouth shut. I refused to let him see me afraid. He said that he was branding me so I would never forget who I really was.

Then he pulled the cigar off and had one of his stupid friends hold it. He took his pants off – his prick was huge. It was huge even when it wasn't standing up straight! He put a pillow under my butt like he always did – he was too fat to do anything else. Then he climbed on me and jabbed his prick in me really hard and just sat there, chugging on his cigar and smiling like he was king of the world. He took a big drag on the cigar and gave it back to the guy holding my arms and told him to put it back on me while he rode me so I would always remember every time I got screwed, I would feel pain.

He took forever, I could feel him fucking me all the way to the back of my guts. It hurt for a really long time after. But I still didn't let him see how pissed off I was.

If I think about it, for the other men, it was mostly about sex. Sometimes rough, but it was about them having sex, I was just a thing to make it work. But this Richard guy, he wanted to hurt me, a lot, make me hate myself. It worked.

When I got my period things changed. Dad told his buddies one day I had started my period, and to make sure nothing stupid happened. I can't really talk about what happened next, it makes me sad. But Dad's warning didn't work.

I also got angry a lot, and I fought back. I would fight and kick and bite and scratch. I ran too. Finally, I could run faster than them and get away. Maybe it all got too hard. I don't know, it wasn't my job. That was *Annie's* job and her story. But I was glad and it stopped. I wanted to make sure no one ever touched me again.

SCHOOL DAYS

School life should have been my escape. It was my territory, my sanctuary from home, and a place where *The Girls* did not venture – at least not blatantly. It was the peace I wished for – most of the time. Where I could be free from the influence of parents who tossed me aside for their own whims or a system of alters who were often more than I could handle. Of course, wishing doesn't make something real, and I often felt the subtle tug of *The Girls* as I went to school. They would share their fears of rejection and bullying as I sat alone, subject to regular bouts of fat shaming. I craved shelter and security, a place of refuge that was not my home.

Instead, I lived in fear of being exposed. The inconsistencies in my behaviour, which I knew was the influence of *The Girls*, and the sordid experiences they had at home, would be laid bare for all to see. Would *The Girls* do something to reveal the truth? Would my relationship with my family finally be uncovered? I spent most of my days hypervigilant, trying to ensure *The Girls* and our home life were not exposed.

But I also wanted to be rescued. In spite of my fears, I secretly wished my teachers would see me and the truth of my life. I wished they could look beyond my fat façade and help me escape. I wanted to be known and find the peace I craved.

In truth, I wanted teachers to help me, but did not believe I mattered enough to be noticed.

My Year Three teacher was a short, stout woman with a stern demeanour. Her beehive hairdo rose above her like a crown, helping assert her control in the classroom. I was terrified that during a parent-teacher night this teacher would tell my Mother I was a bad daughter. I struggled to pay attention, not understanding much of what she taught. I was afraid of what my mother would do once the teacher told her this.

As it happened, my Year Three teacher did tell Mother that I was inattentive and capable of working harder. I'm sure she believed she was simply highlighting something any other parent might use to encourage their child to reach their potential. What happened when we left was another matter. I had humiliated Mother in front of another adult. As we drove home, she berated me over and over. 'Fat, lazy child. Fat, lazy child.' When we were home, Mother made me sit on a chair in my bedroom as she held up flashcards with mathematical equations on them. She hit me each time I got one wrong. I missed a lot of equations that night.

I became a quiet and observant student. My sole purpose was to avoid Mother's wrath.

My Year Five teacher was a middle-aged matron who ruled the classroom with an infectious smile. She was an energetic and engaging teacher, with an enthusiasm to teach us about science. Her laugh lines were as bold as her vivid red lacquered hair. One day she had us dissecting a cow's heart as part of an anatomy class. I knew she would be proud of me. I took my turn and picked up my scalpel. Needing no instructions and asking no questions, with detailed precision I began the process of opening and exposing each chamber, identifying every aorta, artery, atrium, and ventricle. The teacher was astonished at my dexterity and the speed with which I completed my assignment. I was happy she noticed my effort.

Did she ever question how intuitive I was with my dissection skills? How would she have reacted if I told her behind this ability were numerous lessons on being taught how to kill and pull apart animals – birds, mice, kittens. That another alter, named *Animal Basher*, a small child aged five, would have unashamedly explained how she loved the chocolate treats she received as a reward for her attentiveness in killing any and all creatures smaller than her.

How would my teacher have responded to this? Would she see me as disgusting? As a child, I could only wonder, knowing how little I mattered. I was simply another child taking up a seat in her classroom.

To say I struggled with adequate hygiene as a child would be an understatement. I was rarely bathed and had to teach myself how to clean my teeth. I was a ragamuffin, with dirty clothes and face. My hair was a mess of rats' nests most days. I tried to disguise the unsightly mass in a tightly bound ponytail.

I idolized my Year Two teacher. She had fashion sense and oozed an Audrey Hepburn / Twiggy sort of style, her bright eyes framed by a bob of blonde hair and long thin legs sporting the latest colourful stockings. I desperately wanted to look like her but knew my square body, clad in polyester avocado and gold stripes, would fall far short of what she deemed fashionable.

One day, as we lined up to enter class, I felt her long graceful hand fall firmly on my shoulder. I looked down, focusing on the gold buckles of her shiny loafers. I didn't want to hear what she was about to say, fearful my lack of hygiene was about to be exposed. I watched my classmates' faces as she said clearly that I needed to take better care of my hair and use a brush and comb to get the knots out. The snickers from my classmates were deafening.

I dreamt she would offer to help me, to show me the self-care I was never taught by Mother. Could I have told her about the way she brushed my hair while drunk? Yanking and pulling against my head, every movement inflicting pain? Or the time in a drunken stupor, she was unable to get the knots out and grabbed a pair of scissors, snipping and chopping at my head, all the while, telling me what a wretched child I was, and she was sorry she ever gave birth to me.

The sex magazines in Year Six that I carefully smuggled into school in a brown paper bag in the bottom of my school backpack. They were from Father's stack in his bedside table. Excusing myself, I would go to the toilet block, magazine held tightly to my chest, holding my breath as another adored teacher passed by. I mentally prepared myself to get into trouble. But instead, she smiled knowingly and said this sort of material was not appropriate for school. Please leave it at home.

I breathed a sigh of relief but was equally confused by this response and couldn't reconcile it. A desperate part of me wanted her to question me so I could tell her about Father and his friends. About having to practice sex with them and make sure I made them happy.

Those primary school days left me with an acute inability to concentrate for long periods of time. I was only able to read for short periods before the ghosts appeared to remind me of my failings. As a young adult, trying to make my way in the world, mathematics terrified me. Whether reconciling a bank account or converting a recipe, waves of nausea overcame me, reminding me of the humiliation of bygone days.

OUR HISTORY OF FAT

I lived in the world of fat. I was a child who grew up overweight and lived out every shameful comment associated with being obese. From Mother to my schoolmates, I lived in the vocabulary of fat. By the age of six I had learned chubby and chunky were code words for fat and ugly. I was always aware of my mother's watchful eye over what I ate. She hoped, I thought, that I would magically transform from fat to adorable. At school, the comments were hurtful. Snide comments followed me as I walked to class, in class and after class.

I chose a different path. I held fat close, encouraging it to become my intimate friend. Fat was a comfort, accepting me no matter the circumstances. I was constantly navigating the resentment from Mother, and my craving to be accepted by friends. With fat, I didn't have to try, it held me close in its comforting arms.

At school I would see little girls in frocks covered in flowers and lace, laughing and giggling as they talked, wispy hair in clips showing off their pretty little faces. I would sit far away, watching them as I shoved food in my mouth. I would never have beautiful things, but at least I would have fat.

Clothes shopping was, for me, a dichotomy full of hope and rife with shame. I would be thrilled at a few hours with Mother as we walked through department stores hoping for a special moment with her. Instead, I was dragged past racks of beautiful clothes to a small section marked 6X. Big clothes for fat little girls. I felt sick with self-loathing.

With her bag over her arm, Mother would riffle through the selection of shapeless garments, grumbling, 'If you weren't so fat, this might be a pleasant experience.'

Every now and then she would pull a dress off a rack and hold it in front of me and sigh. 'I suppose this will do. Although even this might not be big enough for you.' And she would send me off to the dressing room with a shove to try it on. I willed the zipper to slide closed easily. Or for the last button at the waist to do up without me having to suck in my stomach. I wanted so much to get something to replace the old worn dresses I had been wearing. More importantly, if I had a new dress, Mother might think I was pretty. I would hold my breath the entire time, desperate not to disappoint her.

Most of the time I never got to try things on, instead Mother would come home and toss a piece of clothing in my direction. Mother didn't care if things suited me, or if they were too small. Dressing a fat horrible child was beneath her and a task she barely tolerated.

One time when we were in a department store, Mother was looking in the women's section hoping to find some new dress for a party she was going to. I walked through the kids' clothes, staring at beautiful dresses and fingering the delicate lace. I wandered past a counter and saw an entry form for a free dress. My heart leapt! I wondered if I could win a beautiful dress all my own. I looked up, a nice old man with white hair and beard walked over. I looked at him and he smiled gently. 'Why don't you get your mother to enter you?'

Mother overheard this. I think she was irritated I had interfered with her own shopping. She looked at me and then the man and said, 'I don't care, do what you want.' And went straight back to racks of dresses.

This man, who I was sure was some version of Santa Claus, helped me to fill out the form and then took it to Mother. She stared at him briefly, grabbed the form and pen, and scribbled her signature, then turned back to her own shopping, an exasperated look on her face. The man came back to me with a smile and told me to put it in the container and with a pat on my head, disappearing like Santa up a chimney.

A few weeks later the phone rang and Mother picked it up. 'Hello?' Silence as she listened. Then, 'Really?' I was always curious when the phone rang, and stood a few feet away, wondering what the person on the other end might be saying. Mother looked straight at me as she said, 'Don't bother. It'd be wasted on us. She's so fat it would never fit her. Give it to someone else.' She hung the phone up and walked away.

I stood in the hallway, shed a single tear and told myself this was what I deserved because I was fat and ugly.

I knew fat caused these things to happen, but how could I reject such a dear friend? I always found a way to sneak or hide food away in my room to sooth and comfort me later. Fat never rejected me. Fat accepted me, it wrapped me in layers of unconditional love.

School and Mother became the bookends within which my relationship with fat was written. At school, I learnt self-protection.

I developed a tough shell, armour against the onslaught of beached whale barbs and ugly girl putdowns. From the earliest years I learnt to tolerate the shame and pain of rejection in the vain hope of being accepted. I knew when I was chosen for playground games, it was to make me the target of some sort of joke. I was always the 'weight' at the back of a tug-of-war game, or a slow-moving target when it came to bombardment. Playing see-saw, I would sit on one end, while the other kids clambered on opposite me, hooting and laughing at how many were needed to make their end start sinking slowly towards the ground.

When we took a trip back to England to see extended family, these strangers would make offhand comments about serving me double helpings at dinner. They were kindly, but mean. With a wink and a nudge, they would talk about what a 'big girl' I was becoming. Everyone knew exactly what it really meant. I was the fat black sheep of the family.

As a preteen, my relationship with fat changed. Mother doubled down in her efforts to make me into the daughter she had been denied. It was a dream, a mirage of a beautiful, thin young woman. And it ushered in an era of dieting and even more disappointment.

Mother took me every week to Weight Watchers for the required weigh-in and inspirational talk. These weigh-ins were demoralizing. Fat was my quiet friend, and my closet eating could not be hidden. I would stand in the line for my weigh-in and watch as women looked at me with pity, Mother's words berating me when the scales showed no change. The requisite talks were no better as a litany of speakers discussed how I needed to control my body's cravings (I liked my cravings, thank you very much!) and learned about 'legal' foods -

things supposedly good for my body, but tasted horrible. I was a failure if I did not like mushy greens that felt like slime in my mouth.

I was subject to all of this for one singular purpose – to become the thin, svelte, and desirable daughter my mother wished me to be.

The result of all this dieting meant that there was a brief window, around the age of thirteen, when I was free from fat. It was no longer my intimate companion. *Middle Girl* threw off her comfortable blanket of fat, developing a young woman's figure. For the first time, she actually liked herself.

There is a faded postcard memory capturing this brief moment when *Middle Girl* knew her body was changing. Even more, Mother loved her. In this memory, *Middle Girl* stands tall, posing for a picture for Mother, who is smiling and proud, telling her how good she looks. She wears a sleeveless tunic and pants that accentuate her long legs and growing breasts. *Middle Girl* feels beautiful, and knows she is – Mother said so.

Middle Girl was hopeful that having Mother's love would bring change in her life. She hoped others might like her too, dreaming of parties and friends who would include her in their social activities. She even dreamed that boys might notice her and think she was pretty.

This was a fairy tale, and the truth brought her idealistic fantasies crashing down around her. *Middle Girl* thought that Father and his friends were done with her. She had grown, changed; she thought they lost interest. And they did, for a while (and when I say a while, I mean less than a year).

But as the fat faded away, her womanly figure blossomed and Father and his friends rediscovered their desire to use her. *Slut Girl* became an important ally in keeping the pain away, often sharing these experiences with *Middle Girl*, providing relief when the encounters were too much. It was *Slut Girl* who let them take all they wanted. She pretended to enjoy these sexual encounters in order to survive. But when it became too rough, and even *Slut Girl* could no longer endure it, she would flee, leaving *Middle Girl* to deal with the aftermath. *Middle Girl* was conflicted and ashamed, proving that ultimately, she did have a woman's body.

Middle Girl remembered what a comfort fat had been. So she fed fat, inviting this friend back into an intimate relationship. She was bereft, knowing that by embracing the security of fat, the bulges and wobbles would hide her curves (and she hoped make her less desirable), but would also ensure she would not be beautiful anymore. She became the familiar fat ugly daughter Mother despised.

Runaway Girl began to grow up, becoming more aware of who she was as a young woman. She would sneak Mother's romance books into her bedroom and read late into the night about innocent, voluptuous girls having steamy encounters with dark rakish characters, and find herself in awe of how her body responded. In these dark moments alone in her bedroom she would wrap her arms around her stomach and imagine herself with these men. It was easier to put herself in these fantasies than face the truth of her existence.

In time, *Runaway Girl* was confronted with real womanhood when she started her period. She had crossed the threshold. Everything about her body should have held the promise of a future filled with love.

Then there was a flutter. Mother was watching her, standing across the kitchen as *Runaway Girl* touched her stomach, questioning this strange feeling. Mother's voice pierced the silence as she stormed across the floor and shook *Runaway Girl's* shoulders, 'Slut! When was your last period? Don't you dare lie to me!'

This was confusing. She had lost weight, just the way Mother had wanted. She looked good. But suddenly, Mother seemed to hate her curves. What did she do wrong? Why wasn't Mother happy? *Runaway Girl* rested her hand on this new curve. A bump. Instinctively, she wanted to protect it.

Mother screamed at Father as he sat at the dinner table, grumbling over piles of bills and ignoring everyone. 'You are an idiot, how did you let this happen again?'

Another flutter. Movements of life. *Runaway Girl* knew the truth. Inside her body she carried life. Incandescent joy. This was her naïve girl's glimpse at motherhood. Fleeting wonder broken with the chaos and anger surrounding her.

'Deal with it! I don't want to be embarrassed!' Mother yelled at Father.

Runaway Girl's heart was heavy. This was her fault. A blur of confusing time and space, and then pain – horrible, sad. Final. So much blood. No more flutters as the life she was carrying was brutally ripped from her. Emptiness. The promise of life gone; the wobble of fat returned. Day by day, re-establishing the secure relationship fat had always promised.

ADAGIO FOR LOST THINGS

I love music, it's what I like to tell myself. But if I'm honest, and someone asked me, *do you love music?* I would have to say, *I used to.*

When I riffle through my postcard memories, I remember I used to play the piano, and I remember I was good. After months of begging and pleading, promising I would practice every day, my parents finally gave in and purchased a piano. It didn't matter that it was cheap, old and out of tune. They bought something for me! I was desperate to play, to make beautiful music. They signed me up for lessons and I kept my promise and practised often. It was as much for the love of making music as the opportunity to close the door to the study, hidden away from the realities of life at home. Music was my escape. My pudgy fingers skimmed across ivory keys, working on this scale or that, or picking through melody lines from some funky piece my teacher had given me. I felt like I was in control of something in my life.

Piano recitals were a visceral reminder I was a budding musician. Year after year, I was the last on the program, the best always saved till the end. I would skip up to the large grand piano, dressed in the pink lace dress Mother had made for me, swishing as I sat down to play. This was my moment. I looked pretty, and I knew I would play magnificent music. I looked for Mother's face in the crowd, desperate for her to be proud of me.

In retrospect, I was a dressage pony being primped and prodded to look good and fit a particular image to make Mother happy. My child's mind didn't care. I had on a pretty dress and played beautiful music. I felt special.

I was twelve when reality hit. I was practising late one afternoon, hiding away from the noise in the rest in the house. The door to the kitchen was closed, a makeshift cocoon keeping me isolated and protected. I ran my fingers across the keys, excited to tackle whatever musical challenge my teacher was confident I could face. It never failed to amaze me how I made beautiful melodies by running my fingers across the keyboard.

I heard Mother coming, her monstrous thuds across the kitchen, loud enough to shake the floor as she yelled at me. There was food missing from the pantry, how was she supposed to make dinner when I had eaten everything? I cringed, my heart thumping, waiting.

The door flew open and Mother stood there, bellowing at me. 'One day you will be the world's fattest and ugliest concert pianist, an elephant trudging across the stage to play!' She stomped her feet for effect. 'Your fat fingers will never make their way across a keyboard! You are now and always will be a fat, ugly failure and fraud!'

Self-loathing. Guilt. Overwhelm.

The worst part was that she never punished me. Instead, she ignored me, silent confirmation that I was and always would be a disappointment to her.

This condemnation echoed down through the years, through high school, university and beyond.

My first experience sharing my love of music was when I joined the school band in Year Six. My older brother had been a standout participant when he was in high school and the band teacher noted this when he met me. I felt the comparison straight away, excited to follow in my brother's footsteps. I wanted to play the clarinet or flute, but then the bottom fell from under me. I was assigned the tuba, this large brass instrument which I was sure was to make fun of my size. I knew it, and so did the other snickering students. Ashamed, I chose the safe solution. I dropped band and opted for art instead, wearing a flowing paint smock to hide my rolls of fat, my chubby fingers easily able to wrap around a paint brush.

When I was thirteen, I sang in the high school choir. I loved the way the harmonies echoed around the music room. They literally lifted my heart. Eventually, I found myself sitting on the edge of this as well, as pretty girls sang together in small groups, reaching melodious high notes. I could not reach these heights and instead sang alto, relegated to singing with the boys whose voices hadn't dropped yet. We were a rag-tag group of misfits. I pretended to enjoy it for a while. Eventually, I watched kids who I thought were friends bond over their choir and band activities, neglecting to include me. I began to withdraw, taking comfort in the failure that Mother's words had predestined.

When I went to college, I had my heart set on a degree in education, but I still held a love of music. I would sneak into the auditorium and quietly play on the grand piano. It was a salve to my soul. The head of the music department heard me playing one day and encouraged me to think about changing majors to study music seriously. He believed in me – in my musical ability. This was a new and bewildering concept, spurring on my commitment to practice. I was desperate to recover the love for music I remembered, and which lay behind every chord, run or scale I played. But in the classroom my mother's words of *fat* and *fraud* rang through my head. I was desperate for this professor's continued approval but could not find the wherewithal to understand the music theory required to pass the classes. I was the failure Mother predicted. Finding this love for music eluded me. It was a faint ghost of longing I could not touch. I would hear the constant refrain of my mother's dismissal, *fat elephant failure*, until I gave up, and took solace, instead, in my aloneness.

The sum of these experiences permeated my entire existence.

DOWN THE RABBIT HOLE

Our car was an old white Coronet 440 station wagon. I knew what was coming when Dad said he wanted to take me out for a drive. I wasn't dumb. I would follow him out to the car, asking myself, *why don't you run?* I don't know why I didn't. My brain would go fuzzy, I couldn't think straight. *The Girls* felt exposed and vulnerable. I was in that in-between place, just before the panic of realisation. *What would happen now? Who was supposed to take over?*

These trips began when I was young, a small child of five, with no thought for what lay ahead. As I got older, I became too aware, I held too many dark memories. Beneath my frozen surface, I was roiling with panic and helplessness. *How were we supposed to survive?* All I could do was wait for life on the other side, when whoever had to do whatever they had to do was done protecting me. I would sigh and get in the car, there was nothing else I could do.

I could feel the crunch of gravel under the tyres when we arrived. I knew exactly where we were, the Peters'. A country property, not far from our home. We would drive past the familiar outline of their imposing old two-story home making our way down the driveway to the shed. The outline barely visible from behind the trunk of a gnarled giant cedar tree.

Father would shove my arm and bring me back to reality. I squeezed my eyes tightly, *could I still run? Run fast enough and get to the main road, away from this place?* Another shove, harder this time. I opened my eyes. Father extended his hand. A little white pill. I knew why I needed to take it; it would make things easier.

There had been a time before. Before pills, before oblivion. A time when *The Girls* stepped in seamlessly. Before the driveway. Further back. Before getting into the car at home. There was no need for pills. I just left and they took over.

But then came *Runaway Girl*. It's what she did, she ran. She fought, she bit, she kicked, she screamed; whatever she could to be free. As we got older, and could not just sense, but also comprehend the danger waiting, she would try and run.

This time when I relinquished control *Runaway Girl* took over.

She took stock of her surroundings. She saw a little boy. *Where did he come from?* A blonde kid, no more than two years old, in bare feet and shorts on this sweltering summer's night. Father issued a stern command to stay with the boy as he walked off, talking to a woman nearby. Feeling sorry for the boy, *Runaway Girl* bent down and asked, 'Did your mommy bring you?' He looked at her with big blue vacant eyes and shook his head no.

Then he grabbed her hand, squeezing hard. 'Are you scared?' she asked. He nodded his head yes. Still holding his hand, she stood up. 'I am too.'

Father and this woman went into the shed. *Runaway Girl* looked at the boy, and then did what she always did. She listened to her gut and ran. She picked the boy up in her arms, and ran as fast as her legs would go, trying to get to the main road, where she hoped someone might see them. Her legs felt like dead weights and the road seemed a million miles away. The boy began to cry. She put her hand over his mouth and darted into the tall grass. No headlights, no cars. Nothing. Just dark as far as she could see. There would be no help.

There was a hard yank on her arm. It was one of Father's friends. He dragged her and the boy down the driveway, the boy now screaming. The woman Father had been talking to took the boy and walked away quickly towards the shed. *Runaway Girl* was yanked again, falling on the gravel this time. The man pulled her up and shook her hard, slamming her against Dad's old station wagon. She thought her head might snap off. She wished it would.

Father came over to the car and began to threaten her. He hit her across the jaw. She was used to it; he'd always done it, ever since they were little. Physical pain was always present if *The Girls* didn't do what they were told. He wagged his finger in her face. 'Do that again and you'll regret it.'

He shoved her in the car. She never saw the boy again.

Runaway Girl was done, she never went back. Instead, when I was in our car, eyes tightly shut and Dad would hit me on the arm, I knew not to fight. I was helpless to protect me, *us,* from what was about to happen.

'Take the pill,' he would say, hand stretched out. 'You know it will help you forget.'

I always reached out and always took it. It was easier than dealing with the truth. So I put it in my mouth, swallowed and plunged down the rabbit hole.

Somewhere between the car and the shed door, my world would begin to change, become less real, and I didn't care. Oblivion settled in, and I was free. Internal adjustments made, and the truth of what happened was left for another *Girl* to deal with. Sometimes, in the shed, I could see *The Girl in the Cage* – almost touch her, know the truth of her. But she would slip away too. I gave in to the peace and freedom the little white pill offered. I hated myself because I was free. I left these moments to the others, letting them deal with whatever came after. I suppose in the end it was simply another survival mechanism.

FORGETFULNESS AND FREEDOM

THE ROAD OUT

The vagaries of my life as a teenager until I left home are confusing and unclear at best. The very nature of my life – being MPD – meant there were huge stretches of time when I was not aware of what was going on. A distinct separateness was developing between finding my freedom and the fog I walked through at home. The more freedom I gained, whether it be through outside interests, having access to a car, or being present at school, meant *The Girls* were fast moving to the recesses of my mind, becoming a less tangible part of my world.

Instead, I simply lost time. I knew and owned parts of my day-to-day life but was left with numerous holes in my memory. This growing freedom in my life reinforced a veneer of family, in which both of my parents worked, and I was the last child at home. I rarely ate with them; meals as a family had never been something we did. If I wasn't at school, I kept to my room or walked the streets. I think it was *Runaway Girl's* way of helping to keep us safe and unavailable. I'm not sure. What I did know was my life was fragmented chunks of existence. I thought this was normal.

In this foggy existence, Mother's constant drinking became the norm, and the only place where the world between *The Girls* and my life intersected. Mother went deeper into her art world and our only interactions were angry exchanges. We yelled at each other and she told me yet again that I was a failure and not the daughter she'd wanted.

By the age of sixteen, I developed an ability to navigate moments and days when I felt in control, other days, not so much. Life was real, just not quite safe. I walked through my teen years in a protective hypervigilant state, constantly wondering if something would happen to trigger an argument with Mother. (Father had lost interest in *us* by then.) Or I would just lose time and find myself standing in a parking lot, or at the other end of the school.

There is a picture in one of my high school yearbooks that epitomises for me how I felt about life. In this photo I am standing at the edge, slightly apart from the group. While everybody else was smiling at the camera, laughing with arms draped over each other, I was looking away with a dour countenance. This image is a shockingly accurate indication of how I lived my teenage life. I was detached, alone and withdrawn.

I was an outcast, one of the unpopular kids. In our high school, there was an inside balcony around the common area where the cool kids stood, watching what was happening below. You could hear the loud greetings, humorous interactions and general mischief hurled from the second floor to the bystanders below. I was one of the unpopular creatures, choosing to keep to the bench under the stairs – hidden away from view so as not to be noticed or required to interact with anyone.

My cohort of misfit friends and I didn't extend beyond school. We spent little to no time together once we went home. One by one, even those friends found a new clique, whether it be band, choir or sport, and I felt more and more on the outside. For a while I did have one friend, Kim, who lived up the street. I spent a lot of time at her house after school, listening to ABBA or Heart. We knew all the words to *Barracuda* and loved to dance around her room, singing it at the top of our lungs. But even that ended. As soon as she could drive, she was mobile and moved on to band commitments and other friendships.

At school, I regularly lost time. It was not uncommon for me to find myself panicking, standing at my locker between classes, unable to open the combination lock. I must have still had some awareness of my multiplicity because I would make myself take a deep breath and ask in my head for someone to help – and somehow, I would manage to open the lock. I let myself believe it was just an inner child thing. Looking back, I know it was one of *The Girls* who helped me. Was it a way for them to still play some vicarious part in my world? It didn't matter. I just wanted to be on time for class.

TEMPTED

I was desperate for friends with whom I could find a sense of identity and acceptance. Anything to get me away from home and the Parents. A large family moved in next door; their daughter Sally was my age, so I decided to try and make friends. Sally was nice enough, with striking long red hair and freckles. Her brothers and sisters, however, were overtly self-assured, with a swagger I found both intimidating and intriguing.

Almost every afternoon I would wander over and play jacks with Sally on their front porch. Sometimes her siblings would join us, swearing freely about how angry they were at their parents or how they hated school. There was always something pissing them off. Their language made my skin crawl, but I was drawn to their confidence. I wondered if I could be like them.

They turned me on to smoking. It was the acceptable thing and I felt pressure to conform so I could continue to be part of their inner circle. I didn't have a job, which meant I always had to bum cigarettes from them. They didn't seem to mind, and I felt like it affirmed my place with them. I would laugh quietly as we cursed and took long drags on our cigarettes. I thought I had found a place to be accepted, even if it was uncomfortable from time to time. I was being rebellious, doing something a kid of fifteen shouldn't. It was exciting.

And then came the opportunity to experiment with pot. Tommy, the oldest, asked me if I'd ever had weed before. I said I had. It was a lie, but I was afraid of being rejected by these new friends. He pulled out a joint and lit up. I barely took a hit as the joint was passed around the circle. They seemed to accept my façade; my cover wasn't blown.

A few days later we were walking down to Debra's house. Debra was another girl from school, and a full-on badass. She could always be found in the smoking area outside at school, or home on suspension for breaking something or starting a fight. I shouldn't have been surprised when Sally and her siblings made friends with her. For me, I saw Sally as a shield from people like Debra. I was wrong. When Debra came out of her house she sauntered straight up to me, taking a hit off the joint she held in her hand.

'So you smoke pot,' she sneered.

'I've done it a few times,' I said defensively. My legs turned to jelly. I was cornered and called out.

'Fuckin' bullshit. There is no way you've smoked weed.' She handed me the joint. 'Prove it.'

I took it from her, I'm sure my hands were shaking. I held it up to my lips and took a weak drag.

'Oh, you are so full of crap. I don't believe you.' She looked at the others. 'She's full of shit you know. She's lying.'

What Debra said was law. They teased me for a minute and then left me out on the lawn. Shoulders slumped, I walked home, rejected by yet another group of friends when I so desperately wanted to be accepted. I sighed. This was normal for me. I was isolated as a child and never really had any friends, so as a teenager I almost expected the same to happen. But that didn't make me any less lonely.

UNEXPECTED GRACE

Teachers were always busy and overworked, and certainly didn't take any interest in me, almost invisible on the fringes, and usually with poor grades. I was surprised then when the journalism teacher did the opposite. On a whim (another thing very out of character for me) I signed up for Yearbook as an elective. I found myself in love with writing and laying out images to tell a story. It was fun and something I did well. This teacher registered my interest and invited me to work on the editorial staff. As she proudly told me, I was the youngest, most promising student she had ever invited onto staff. I was thrilled to be noticed. I received several state awards for my page design layouts. Being able to do something well was a thought I had never let myself consider before. This was the highlight of my academic life, a teacher who actually invested in me.

Which is why, when the announcement came over the school PA that there would be try-outs for a play, I was surprised that I wanted to give it a go. Maybe it was the fulfilment I had found with the Yearbook that gave me the courage. I wanted to believe I could do something more. I nervously attended the auditions, sure

I wouldn't get a part. My heart leapt when I looked at the cast list posting the next day. I would be playing a maid in the one-act high school remake of *Taming of the Shrew*. It was a small, funny part with a few hilarious lines. I had so much fun. This unexpected willingness to move outside my comfort bubble was a significant moment in my life, it reinforced my freedom. I was beginning to create my own life outside of home and the Parents.

Amongst the cast were two other students, Brad and Dave. Athletic, friendly and smart guys, two years ahead of me in school. I was surprised they befriended me. They would talk to me at rehearsals, treating me like anyone else. Rehearsals were often long and outside school hours. It meant I was away from the never-ending tension of home life, developing a new circle of friends. Brad and Dave would wave and say hi at school – to them I wasn't an unwanted misfit. They were simply friends. I was a moth to a flame, chuffed at their interest in me and drawn to their generous spirits.

It was against this backdrop of real friendship, something beyond my comprehension, that I was introduced to the concept of faith, God, and unconditional love. Both of them told me how God had changed their lives and what He meant to them. Of course they struggled, but God was their rock, the one thing they could count on. Having learnt to instinctively distrust everyone, Dave and Brad's willingness to walk alongside me, a school reject, without judgement, was living out this mysterious 'God love' thing they talked about.

They invited me to church, opening my eyes to other normal relationships. With Dave and Brad by my side, I would attend church and experience a community in which people cared for and supported each other. I made friends. It didn't matter that I was ugly and fat.

These new friends wanted to talk to me about God and what He could do in my life. It was something else completely. For the first time in my life I felt safe.

Brad and I were talking outside school one morning when he challenged me to look seriously at faith and what it could mean to me. We sat down in the grass at the side of the school. 'You know, God is more than a church or a community. It's about a personal relationship with Him. No matter what problems you might have, He will be there for you - if you trust Him. Do you think you could do that?'

I thought about the people I'd been introduced to, and how kind they were. Even more, they had a peace I yearned for. I wondered if this relationship thing Brad was talking about could be real. 'I think so. Maybe.'

'If you commit your heart to Him, He will take care of you. He will change your life and give you a new perspective.'

I nodded. I was unsure, of course. But the thought I could trust in God seemed too good not to try. The love I was experiencing from these friends was filling a deep yearning in my heart. And so it was, days before my sixteenth birthday, I embraced Christianity, accepting Christ into my heart.

When Father came home from work that day, I was standing in the kitchen. He put his briefcase down and let out a sigh after a long day at work. One look at me and his countenance became dark and menacing. I couldn't explain it. It was a seismic shift. He knew something had changed for me – I was no longer at his, or his friends' mercy.

They never touched me again.

When I reflect on that period of *our* life, I can see how I subconsciously began to change the way I dealt with being at home. I found a strength and security, feeling more sure in who I was. And while *The Girls* were not a part of my conscious life, I am sure they felt safer and more secure too. I knew things could be different and began pulling away from my family. It was the beginning of an inner fortitude, propelling me into new relationships and a life in which abuse was not the norm. I immersed myself in this world of faith and God, in which who I was, with all my faults and failures, was accepted. The seeds of self-worth had been planted.

HALF LIFE

This newfound sense of worth enabled me to take baby steps deeper into my church community and away from the emotional minefield at home. But it didn't solve everything. I wasn't being abused anymore, but like a ghost half-life, my past wouldn't, or couldn't leave me alone. *The Girls* were still anxious and stressed. So I did what I had learnt to do – I dissociated. I simply pulled the curtain down over my history and forgot. I left *The Girls* to hold our past, while I tried to find some way to live a life that was simply – more.

In school, I became more involved with the journalism group, which also buoyed my sense of worth. I became a senior section editor and continued to receive awards for my work. I also focused on the stage, gaining parts in several plays, and performing poetry and prose at numerous area competitions. I hid my family life from everyone I knew and it was these activities which got me through.

At home, I lived with a simmering current of unease. I was terrified of any possible relationship with the Parents, of any demands they might place on me. As I looked to the future, I didn't want them to be involved in my life in any way. My goal was simple; finish school and leave them far behind. This is what fuelled my days as I began dreaming and thinking about a life of freedom without them.

My childhood was gone, hidden behind a thin gauze of growing anxiety and conflict. Memory fallible, the past disappearing.

TWO HOUR WINDOW

During my last year of school I would come home after class and park my old forest green Toyota Celica in our driveway. I relished those hours before my parents would get home from their jobs. This was my two-hour window, a sanctuary between the chaos of school and the insanity of parents, a place to be free.

    I had a routine. After I parked the car, I would walk to the mailbox and go through the contents. I was always curious about the junk mail and I wondered which of the numerous bills would cause Father to get angry. How would he demonstrate his fury this time? Would it be the quiet mutter as he drank his whisky and wrote out cheques, or would he yell because of some indulgent purchase Mother had made? At least once a month after dinner he would take over the dining room table, lay out various check books and reams of paperwork, where he would sit late into the night, grumbling under his breath. Both Mother and I knew to avoid him on bill night.

    One day I stood in the driveway, riffling through the various envelopes and froze. In my hand was a private letter from my high school, addressed to my parents. My gut slid up into my throat, nerves spasmed through my body. I couldn't think of anything I'd done wrong. Had I failed another class? Lost time? Been truant?

I desperately wanted to open the envelope, I needed to know what was in it. My fingers hovered over the gum seal on the back. I knew it was a federal offence to open mail not addressed to me and I was hypervigilant about obeying rules. I weighed up the options. On one side, the truth of another school failure and the retribution from the Parents, on the other, the ludicrous fear of federal prison. What I learned was that I was more afraid of the Parents than the law. Without hesitation, my fingers teased open the envelope. If I was gentle enough, I might be able to reseal it.

Dear Mr and Mrs ... I am pleased to inform you that your child will receive the Journalism Award at the Year End Assembly ... you are invited to attend ....

If my anxiety had been hovering at nine, it rocketed to twenty. This couldn't happen. Instinctively and without any hesitation, I ripped up the letter, pushing the shreds deep into the bin. My arm went elbow deep into the filth, ensuring these scraps of my other life were buried and unrecognisable in the stench of the garbage. Closing the lid, I could feel my heartbeat slowing down, normalcy returning. I breathed deep, satisfied another secret was hidden away. This was my solution for surviving. Remaining small and unnoticed meant I was left alone.

In the end, I was alone at the Year End Assembly. I received a Certificate of Achievement and a $50 check for my commendable work in the area of journalism. I mentioned it in passing later to the Parents, in case they heard about it from one of their friends. Father never acknowledged me. Mother, deep in her painting, said, 'Isn't that nice. I never knew you liked that sort of thing.'

RUN AWAY

I turned eighteen, graduated from high school, and enrolled at the University of Texas, a large institution with over 60,000 students in my hometown. I set my sights on becoming a journalist. I applied for and won a position on the University yearbook. It was a prestigious appointment, awarded on the basis of a letter of commendation from my journalism teacher and samples of my work. Even the supervisor acknowledged they didn't often make such appointments to first-year students. I was elated.

What I couldn't anticipate was how the academic rigors of university life would overwhelm me. I struggled with study and grades in high school, and the commitment required for tertiary study eluded me. After my first term, I was placed on academic probation. My grades had to improve or I would be asked to leave school. Shortly after this, I received notification from the Yearbook supervisor that I was being dropped from staff but could reapply once my grades improved. Deflated and overwhelmed, there was no improvement in my grades. I dropped out completely at the end of the term, giving up on a career built around journalism and the written word.

I worked for a while in a factory, making gadgets and gears. I clocked in and clocked out, a shift worker. The pay check gave me some financial freedom, but my new-found self-belief was shattered. I kept thinking I was a loser, incapable of accomplishing anything.

When I was not with friends or church community, I went out. Going to movies, driving around, up and down streets, anywhere. I preferred my own company, or this is what I told myself. I became a loner. Memories of my years of abuse were gone, held away from me in dark parts of my mind. But what I was able to forget was replaced instead by anger and emotional explosiveness, coming out of nowhere. Mother and I began having monstrous arguments as she tried to retain some sort of control over me, demanding I run errands for her and take her places. These arguments often took place in our kitchen, her playing the wounded puppy, me the screaming alley cat. I was sick of her demands and just wanted to be left alone. She would revert to manipulation, cajoling, and telling me she loved me. It fuelled my desperation to get away from her and the leech I felt she had become.

I attended a young adult Bible study group on Friday nights, and church on Sundays. This was my respite and only source of positive, nurturing engagement. One young couple in particular took an interest in me and I would spend evenings and weekends at their home, studying the Bible and feeling relaxed in their safe company. They were only home for the summer break and would be heading back to Colorado to continue their studies at a Bible college at the foot of the Colorado Rocky Mountains. 'Have you ever thought about doing further study in the Bible?' they asked one night over dinner. 'You could get a college degree and learn about the truth of what the Bible says. And see what God wants for your life.'

The idea of studying the Bible and exploring my faith in a deeply rich environment was intriguing. But even more appealing was the opportunity to get away from the Parents, the arguments and residual influence they tried to have on my life. It was the freedom I craved and I jumped at the opportunity. I wanted to make my own way in the world. I gave no thought to the academic demands required. It didn't matter because I would be free.

So it was at the age of nineteen, behind the wheel of my old Toyota Celica, I ran away. The car was stuffed to the brim with personal belongings, clothes, a few books and my favoured stuffed toys, a small dewey-eyed puppy and a yellow and lime green snake.

I left behind a home I would never return to, other than the odd Christmas or summer visit. I was free. Or so I thought.

In the midst of this newfound independence, *The Girls* and the truth of my system remained hidden from my awareness. I was living my best life, without the constant fear of parental engagement. I made new friends, living on campus and socialising. I often went to the student union for coffee and a game of pool. *The Girls* were well and truly locked away in the deep recesses of my brain, as were any memories of abuse.

Instead, I lived with anxiety about my family, a constant presence at the back of my mind. But I refused, or was unable to look at it, reminding myself this was now my life, new friends in a new environment, without the interference of home. I'd run away, I'd done it. I had successfully suppressed my past, with no thought as to the ramifications this would eventually have on my life.

CURSED FREEDOM

I hoped when I moved away from home, I would find a place where I could pretend to be normal – where the unsettling dark shadows of a past I felt, but had forgotten, would not haunt me.

I lived in a dorm, no more than an army barracks, at this small Bible College on the backside of the Flat Irons outside of Denver, Colorado. I shared a bathroom with half a dozen other girls, and a common room where we hung out.

My roommate was Tracy, and we couldn't have been more different. I was a slob, couldn't care less if the bed was made or things put away. But when I went to class, my clothes were tucked in, ironed and clean – I met the school's rigid dress code. Tracy on the other hand, would roll out of bed ten minutes before class and didn't care what she looked like. But her side of the room was fastidiously tidy. We had several arguments over this; I think secretly, I enjoyed irritating her. As a local, she was often out with friends. I was content to stay in our room listening to a mix of Tina Turner, Bon Jovi or Lionel Richie, with a bit of Bach or Beethoven on the side. Tracy and I tolerated each other. It was a running joke in our dorm.

I was intent on studying primary education. I didn't really have a passion for it, but I knew it would be a guaranteed job. Instead of studying though, I would be drawn to the school auditorium, tinkering on the grand piano. These late nights reminded me how much I loved music, and that it had always stayed with me in some form or fashion. I treasured these evenings alone in the school hall, losing myself in a world of music.

One of the music professors heard me playing and encouraged me to look at studying music as part of my degree, and to think about combining music and education. He was another teacher who wanted to nurture my academic life. This encouragement led me to eventually change programs.

But I was still not prepared for the rigors of study. I couldn't focus. I tried, but discovered studying was indeed hard. I would stare blankly at a text on Ancient History, unable to find a reason to get the assignment done. I would tell myself I was stupid and couldn't do anything right. I tried to give myself a break, but I was barely passing my classes. I ignored these tell-tale signs that something was amiss.

In spite of this, my life was much more up than down. I made friends, and even got a job in the campus kitchen to help pay some of my bills. This meant when the Parents called, I didn't have to ask for money and could skirt around any obligations to them. I was getting to know other students who were just as wide-eyed and wondering about the road ahead as me. I almost felt normal.

I noticed boys for the first time, made friends with guys and even had a not-so-secret crush on one or two. But in my heart, I knew I was not desirable. I was fat and ugly. Thinking this way triggered memories of me as an obese child, which was another aspect of my past I had successfully pushed away. And true to form, boys did not look at me in any sort of romantic way. I was a mate, a buddy, a pal. Watching all the other girls go out on dates, I accepted this as my destiny. It was easier to stay in my dorm room, isolated, eating chocolate or candy or whatever I could find to shovel into my body to help me feel better about myself. I liked fat. Fat was my friend.

I would get regular calls from the Parents. I was fine, they were fine, everything was fine. But of course it was a pretence, as if we were playing the game of happy family.

'Coming home for Christmas?' Mother would ask.

'Sure, for a week or so.'

'It will be so lovely to see you.'

Out of a sense of obligation, I did go home at Christmas. But these few weeks were the limit of my endurance. The more time I spent away from them, the more they seemed to cling to me, especially Mother. When I was around them my anxiety was ballistic, and I couldn't explain it. It was as if my body held some visceral knowledge my mind could not access. For the most part, I shoved the discomfort aside. It made me edgy.

I returned to school and started skipping classes and distancing myself from friends.

I went home during the first summer break. But I made sure it was a short stay and quickly rejoined the handful of students who stayed on campus for the summer. We would occasionally meet up in the student union for a game of pool. But while I was away from the Parents, apart from church, I still led a self-protective solitary life, working and taking hikes across trails where I would drink in the warmth and beauty of a Colorado summer.

During my second year, things changed. I moved into a new, small dorm, a house in effect, and had my own room. I still struggled with academic life but decided to pay attention in class and study harder. I did try, but would still get angry and frustrated because no matter what I did, it seemed I just couldn't focus. It was impossible.

Then I met Kate. I was walking towards my house on a beautiful sunny day at the start of term and saw her sitting on the steps of her dorm. She was a new student, so I said hi. She looked at me, her blond curls blowing in the wind, long legs stretched out in front of her, soaking in the warmth of the sun. Her eyes smiled before she did. We exchanged pleasantries. She had transferred in from another school in the Midwest but was Canadian. I asked her where she was from.

'Calgary,' was her flat response.

'In Alberta, right? My family once looked at living in a place just outside of Calgary.'

She gave me a quizzical look.

'Medicine Hat, just outside of Calgary, yeah?'

'Yes, it is.' She seemed surprised.

'What?'

'Oh, it's just not many Americans know Calgary is even in Canada, let alone that it's in Alberta, or that Medicine Hat is nearby.'

'Oh well. Guess that explains it. I'm not American. My family migrated to the States from England when I was young.'

We both laughed, and then she slid over and invited me to sit next to her. We talked about classes we were taking, who she had met, the school she had come from and what life was like in The Great White North. We found common ground while enjoying the sunshine. This instant comfort of easy conversation would prove to stay with us. This was the start of what became a lifelong friendship.

Kate was a quiet extrovert, academically astute, fastidiously neat and tidy and not afraid of anything. We couldn't have been more different, but it didn't matter. She said I was interesting, I told her she brought out my adventurous side. We spent many late nights in the student union, playing cards or pool. We were honest with each other (brutally at times). She had a way about her guys found intriguing, I told her she attracted boys like a moth to a flame. I was horribly jealous, but our relationship survived. Others were surprised at our bond because we were such opposites. I didn't see us as opposites, but for whatever reason, Kate and I just clicked.

A highlight for us in those early years was a trip to the Philippines. A missionary group came to the school, talking about the work they were doing and the opportunity to spend an extended summer in the Philippines, working and living with the locals. Kate and I caught up after class the same day and couldn't stop talking about the opportunity. We were both excited about the prospect of living and working deep in another culture. We applied to go, and when approved, chose to work on separate teams, coming together in our breaks to share the diversity of our experiences. These mini breaks were precious moments of re-connection and storytelling for Kate and me. We were both posted to the island of Luzon. Kate worked in Baguio, a city in the mountains, while I was in a beach-side rural area called Dagupan City. We worked in churches, talking about faith and helping practically where we could. We both came away with memories that were etched on our hearts.

I fell in love with the Filipino people, determined I would one day return to live there. I had slipped easily into the relaxed lifestyle.

But it was the needs of the children which haunted me. So many had no home, no parents. These children mostly lived on the street. They had the right to a family. My heart was full of love for the Filipino people, and I was determined – or perhaps, had the dream – of one day adopting a child from the Philippines.

Kate was an important part of the ups and downs of my college life. I loved the way she made me laugh, a lot, something which wasn't a part of my life growing up. My friendship with Kate allowed me to see the possibility of such a thing for my future relationships. Laughter and joy.

Still, nothing could stop the anger inside me, a molten volcano of emotions I could not control. I would get frustrated at the rules and regulations of the Bible College, from curfews and study hours to the demerit points if I didn't leave my room neat and tidy or failed to complete my communal chores. I wanted freedom, but instead, felt controlled. I would get angry and lash out at housemates for no reason. I would wake up in cold sweats from nightmares I couldn't remember, or I simply couldn't sleep at all. I would run away, leaving campus after curfew, not letting my resident adviser know where I was.

I wasn't surprised when I was called into the Women's Dean's office. She had recently taken an interest in me and would ask how I was doing when she saw me on the school grounds. Kathy was a nice woman, but intimidating. She had authority, and I found this unsettling. It didn't help she was perky, pretty and dressed impeccably. I couldn't help but compare myself to her. Guaranteed failure.

Kathy was not one to beat around the bush. I had broken rules, and she was worried about me. It seemed I was having anger and authority issues, was there any way she could help? I said I was sorry and would get my act together. Then she got to the point. Because I had broken several school rules, they wanted me to see someone. By which she meant a counsellor or therapist, someone who could help me understand my behaviour. It was in my best interest, she said, and she was sure in the long run it would help. Kathy slid a piece of paper across her desk with the name and phone number of someone to call.

I was seething inside. I had moved away from home but was still trapped by rules and expectations. I couldn't see that Kathy was trying to help me. I was confused. I thought I had escaped the emotional bondage of home to live some great new life. But I was still a fraud and a failure, even as I moved away from the clutches of my family. I did not understand that the murk of my hidden past was affecting me. I was in limbo. Safe, but still living in fear.

SHRINK #1

I went to therapy, not because I wanted to, but because I feared being forced to leave College. This would mean I had to go home. I would lose my freedom. I chose the fear of therapy over the threat of going home.

At the age of twenty I began a relationship with the therapeutic community which would last a lifetime. I walked into Shrink #1's office for the first time, terrified, not knowing what to expect. I made assumptions that the school had told him what a complete screw up I was, believing he would be determined to undermine me. Choosing to see this man, I thought, was setting myself up for a life of continued failure.

I was wrong.

Shrink #1 was a nice guy. He was tall and lanky with deep laugh lines, smiling eyes and a long beak of a nose. His mature age was only given away by his salt and pepper hair. He was a truly gentle soul. He asked me for a hug at the end of each session. Apparently, that's what you do, or so I thought. I was uncomfortable the first week, but soon adjusted to these hugs with no agenda, no requirement for anything at all. He was simply being kind.

We would talk regularly about the pressure I was feeling from the Parents and my inability to focus on my studies. And, apart from Kate, my inability to have any deep friendships. I am sure he identified my trust issues and was simply waiting for me to engage. I had no memory of my history, so instead I was pissed off at the world for reasons I didn't understand. Round and round on a carousel, turning and turning at the same continuous, monotonous speed.

He encouraged me to participate in a therapy group he ran, assuring me it was an opportunity to realise I wasn't alone in my struggles. I joined the group, but always felt uncomfortable in this room full of misfits and undesirables. I was convinced I was the only sane person. I got along with a few people, but they weren't friendships which lasted.

However, I did get to know George. George was flamboyant and had a strong Italian streak which meant when he talked (and he talked a lot), he spoke with his hands. We would hang out, go to movies, and have the odd drink at his Denver inner-city very hip art deco apartment. We sat around for hours as he used me as a sounding board to talk about his gay lifestyle and the relationship issues he was having. In the end he started telling me about an abusive relationship he was in, and how it related back to his own father. I was amazed at how he tied all his relationship and identity issues to his father. I listened, because that's what friends do right? It was easier to stay quiet as he talked so casually about his family dynamics, when in truth, it made me uncomfortable. George dared to ask if my own anxiety over my family could be related to an abusive history. I dismissed this summarily, but quietly I wondered if there could be some truth to it, afraid to admit what wrestling with this might mean.

As I think about these early years in therapy, I wish I could have told myself to hold on. To seek healing, rather than running away from a darkness I could not identify. I would have said therapy is a brave risk, a choice to gradually move toward wholeness, where I could understand who I was and begin to believe in myself. An intrinsic hope, knowing there could be more – more joy, more purpose – just more. Daily, gradual, baby steps in the healing process.

For the lucky ones, the healing process is straightforward. Identify roadblocks. Wrestle monsters. Slay dragons. Locate inner strength. Move on. This would not be my path. My relationship with therapy would be lifelong. I did not know when I started how deeply wounded my soul was. For me, therapy would not be a straightforward journey.

Anxiety and anger were my intimate friends – because they were familiar. My foes, instead, were those people who tried to care about me – they were the monsters in my life. Trust was not something I was capable of. The belief had been seared into me that no-one – *no-one* – could really be trusted. Layers of pain I was yet to remember, beasts of chaos leaving me hypervigilant – these were my dearest friends, simply because I knew them so well.

My soul had been so decimated, just choosing this process of therapy was its own horrific hell.

The group wrapped up and we went our separate ways, each of us still an oddity. I fulfilled my obligation to the school to seek help and made a solid attempt to control my anger, stay in class, and not disappear without warning. I assumed this was the whole purpose of seeing Shrink #1. But from my perspective, nothing changed. I ticked off the requirement to get help, which meant I could stay in school – and this meant I didn't have to go home. I retained my freedom.

BROKEN DREAMS

I wasn't capable of the commitment required for academia, and eventually left school one course short of a degree. Between the classes and expectations of emotional growth, it was all too much. I told myself it didn't matter, pretending I didn't care, but really I thought I had failed completely and was ashamed. While others were furthering their education or working in ministry, all I wanted to do was find a job and make money. I thought this would give me the freedom to cut the strings of financial assistance that kept me tied to the Parents.

I stopped therapy when I left school. Shrink #1 met a need. I appreciated his compassion, and in retrospect, I did therapeutically attach to him. But trust was at the heart of my problems, and kept me from getting anywhere. I wasn't prepared to delve further into the topic of how uncomfortable discussions about my family made me. It was no surprise that after sessions when he enquired specifically about my family I felt slightly unhinged.

After I left college, I stayed in Denver, cementing my freedom and continuing my affair with the Colorado Rockies. I loved the snowy, blustery cold winters in front of fires, and hot chocolate to warm me through. I kept up the relationships with people I knew from church when I was at college, and now I was out of school, got involved with the young adults' groups. We enjoyed punk music, and sing-along versions of the *Sound of Music* at the local midnight theatre. A few of us would go regularly to the movies or out for drinks and dancing. I made friends with a girl called Jane. We had a number of similar interests and shared a love of having friends over. She was slightly older than me, very relaxed and easy to get along with. I really liked her. It was an easy decision for us to move in together.

I found entry-level office work in a claims department of an insurance company. It paid the bills, just. My immediate supervisor was a woman named Myrtle. She was older, with a negative, dour personality. She took great joy in nit-picking everything I did. I came through the doors each day stealing myself for the inevitable dressing down I would receive. I did everything wrong in her eyes, and her management style could only be described as controlling. The phone had to be answered within two rings, and if I wasn't at my desk, I was expected to run and get it. No more than four case files could be waiting to be filed at any time, and my palms would sweat when she would examine case files I hadn't set up exactly right. Do it again, I would be told, with an exaggerated sigh. If she could find nothing to complain about, there were always the grunts and glares that reminded me I was not performing as required. There were days when I was running from task to task, just to keep her criticism and disapproving looks at a distance. I moved on in less than a year, to another insurance-related position, something where I earned slightly more money and was mildly appreciated.

Life went on. I still went out with friends from church, and Jane and I would socialise and have friends over, often while watching our beloved Denver Broncos play football. But the one thing my social life didn't include was men. Sure, they were friends, but there was never any romantic attachment. I had long ago accepted I was the ugly fat girl, who now apparently also had unresolved emotional problems, so I'd learnt not to expect any interest from the opposite sex.

During this time, I began to understand just how anxiety-ridden I was. I constantly worried about doing something to offend Jane. We navigated house duties, noise and keeping the house tidy, but I worried when she was distant, wondering what I had done to upset her. These things were always lingering around the edges of my mind. I wondered when I would be asked to move out. She was a paediatric oncology nurse, and the emotional pressure she was under at work didn't cross my mind. It didn't occur to me that working with children who had cancer would be hard on her and she just needed space to process. I couldn't see beyond my assumption that whatever was going on was my fault.

Kate returned to Canada. We talked on the phone often, regularly sending each other letters and cards, with photos or some little trinket reminding me of our friendship.

I took a trip to Calgary to see her one March, just before my twenty-fourth birthday. After a short stay in Banff to see the sights, we took off to Jasper, and spent a week hiking glaciers, roaming streams along the base of snow-covered Mount Robson and visited Athabasca Falls. The wildlife was stunning, from elk on the lawn of our hotel, to goats and sheep perched precariously on the side of a mountain. We also saw several black bears waking up from their winter hibernation.

But it was a lone grizzly bear which topped the trip. It was our last day, and we were doing a slow scenic drive down Highway 93 on our way back to Calgary. We noticed some cars had pulled over, so we joined them. Sitting in the middle of the road was an immense grizzly sunning itself, soaking in the warmth of the asphalt on this early spring day. Kate pulled out her long-distance lens so we could get a better look. Its claws were huge! This brown behemoth opened his eyes at one point, looked around, got up, and sauntered casually to the side of the road. He stood there for a few minutes and waited as a road train thundered past. Then he walked casually back to the middle of the road and sat down for another dose of Vitamin D. It was exhilarating to be up-close and personal with one of these creatures. Being with Kate and experiencing the beauty of the natural world was a breath of fresh air, one of those rare moments in my life when I felt I could really relax.

Holidays were always on the agenda for Kate and I. We tried to alternate locations. One year I would go to Canada, another we would head off somewhere unusual in the States. We always made time for the beaches when we were away. On Sanibel Island in Florida, we collected seashells by the dozen, seeing who would find the catch of the day – one shell which stood out from all the rest. We even went to the Cook Islands in the distant South Pacific, where we soaked up the culture, sun and sea.

Whatever we did, wherever we went, Kate and I had deep discussions about music, religion, and politics – and even my strained relationship with my family. Nothing was off limits. We laughed and enjoyed each other's company. She was the sister I never had. We spent many hours over dinner and drinks, discussing the intricacies of each other's lives.

Kate and I would reminisce about our summer in the Philippines. I wanted to go back, I would say to Kate, and anyone who would sit still long enough to listen. After coming back from the Philippines, I was sure I would not live the rest of my life in the States but would end up somewhere overseas. I couldn't explain it, it was simply something I knew as a gut truth.

My heart kept coming back to this belief I would live overseas. I applied to become part of an overseas mission organisation I admired, known both for its work translating unwritten languages to text, and its social justice projects with disadvantaged groups in developing countries. Their missionaries would go deep into tribal settings, where they would focus on providing Bibles in the local dialect. Religion aside, this was the only group I knew of who worked in the area of ethnomusicology, studying the significance of music in a language group's culture. Once a language had been translated to written form, the organisation would send in people to record the group's indigenous music so it could be preserved, along with their traditional stories. While I had failed at a music degree in school, I still had an intrinsic love of music and I think I saw this as a way to use that to help others.

The application process was arduous. I filled out reams of paperwork. I had to make a self-evaluation of my strengths and weaknesses, list any medical conditions and name the people to contact in the case of an emergency – all pretty typical requests. I had to write a short autobiography - which I kept quite light, skirting around uncomfortable facts about having been in therapy, or anxiety related to the family. A statement of faith and religious values was required as well as five references, including one from a pastor.

Then came boot camp. I drove out to California and spent six weeks with other applicants. Some were interested in career work, others in short-term two-year projects. All of us were keen to serve in developing countries. We lived in small bunk houses and came together for meals. We dived deep into studying the Bible and did group activities to see how we would function as part of a team. We also studied pidgin English, used by locals in many parts of the world, to see how adept we would be at learning new languages. The academic nature of this terrified me.

This was something I seemed to be drawn to, engaging in activities which despite my past failures, I had to try. I wish I could say I had hope, or the tenacity to overcome these historical failings. But I didn't. I think I chose to attempt things that I'd failed in the past, hence trapping myself in a cycle of worthlessness, ensuring my failure followed me. I still couldn't connect the dots between my buried history and the need to fail and despise myself.

In the last week of boot camp, I had an interview with the Human Resources Director, a man named Ken. The purpose of this was to go over my application, discuss any questions the organisation or I might have, and to clarify what the next step would be after I left camp. This should have been a straightforward process. Ken invited me into his office and we went through my application. Everything was in order – my statement of faith was accepted and my academic record, while not the best, would not be a hindrance. And then he asked about my references.

'Did your referees agree to write these for you?'

'Yeah. They all said they were happy to do it.'

Ken was looking at the papers in front of him and then put them down and looked at me. 'I have to tell you, I've never seen this before.'

'I'm not sure I understand,' was all I could muster.

'All of your referees have basically said the same thing.' He paused and gave me an apologetic look. 'None of them feel like they know you well enough to provide a reference.' He flipped through his notes. 'Some of them have made brief attempts at answering some questions, but for most questions, they've simply said they don't know.'

'What?'

And then, thoughtfully and carefully, 'All of them have said, in their own way, they did not feel like they knew you well enough to answer the questions.' Another pitiful look. 'I'm so sorry.'

I went numb. I felt like I was watching my life fall apart.

'We sat down as a committee,' he continued. 'And we don't feel it would be fair to you to accept you into the program while you have, well, unresolved issues.' And then, as if to hold out a carrot, 'But please, once you feel like you are in a better place with your life, and perhaps after you have talked to your referees for clarification, feel free to reapply.'

I walked out of his office blindsided. It took a while for it all to sink in, then I gradually began to let myself feel betrayed by people I thought were my friends. People I hung out with and knew me personally, these people who had said to my face they were happy to be a referee. I was angry. They were cowards. How could they do this? I did eventually find the courage to ask one of them why they hadn't been honest with me. I didn't get a straight answer. All they could say was they understood what they had done and were deeply sorry they had hurt me and hoped I could forgive them.

I did not understand the root issue behind what had happened. Even without consciously acknowledging my history to others, I still lived a semi-dissociative life which meant people around me didn't really know who I was.

This experience hounded me. I tracked back through my life, trying to figure out what was wrong. My childhood was a mystery. There were niggles of darkness and barely visible memories of Christmases past and the odd holiday. I told myself that people just don't remember their childhood. I was sure this was all part of becoming an adult and establishing my own identity. Nothing unusual.

But the inability of these people to give me a reference made no sense. What did it mean that they felt they didn't know me well enough? I had never seen myself as distant and aloof. If anything, I was the opposite – too open, too emotional. I was hurt and wounded. But I knew I didn't have the right to feel that way. Something inside reminded me I was a failure, and I knew it. So, which was it? Was I betrayed by people who couldn't be honest with me, or was I simply a horrible person? I did not understand and could not talk about it to anyone. I simply sat with it and let it eat at me, unresolved.

And so it was, after a few false starts and broken dreams, I left the glorious Colorado Rockies and landed in the endless flat landscape of North Texas. I had made arrangements to live in Dallas after boot camp, with the assumption I would be starting my training at their Dallas headquarters. I had no intention of going back to Colorado. I could not face those people who had betrayed me. I spent the drive between California and Texas mulling over this rejection, trying to pick apart my failures. But it was the same old story. I was a fat, ugly, anxiety-ridden person who would never be good enough. And now I had the references (or lack thereof) to prove it.

TAKE TWO

I was a planner. I liked knowing what was happening and when. It felt safe. So I put a plan in place before leaving boot camp. I stayed with friends in the Dallas area, getting involved in their church, and social circles. I looked forward to the respite these new surrounds and friends could offer. I had no intention of admitting my failure so I kept my story simple, without sharing how I had been rejected. I was mulling it over, I would say, still trying to decide what I really wanted to do. I said it with enough confidence to convince everyone around me, including myself.

I landed on my feet almost instantly. I was approached by a woman at church. There was a job opening where she worked, a medical mission organisation. Maybe I would like to apply for this role? It would be working for one of the regional directors named Steve. Why not? It was a tangible social justice group making a difference in people's lives. I waltzed through the interview process. Maybe this would be the opportunity to redeem my life, I told myself.

I also found a roommate, moving into a well-located apartment near work. Audrey and I met at church, she needed a roommate, I needed a place to live. It was a good solution for both of us. Audrey's job required her to be clothes conscious. I was fascinated by the way she transformed when she put on something stylish. She was immediately confident and professional. She showed me catalogues full of beautiful clothes, saying my weight didn't matter, page after page of fashionable clothing for larger women. Suddenly I had a closet full of chic suits with shoes to match, and a credit card bill to prove it. I was not good at managing money, and like everything else I couldn't handle, simply ignored it. I kept telling myself I looked good, so it didn't matter.

I enjoyed my work, my boss and my co-workers. I told myself perhaps this was my calling, answering phones and typing letters, knowing my background work supported real change by medical teams across Central and South America. My boss, Steve, was not only a dynamic speaker, but a generous person as well. He invested in medical students, encouraging them, challenging them to consider using their skills as medical missionaries. I was part of something bigger than me that was changing lives and making a difference.

Between church and my work, I was settling into a new life. The missing piece of the puzzle was family. I failed to appreciate the pull they would have on me now I was back in Texas.

I lived four hours from them, so it was impossible, rude even, not to see them. I would talk to them on the phone, hearing the same old question: when would I come for a visit? They missed me, they said. Both of my brothers lived in the area now. Surely I wanted to see them and my niece and nephews as well? I forced myself to drive down, keeping visits short, a weekend at best. This was how I controlled my circumstances. The entire visit would be spent wanting to escape Mother's suffocating clutches. I would imagine her bony hands wrapping around my arm refusing to let go. It was a terrifying feeling. With Father, well, I was just uncomfortable.

I was not sleeping well, binge eating and getting angry, a lot. I was trying desperately to control my life in Dallas, find something, at least, that made sense and gave me some stability. In the midst of this, I received an envelope from the mission group which had rejected me. Enclosed were the references and an official letter stating what I already had branded on my heart. I wasn't good enough, I should come back later when I had my shit together. That was how I took it. Although the words were more considered and sensitive, it didn't change the fact I had been rejected.

I became friends with Tina at my office. We were similar ages and had fun going to movies, followed by deep, meaningful conversations about God and even, to a certain extent, family. I desperately wanted to trust her. We talked about our mutual desire to work overseas. I told her I wanted to go, but gave her my safe answer: now didn't seem to be the right time. Part of me wanted to believe my life didn't have to be about failure, and if I shared the humiliation of this rejection, someone might care. I took a risk and showed Tina the paperwork I'd received and told her the gist of my story.

She barely looked at the paperwork and said, 'Come with me.' She grabbed a metal garbage bin and a book of matches, and we went outside. She put the bin on the driveway and gave me the matches. 'Burn it.'

'What?'

'Burn the paperwork. It's your past. Focus on the future. Burn it and put it behind you. You don't need it in your life.'

I did what Tina said. We celebrated with takeout Chinese and talked about the future. I wanted to believe it was that simple. That with a puff of smoke, something that had destroyed me could be gone.

It was time for my first employment review. I was sure it would be a breeze, Steve was relaxed, and always saw things as a team effort. We talked about how my work was fine but could use some quality checking. (Editing was not my thing.) I got along well with the people he brought into the office and made a good impression, an extension of his own care for others. I had learned the ropes quickly and he appreciated my efforts.

Then he put the paperwork down and asked me a simple question, 'Have you ever thought about seeing a therapist who could help you?' A pregnant pause. Was some sort of deja vu going on? He continued, 'Others have mentioned you have anger and self-management issues. I was wondering if you had thought about seeing someone to help you?' He said it so thoughtfully and kindly. Apparently, I was short and demanding with staff, not showing enough kindness. I really needed to learn to hold my tongue.

My heart sank. I was devastated. How could anger and authority issues still be affecting me?

What I hadn't understood was how being near my family triggered my outbursts. My body knew it, my emotions knew it, my brain hadn't put two and two together. All I could see was that I was being judged and condemned as a failure, again.

Steve continued. He was generally happy with my work and

delighted to have me as part of the team. He handed me a piece of paper with the names of a few therapists on it. It was as if I was back at Bible College, trapped, caged, again. These were people he knew personally and believed they could be a great support for me.

This time, there was no requirement to do this to keep my job. But there was an expectation, because after all, didn't I want to grow and mature? My boss, an authority figure in my life, had identified and ripped back the curtain on issues I thought were long gone.

SHRINK #2

And so it was I found myself in the office of Shrink #2. He was a short, balding man with a dark beard, who wore a suit and tie. Beyond this conventional, if not stereotypical appearance, I would soon learn he was a mixture of kind and direct, with a strong dose of Freud thrown in.

I was much more suspicious this time. Therapy hadn't fixed me before, why would it now?

'I'm here because my boss thinks I have anger management issues.'

'Okay. Why don't you tell me about that?'

'I guess I get angry. A lot.'

And then nothing. Silence. Some weeks I could spend an entire session not saying anything, refusing to engage in the process. Yep, anger management issues.

After several weeks, he quietly suggested, 'Do you ever write?'

This was different. 'I used to, but not anymore.'

'Would you be willing to try something for me?'

I shrugged my shoulders. It was the closest I could get to begrudgingly acquiescing to his request.

'Could you write how you're feeling in a notebook? A journal maybe? Just write what's going on each week and how you feel. Then you could bring it in and let me read it, so I can understand what's going on. So I can help. Would writing be something you could do?'

How could I say no? 'Okay. Maybe.'

#2 hit on something. I bought a small notebook and started to write. At first it was innocuous, small insignificant things happening each day. But gradually, something began to blossom and I started writing about my fears, random thoughts, anything really. It felt liberating, getting this inner turmoil on paper and out of my head.

I began writing like a madwoman, putting down all sorts of thoughts and feelings in this little book I willingly shared with #2. In fact, I looked forward to showing it to him. Somehow, through this journal, I was communicating those things that were important to me. Just the process of writing was freeing. I wrote weekly, daily, sometimes morning and night. Capturing on paper those things which caused me to become unhinged. I wrote about family, about unexplainable anxiety. I wrote to help #2 understand me. I made this attempt because I wanted to believe maybe, just maybe, things could change.

#2 remained ever stoic. His countenance was reliable and consistent, something I had come to expect each week. I kept thinking he would get bored with all this nonsensical writing, but he plodded through, asking for clarification if he couldn't read my somewhat illegible handwriting, and then ask me questions. Insightful and thoughtful questions based completely on what I was writing.

What became evident was the pattern of emotions and experiences I was having. Moving back to Texas, the phone calls and pressure by my family to spend time with them was putting me in an emotional tailspin. I was on a carousel of family and anger, family and fear, and family and more anger. #2's goal was to try to not only control the speed of this carousel, but help me find a way to get off it as well. It wasn't really working for one simple reason: I couldn't predict when my anger and anxiety would overtake me. This was a mystery yet to be unravelled.

I was out driving one day, on one of the long meandering drives I would take to clear my head. I don't remember if I was thinking about work or family or just listening to music, but my mind was distracted. And then I had an unexpected sensory experience. I was so completely overwhelmed I had to pull over to the side of the road to recover.

I felt like I had a sticky, gooey mess all over my face and shoulders. I panicked and tried to frantically wipe it away; it was like someone had ejaculated on me. Looking at my hands, I knew it wasn't real – but it absolutely felt real. I used anxiety techniques #2 had told me about to try and centre myself. Deep breathing ... in, 2, 3, 4 ... hold 2, 3, 4 ... out 2, 3, 4 ... repeat. Identify objects around me which I could see, smell, and hear. I was terrified for reasons I could not put a finger on, but the exercises were helping me feel safe again. I went home and wrote this experience out in detail, page after page in my journal about how it felt, and how confused it made me. It was as if by putting it in writing, I could allow myself to forget about it until I went to therapy, where #2 and I could unpack it.

My self-protective armour began to melt away. Suddenly, #2 and I were talking about abuse. He never pushed, just sought clarification regarding the things I wrote in my journal. Like a weaver of fine tapestry, we were trying to pull the threads of this mysterious rug of my life back together, make sense of what had happened. But there was still no detail, nothing I could remember to indicate that I had been abused. It was all still a mystery. I kept on writing.

I became inseparable from my journal. It was as if a three-way relationship had started between my journal, myself, and #2. I always found the space and time to write. I was creating something to help me understand who I was and what was ripping me to shreds with these questions about an unknown history. I spent late nights at my kitchen table, classical or jazz piano playing over the stereo, candles my only light. I wanted to feel safe and cocooned, create a mood to give me the space and openness to discover unknown secrets in my soul. And, if I was really needing to pour out my heart after a particularly difficult day or inexplicable outburst, I would end up on the floor next to the speakers, Barber's *Adagio for Strings* strumming through my head, inspiring me as I wrote, trying to find something to make sense of the dark recesses in my memory.

Poetry was flooding out of me. I had a vague memory of being very interested in the lyricism of this style of expression when I was in high school. It was a torrent now. Some were a painful expression of how much I hated myself, while others held the promise of hope. I found a renewed sense of my spiritual self as I wrote this poetry, not reliant on the dictatorial mandates of a rigid God, but built around my own personal relationship with Him, and what He meant to me.

Writing became an intrinsic part of my self-expression. I did not trust anyone with it, apart from #2. It was validating for me to have him read and discuss things with me. And even though there was no concrete memories or detail of abuse, I began to trust #2 to guide me through the process, whatever it might look like. This trust was a new experience for me, and I felt myself opening into deeper, hidden wounds the more I trusted him. I realised it was not so much about trusting #2 – although that was essential – it was about trusting myself to process the things we were discussing and rather than being trapped in them, move beyond them.

I Saw The Breath of God

I saw the breath of God today.
Caressing winds, marking seasons change.
Quietly kissing mountain meadows, tugging
tender on columbine blossoms
and dogwood petals.
Prying loose the glorious beauty that is,
turned to lingering memories of summer sunshine.

I saw the breath of God today.
Bright green aspen trees shedding summer coats.
Instead, brilliant shades of red, gold and rust
boldly declared the handiwork of their Creator.
Mountain sides burned their patchwork blaze.
Winter's white blanket descends on Creation.
This quiet, cold, bitter breath of God,
Frigid concealment of all signs of life
and the living.
Dark stillness, fresh snow gleaming,
Crisp vivid images of ice, dancing frantically,
knowing too soon, the sun will burn away winter's shroud,
their dance of ice stilled.

I saw the breath of God today.
A single blade of grass, struggling bravely
to burst through winter's frigid hold.

SPLIT

Streams breaking through icy blankets,
Slowly, then plunging wildly
down mountain sides, through valleys,
on this budding spring day.

I stopped today.
My thoughts lingering on the beauty of God.
The forming of a petal on a newly budding flower.
Life breaks forth each spring,
no regret, only joy and abandon.
Waiting to eagerly experience the sun's warmth
or refreshing spring rain.

And I wondered.
If He did all of this because He loves Creation,
How much more certainty have I in
His tender care for me?

TRUTH WILL OUT

I began to have unsettled dreams. Some held bizarre imagery of sex with machines, making me feel deeply ashamed. Things I was unable to share with #2, fearful of his rejection. But there was one recurring dream I couldn't shake. It wasn't about sex, but about a girl. In this dream, I was lying down, unable to fall asleep. I looked down, and next to me was a girl with her eyes closed. I could feel her body against my leg, the sense of physical contact quite visceral. This was unsettling, not because I was embarrassed, but because I was drawn to this child – I was curious about her. I finally wrote about it in my journal. My gut told me this was significant and needed to be discussed in therapy.

I sat quietly while #2 read my journal. This dream was on the fourth page of my weekly writing and I counted as his fingers turned each page, holding my breath. He stopped on page four, paused, and then moved on. This time, when he was finished, instead of returning my journal to me, he held it in his lap.

'Interesting dream.' Straight to the point. 'Often times we have dreams as a way of speaking to our inner child.'

'No,' I said. I was frustrated, I thought he was blowing it off. He didn't get it. 'This girl in my dream felt *real*.' And then to help make my point, I slapped my leg. 'I can feel her, right there.'

He was writing on his pad. Then he looked up. 'Can you describe her? This girl?'

I was confused, why was what she looked like important? I looked closely at this sad creature in my head, 'I dunno. Maybe eight or nine years old. Not sure.'

'Look closely, what is she wearing?'

'Filthy old clothes, a dress I think, with rips and holes.'

'What does she look like?'

'Her hair is brown, all knotted and tangled. There's dirt on her face.' I told him how she was clinging tightly to my leg and would stir occasionally, let out a whimper and then fall back asleep, exhausted.

#2 continued with his pointed questions.

'Does she look like you?'

'No. Not at all. Well, maybe a bit. She's pudgy.'

'Do you recognise her clothes? Does the dress look familiar?'

'No.'

'Do you recognise the location in your dream?'

I hesitated. 'No.'

'Are you sure?'

'Something feels familiar about the place, but no, I can't identify anything.'

'Does she have a name?'

My voice disappeared in a way that hadn't happened to me since I started writing. My vocal cords finally scratched out an answer, 'Yes.'

Gently, he asked, 'Can you tell me what it is?'

'*Middle Girl*. Her name is *Middle Girl*.'

He had enough information for this session. He handed me back my journal and said quite casually, 'Maybe you could try talking to her at some point? But only if you want to. I could talk to her too if you like.' Our session was done, but my brain went into overdrive contemplating the strange idea of talking to this sleeping fictitious child haunting my waking dreams.

In our next session, it was clear from the writing in my journal I had not tried to wake this girl or talk to her. The idea terrified me. Not so much #2.

'Did you think about my idea of talking to *Middle Girl?*' I cringed as he used her name. It made her something tangible, something more than a dream. 'Yeah, I thought about it. It just seemed too weird. And I didn't know what to do.'

'How would you feel about me talking to her?'

I wasn't sure I liked this either. It felt like it would be opening a box of secrets I wasn't supposed to know about. 'Not sure.'

'I can walk you through it, if you like.'

I sighed, running my fingers over the beige cushion on my lap and counting the seconds as they ticked past the clock on the wall. I always sat in the farthest corner of the couch with this cushion in my lap. Then I did the same thing over again.

Finally, I stopped. What he was asking seemed utterly bizarre yet made complete sense.

'Okay,' I said.

This time #2 sighed. He leaned back in his chair.

'Just look inside. Can you see her?'

'Yes.'

'Is she still sleeping?'

'Yes.'

'Why don't you try and touch her, as if you're trying to wake her up.'

I looked at her in my mind and put my hand on her shoulder and gently shook her. It was as easy as that. Suddenly she was awake, staring at me. And then she was staring at #2, through my eyes. #2 was looking at me, but not really, he was looking at her. I stepped aside and pushed her forward. Her breathing became heavy; she fidgeted with the tassels on the cushion in her lap, hunching her shoulders. With her body language, she was trying to make herself small, so she wouldn't be noticed.

'Hello,' #2 said in a soft voice.

She glanced at him briefly out of the corner of her eye, saying nothing.

'Are you *Middle Girl?*'

She nodded yes.

'I'm a friend of Annie's. Do you know Annie?'

Another nod yes.

'I'm wondering if you'd like to talk to me? About anything at all? Annie talks to me about her life and the things that happen. Would you like to talk to me too? Sometime?'

She looked around the room, fidgeted with the pillow, nervous, unsure. No answer.

'Well, that's okay. Just know you can talk to me whenever you want. Maybe just tell Annie. You could tell her, and she can let me know. I like helping people, and if you need help, it's what I'm here for. But only if you want.'

And she was gone. I felt a slight adjustment in my body, like everything re-centred, and then it was me.

'You okay?' he asked.

'Okay. I guess. Kinda weird maybe.'

'I just wanted to introduce myself to her. So she can know who I am if she wants to talk about anything that might be bothering her.'

'Yeah, okay. What do you mean? Are you talking to my inner child?'

He put his pen and pad down on the floor and said, '*Middle Girl* is not your inner child, but instead something called an *alter*.'

Then he asked if I had ever heard of something called Multiple Personality Disorder (MPD). What #2 explained was that sometimes, when children experience trauma, they simply go away in their minds, leaving someone else to deal with the experience. Victims of trauma often dissociate as a means of self-protection, but children have an innate creative ability to fragment their existence to the extent other distinct personalities can take over the body.

He said if *Middle Girl* had memories of any childhood trauma, it would be important for her to be able to work through them. It also made sense then, why I couldn't remember any trauma, apart from one fuzzy image of being ejaculated on. Those memories were being held somewhere else, by someone else. He encouraged me to educate myself about MPD, it would be an important part of my healing process. Read books, find articles on the subject, anything to help me understand what this meant for me.

#2 eventually did get *Middle Girl* to talk to him. In the end, it wasn't hard. She was afraid of a lot of things, but #2 didn't scare her. He was able to talk to her about her fears. She was always afraid 'they' would get her if she said anything. But she could never explain who 'they' were. Bad guys, big men, who would hurt her. This hurting was not something she was willing to explain.

And then one day, out of the blue, *Middle Girl* said, 'They hurt the other girls too.'

#2 explained this meant there were other alters. It was quite common for someone who was multiple to have a system – a group of alters to handle difficult circumstances. I had barely started getting my head around the fact this girl living in my head wasn't simply a manifestation of an inner child concept, but a concrete adaptation who lived through a traumatic childhood. And now, suddenly, there were others? Frankly, this seemed unhinged, psychotic even.

Week after week, #2 began to split his time in our sessions between talking to me, so I didn't become completely untethered, and talking to the girls about their lives. *The Girls.* This became the name for an ever-growing tribe of alters who apparently held everything about my history locked away in their minds.

Middle Girl became an immense resource of information. Not so much about her history of abuse, although she certainly did have her own story. She was more inclined to talk about how the system, *The Girls*, worked. She referred to the place where they lived as a house. This construct allowed them to exist together. When I looked in my head, I started seeing this house, an old country home, a bit run down, surrounded by a large field of yellow daisies, out in the middle of nowhere. My research and discussions with #2 indicated this house was some sort of representation of how the system of alters functioned and related to each other, and well, me.

I worked very hard during this time at having a life outside of therapy. I had my work, I focused on the odd holiday with Kate, did things with other friends and went to movies. I needed this *normalcy* to keep me connected to a life where deep processing of this crazy-making going on in my head wasn't required. Which is exactly how I saw it. I was convinced if anyone knew I was this thing called MPD, I would be labelled as insane. I kept it quiet, only occasionally telling my closest friends about being in therapy. If pushed, I would say I was seeing someone because of a history of abuse and I had PTSD. (Which was true – MPD is a form of complex PTSD.) But I never talked about MPD. I was afraid our friendships would be defined by this diagnosis and my friends would agree with my fears and see me as crazy.

My journal became *The Girls'* journal. They felt they could write (through me) about things that happened to them which could then be discussed with #2. They would scribble or draw, and some would write with their left hand (because they were punished for using their right). *The Girls* varied in age and in the experiences they had lived through. What was becoming clear was that life for *The Girls* was not linear. They lived, they *existed*, for specific purposes and roles. It wasn't just a father and mother who had emotionally and physically berated and tortured them, but Father's friends as well. #2 patiently, thoughtfully, listened to their stories and allowed them to process their pain. It was a slow journey, both for *The Girls* and me.

For them, the space in therapy was a new and hopeful experience, where they could explore the possibility of trust by talking to #2. Despite all they had been through in their short existence, this was someone with whom they could share their pain, who wouldn't hurt, ridicule, or betray them again.

I held their pain at arm's length. I told myself this happened to them, not me. It was my daily mantra and a way to not be consumed by the trauma they were sharing. My logical brain knew it was, in the end, all a part of me and the mechanism my brain used to survive.

But still, these were not experiences I could, or wanted to own. They were *The Girls'* experiences, not mine. I preferred instead to deal with the things I could control: how to navigate a relationship with my parents, or my continued bouts of anger and anxiety. I could not, or would not see the connection between *The Girls'* stories and my life. It was easier, safer really, for me to keep them off in their house and rooms, confining their existence to therapy and journal writing. Everything else was my life. This was how I survived those early days of beginning to understand who I was.

GETTING ON WITH LIFE

Despite my fairly active social life, I sensed I had to find some new focus so as not to get completely consumed by therapy and *The Girls*. It was far too easy for me to get lost in their lives and our shared past. My entire existence could have become about them and discovering a history I had forgotten. The fact we had survived was overwhelming. When I thought about *The Girls,* when I tried to get to know them, it was like stepping inside their open chests, laid out bare and vulnerable on a surgical table, their inner workings confronting me. If I wasn't careful, all of my waking moments would be about them.

My job wasn't complicated. It didn't really demand any more than my time and a modicum of effort. This low stress helped in my healing process. What I hadn't expected was for my boss to be promoted to General Manager. He decided to keep the person already in the role of Assistant, because of her experience inside the organisation. Understandable decision. But it meant I was relegated to being an assistant's assistant. I got the scraps. I wasn't demoted, but it felt like it. My work seemed even less challenging, and this allowed me far too much free time to contemplate *The Girls'* history, when I should have been focusing on friends and having fun. I needed a change.

In the middle of all this introspection, my friend Tina, the one who had helped me burn my references, told me about a vacancy in her church. It was as an assistant to the Minister of Music in a very large church in Dallas. I held my breath. Could this be what I was looking for? An opportunity for me to explore my love of music and work in ministry?

As with most things, I discussed the possibilities with #2. He thought it would be a great opportunity. Then #2 told me this was where his family went to church. And in fact, he was involved in the music program. He wanted to make sure I knew this, because there would be a good chance our paths would cross in the halls of the church, outside of the safety of the therapeutic setting where I had him confined in my mind. #2 was absolutely fine with the idea, and I would simply need to decide how I wanted to handle seeing him from time to time.

He also warned me about the person who would be my boss if I got the job. Carol was the Minister of Music, a creative who had climbed the ranks to be a woman in a senior position in ministry. She was known for being demanding and temperamental. She worked hard and expected those who worked for her to do the same. But she was committed to excellence in what she did and lavishly rewarded those who worked with her. It sounded exciting, exactly what I needed to keep my mind from wandering to *The Girls*.

I decided to interview for the position. Carol was exactly as #2 had described. A strong woman, bordering on flamboyant, with a passionate love of the creative arts. She would gesture enthusiastically as she talked about her special programs, as if she were conducting an orchestra. She painted a picture of the work she and her team did. It was a job that would require immense flexibility, but the trade-off would be worth it. It was a mix of event management, program coordination and being piano accompanist for the choir and various ensembles Carol worked with. I knew I would fail dreadfully when it came to playing the piano for my interview. Hadn't Mother told me over and again what a failure I was at piano? I went in very nervous and this self-fulfilling prophecy came true.

But at the end of the day I still got the job, with one caveat. Carol had found someone else who was an amazing accompanist and so the job would be divided between the two of us. It simply meant a smaller pay check. I breathed a sigh of relief. Maybe this would work out after all. Sharon would be the pianist, and I would do the event planning and project management. Sharon and I became fast friends. We complemented each other, and therefore, complemented Carol. We were a trusted part of her inner circle and would help her manage the department and run musical events.

It was just the fresh start I needed, a dynamic job in which I could focus on something besides therapy, *The Girls* – and a gradual unfolding of a history of abuse I was still not prepared to wrestle with.

Vacant Places

Shed a tear for vacant places – a childhood lost.
Joy from mysterious tree-climbing escapades
Fairy princess dress-ups and icky gooey mud cakes
Swings and roundabouts
Silly upside-down messes
A cacophony of colour as loud as the big outdoors
Being scooped up by safe arms in delightful glee.

Shed a tear for vacant places – a youth robbed.
A place where nubile dreams bloom
A sense of self and possibilities of life and love grow
Boys and kisses, tears and heartbreak

Held close when the world crumbles,
Tomorrow will dawn brighter,
Knowing someone believes in you.

Instead, vacant places become filled with fear.
Recounted with ease and formality,
a well-worn shirt that knows our form too well.
Moments, days and years lost.
Trust betrayed.
Rabbit holes and dark secrets,
Isolation and fear.
Self-loathing the new normal.

Expectations of a parent's touch turning to rage
the emptiness of being alone.

I have no more tears to shed for vacant places.
They are lost, somewhere
between the cracks of childhood and youth.
Where hope faded,
and a promise of tomorrow is gone.

DESPERATE ACTIONS

I was desperate for some sort of validation that these overwhelming images were real and not just deluded figments of my imagination. In therapy, #2 and I talked constantly about memories *The Girls* would share, things I didn't want to know or acknowledge about the Parents, things which were warped and sinister.

I felt guilty and ashamed. How in the world could I think this of my parents? Sure, Mother was clingy, and Dad was distant, I didn't care. They were inattentive parents. So what? Shouldn't I just grow up and get over it? But this, to slap them with the label of child abuser seemed too much. I didn't want to judge or condemn them. But I couldn't deny it felt like pieces of the puzzle were fitting together when *The Girls* talked to #2. This questioning, this need for truth, was causing me as much anxiety as the pictures in my head. I became desperate for some sort of confirmation and wondered if my brothers would give me any insight.

I relied on #2's perspective. The harder I worked in therapy, the more *The Girls* processed memories, the more I felt stuck. He assured me this was an important part of the healing process. But it didn't change what was going on in my head. The Parents would leave messages on my answering machine to which I would not respond. I was afraid of them – or more accurately, *The Girls* were afraid, and this left me paralysed with anxiety. They were worried about me, the message would say, they just wanted to know I was okay.

This pressure to go home would bring on waves of subterranean anxiety. I made trips home out of obligation. I kept telling myself that this was what any good child does. I acquiesced as little as I could, making excuses that I could only spend one night as I had obligations back in Dallas I needed to attend to. This was legitimate, given the scope of my work. It was an excuse I appreciated immensely. When I was home, I made sure I was busy, doing grocery shopping or making a meal. I was keeping up appearances that I was an engaged daughter because it was easier than admitting I wanted to run as far away from the Parents as I could. I would be a basket case the entire four hour drive back to Dallas.

My brothers and their families had both returned to live in Central Texas. I had seen each of them a few times while I was at school, but our interactions were limited to holidays and special events; we never spent any real time together other than that. These occasions, at least, were full of life and laughter with their spouses, and a gaggle of nieces and nephews running around. But beyond this, we hardly spoke. There was a natural distance which was, well, convenient. Picking up the phone and having a chin wag with my siblings was not something we did on any sort of regular basis. We saved it for our catch-ups during the holidays.

Inevitably, the idea of approaching my brothers and asking for their perspectives came up with #2. He was supportive, but cautious.

I knew I relied on #2 for a great deal, and he had become a father figure in many ways. I decided I would be straightforward with my brothers, say I was remembering abuse at home, and did they have any similar recollections. #2 was very clear: if they didn't have any memories, I shouldn't push it as it could have long-term ramifications. I didn't ask what this meant, and he didn't explain. I simply accepted what #2 said as truth.

I called my brothers, and both were surprised, even shocked. Neither had any recollection of abuse. One did acknowledge there was enough of an age difference between us for them to not be aware of anything going on. But no, for them, there was no abuse. My second brother was angry that I could imagine our parents having abused me. He suggested I had a sick mind for thinking they were capable of such things.

I was naïve about my expectations. I assumed they would affirm my suspicions, and hence my life. I couldn't have been more wrong. On #2's advice, I made no more attempts to contact them. It was a safety issue, he said. I was easily persuaded.

In retrospect, I wish I'd discussed making these phone calls more with #2 before jumping into such a complicated situation. My heart was destroyed. I felt like these calls meant I had effectively lost my brothers. In the end, they thought I was a horrible person. What would happen when we saw each other at holidays? Would I be able to look them in the face and not feel like a traitor? I knew the things I saw in my head were true, but how was I going to put this aside when I was with them? Was there any chance of reconciliation? This outcome was not what I expected.

After this, I was not sure I could visit the family. I assumed my brothers would be less than happy with me. I knew seeing my family after this would be terrifying. I would have to hold *The Girls* in check, and not let the anxiety and fear bleed out, while I tried to be a dutiful daughter. The very idea ripped me apart.

I discussed this with #2, and eventually wrote the Parents a very short, direct letter. If I said too much, it could open the door for them to ask questions. This was something I was desperate to avoid.

Dear Mom and Dad,

I am writing you this letter to let you know I need space. I am going through a few things right now which are very difficult and just need time to work it through on my own. I promise you, when I am ready to talk, I will be in contact. But until then, please give me the space I am requesting.

Annie

They honoured my request, and I breathed easier. Therapy stabilised. I was starting to be in control of my life.

Over the course of the next year, I discussed several times with #2 the idea of confronting my parents. As we worked through how this might look, the issues of safety, boundaries and expectations came up.

Safety and boundaries. I needed to feel safe, however this was done. *The Girls* needed to feel safe. There was safety in silence. I needed to decide how much I would say. Saying too much would give them control, I needed to be the one in control. I would set the agenda and terms for this confrontation.

My expectations? Of course, I wanted them to acknowledge what they had done. How did I imagine it would look? An apology?

Would they ask forgiveness? And the biggie: could we become a happy family? Would we be able to make up for all those lost years? But what if they if they denied the abuse? Worse, what if they didn't respond at all? #2 and I went through these various permutations to help me prepare for what might happen.

I wrote a second letter to the Parents.

Dear Mom and Dad,

I am contacting you as I promised I would.

I have been seeing a therapist for a few years now, working through some important issues in my life. I am finally at a place where I am willing to discuss this, if you want to. There are some specific boundaries I need for you to honour.

The first is for us to meet at my therapist's office. The second, you pay for the therapy hour. And finally, for you to have no expectations for a restored relationship. This meeting is for me to share with you my journey, and what I have learned. This will have no bearing on whether or not I am willing to see you again after this meeting.

If you are willing to abide by these boundaries, please feel free to contact my therapist and make an appointment, I have included his name and number at the bottom of this letter.

Annie

#2 and I reviewed the letter before sending it, he approved. I asked how often he helped clients this way. He said he had only had one other client brave enough to confront their abuser, and saw it as a sign of immense strength. I skirted the sideways compliment, taking his affirmation to acknowledge instead that I had communicated myself well. He reminded me at the end of the day, it was my choice whether or not to send the letter. I stood in front of the post box quaking, questioning my sanity. In the end, I dropped the letter in the chute.

I then headed out on a desperately needed holiday with Kate, making every attempt to forget about it while walking sandy beaches and laughing with my best friend. While we did talk about my letter on the odd occasion, this holiday was breathing space to help me relax and remember I was free. I was in charge of my life.

I walked into #2's office after my holiday and had barely sat down when he said my parents had called and booked an appointment. I clamoured with nerves, fears and questions. It was too late to back out now. My date with the gallows was confirmed and nerves of steel would be required.

I arrived early on the appointed day, not wanting to run into them in the waiting area. The receptionist ushered me to the playroom used by the group's psychologists, where we would be meeting. Four chairs were already set up in a circle, I noted the distance between each chair allowing for necessary personal space. The receptionist said #2 would let me know when they arrived. I paced, looking at the stuffed animals and building blocks regularly used with children. I wondered if any of *The Girls* would enjoy therapy in this room. I was willing to entertain any thoughts to keep the impending confrontation at bay. #2 walked in a short time later.

'Your parents are here.' His hand was on the doorknob. 'How are you feeling?'

I managed a weak smile. 'Terrified. But let's do this.' #2 nodded, and I followed him into his office while he escorted the Parents to the meeting room. The weight of these years was coming to a head.

I walked in behind #2, skirting chairs, giving them a wide berth. The extent of the small talk was a blur. General vagaries about the trip up, normal polite conversation. I noted how old and frail they seemed. Mother's face worn and wrinkled, Father's hair had gone from salt and pepper grey to white. They were both slightly hunched over and looked tired.

Mother was the first to speak. 'You look good, healthy. Have you lost weight?'

Her statement was like a smack across my face and grounded me. Her smothering, sickly, needy ways, and the not-so-subtle dig at my weight. As if she was apologising while trying to cover up the vast chasm between us. Father remained quiet, simply staring at me.

After an excruciatingly uncomfortable silence #2 began the real conversation. 'Annie has been working with me for a while, and decided she wanted to talk to you about the distance she has put between you.' He shifted in his chair. 'But it is important, as Annie shares with you, for you to listen, and not just talk over her, or cut her off. If we can all do that, we can have a productive discussion. Can you agree?'

They looked at each other and then Father shrugged his shoulders. 'I don't see why not.'

#2 looked at me, 'Okay Annie. Why don't you start then.'

It felt like my voice had been stolen from me. I felt stupid, like a small child who had done something wrong, refusing to make eye contact. I was the one who wanted this – to find the truth. I sighed, finally looking each of them in the eye. 'I've been struggling because I've felt a lot of stress in my life, and so I started seeing #2, wanting to work through my anxiety. I chose to break off contact with you because I felt a lot of pressure to spend more time with you, which was a big part of the stress I was feeling.'

Mother leaned forward to say something and Dad put his hand on hers to stop her so I could continue.

'#2 and I talked a lot about the anger and pressure I felt. I started seeing things in my head, snippets of memories, all about abuse. Things that have made me realise I had been abused as a child, by both of you.'

There were instantaneous gasps of shock from both of them.

'How could you think that of us?' Mother cried. 'I know we weren't the most attentive parents. I know I asked a lot of you, but there is no way we would hurt you.' She looked at me, bewildered and hurt. 'How could you think that of me?'

I shrugged my shoulders. 'It's just what I remember. And I wanted to ask you about it. To find out the truth, hear what you had to say.'

She turned to Father 'Say something. What do we do?' She was pleading, her long, wrinkled fingers grasping his arm.

Father gave me a dark menacing stare, and then turned to #2, pointing his finger. 'We will get you for this, for messing up our daughter's mind. This isn't over.'

There was nothing else to say. We were done in less than 10 minutes. I walked out without a word, knowing I was choosing to never see them again.

As I waited in #2's office for our debrief, I looked out of his 4th floor window down to the ground. I watched my parents walk out and cross the car park. I looked for some sort of sign, showing me they were as grief stricken as I was. A stumble or slumped shoulders, anything to show their anguish. Ludicrously, I hoped they would be as devastated by this meeting as I was. How could I have a relationship with people who could not acknowledge what had happened?

During our debrief I was dumbstruck and terrified. My body was shaking. The fact Father had threatened #2 was, in both our minds, confirmation of their lies. There wasn't much to say. #2 encouraged me to go and rest, take some time to process what had happened and write in my journal. We could talk about it at our next session.

I had desperately wanted this confrontation to be freeing, for those chains of anxiety and anger to fall away. I wanted to be at peace with my circumstances, understanding I had a whole life ahead of me to enjoy. But instead, I felt regret, thinking I should have somehow found a way to make it work with them, to forgive them, embrace their frailties and move on.

In my mind, when I left #2's office I was an orphan. I had no family, no security. Because of the choice to confront them, I was alone, solely responsible for navigating the road ahead of me.

DO NOT DOUBT THIS

I had the rest of my day post parent confrontation, planned out in detail. I drove home, stood in the middle of my apartment, and looked around at my walls, covered in photos of precious memories. Reality seemed surreal. I was still numb, holding the previous few hours at arm's length. Was it real? Why had they denied it? How was I supposed to cope? These questions were like a small pickaxe tapping at my brain. I picked up one of my cats and held her close to my face, letting the soft thrum of her purr work its magic, grounding me. I heaved a sigh and changed into my swimmers, grabbed a towel, and pulled Rod McKuen's *Alone* off my bookshelf. An American beatnik poet who always spoke to my soul, I needed the solace of his words. I would spend the rest of the afternoon poolside, forgetting.

But first, a phone call. Wendy was the wife of Dave, one of the guys who had befriended me in high school. We'd kept in touch over the years, and I'd told them about the abuse and the MPD. Wendy was an intense, direct, no-holds-barred sort of person. They lived in Missouri. I think that distance made it easier to share my life with them. I had promised her I would tell her the outcome of the meeting with the Parents. I told her everything I could recall, and how I felt betrayed and alone. Wendy proceeded to share an important truth.

If my child accused me of abuse, and I hadn't done it, I would stay until I was blue in the face trying to convince them they were wrong. I would not leave, I would not budge until they knew I loved them. I would do everything in my power to change their mind. Your parents do not love you. Do not doubt that fact. You may question some of the things you remember, but this confrontation has shown your parents do not love you.

PERSISTENCE IS A VIRTUE

I continued working with #2, pulling together the puzzle of my life. Writing in my journal, for both myself and the alters, was a cathartic experience. For *The Girls*, they were able to put into words experiences they had gone through, giving a voice to their trauma. For me, writing gave me the opportunity to process the information that was coming to the surface. I was remembering who I was, and more importantly, *why* I was.

I began to realise I was not the person who was born. The child, Maggie, had gone away long ago and left me in charge of the body. Trauma. A boat trip, I think. The images were not clear, but the child who was born, she was the core. She was gone, and then I became. This was a strange truth for me, it made me feel less real. I didn't talk to #2 about this. I was scared and sure it would make him think less of me. We focused so much on my life and owning it, that I was terrified he would suddenly see me as just one of *The Girls*, relegated to some secondary role while he tried to figure out who and where the original core was. I kept this kernel of truth hidden away.

I knew I was the system administrator. There was no other way to describe it. I knew of the experiences *The Girls* had gone through, but they were not my own. There was a delineation between the relationship with each Parent. *The Girls* held the abuse at the hands of Father and his friends. My domain was my daily life in the arms of Mother's wrath and disgust. I was the vessel *The Girls* lived through, allowing them to come and go as required. As #2 told me, the very nature of MPD meant I didn't remember what happened. What we were trying to do in therapy was give a voice to *The Girls'* pain, and hence give me the opportunity to live a complete and healthy life. My deepest desire was for my life to be more than the anxiety and hyper-vigilance I had learned to live with.

Journaling and writing became my sanity. I filled notebook after notebook with tales and clues of a life that had been hidden. I treasured these journals. They were something tangible I could look to for truth. These words became so important I dreamed about sharing them as a published story. Sharing my life with others, surely it would help those who were hurting? Educate people who didn't understand MPD? I began the slow and painstaking process of converting each journal to an electronic format. Spending long nights at my office, transcribing, making notes, recalling sessions, all of which I could use as a reference one day, if I ever chose to write about my life, *our* lives.

The other thing happening for me in therapy was learning about and understanding triggers. This was important. It meant I was taking control of my life rather than letting life happen to me. I was learning to manage the many triggers which in the past had ended up in anger and anxiety. With the help of #2, I was starting to identify those issues. This worked, not always, but sometimes. It was an education process after all.

I chose to persist and own this life. I decided it didn't matter to the core. Maggie had retreated, to protect herself. This was my life now, and with the help of #2, I would do the best I could. I took ownership.

FRACTURES

I was grateful for my job. It demanded a lot of me both mentally and physically and I could lose myself in it. But my role working in the church meant being surrounded by male authority figures. Men ran everything. We had a congregation of over 4,000 and more than a dozen pastoral staff, including my boss, Carol (one of only two female pastors). Carol often voiced her frustration behind closed doors about the church's old-fashioned male leadership. Men dominated at every turn, starting with the church's interpretation of biblical principles, which underpinned every decision within the church. This meant controlling male authority figures were constantly in my face, which was a trigger. Men were trying to control my life again, and I had to manage regular outbursts of anger and bouts of anxiety. This struggle was often a part of my therapy with #2. History told me if I allowed those feelings to run, I would be reprimanded, so I knew better than to go there.

By this time, however, I was armed with the knowledge of *why* these feelings of anger with authority would overcome me. I wish I could say this knowledge gave me the strength to deal with it. It didn't, at least not completely. I would watch meetings go on behind closed doors, knowing I would hear about important decisions second hand. Mostly, it was simply the authoritarian way the men spoke. They were in charge, we were to do what we were told. It was enough to make me seethe, but I kept it to myself. Baby steps, I told myself, consistent, persistent.

In the course of my work, I developed relationships with two of these pastors and their families. Truth was, they weren't all bad, and I knew that. I would be invited over for dinner to share, if only peripherally, in their families' lives. I felt comfortable enough with them to eventually open up about my history of abuse and being MPD. Harry and his wife Beth were compassionate and caring and this revelation seemed to make no difference in how I was treated. I didn't want pity, I just wanted to be able to talk about my life with someone other than #2. Their home was a haven where I babysat their kids and spent holidays feasting with them and playing games.

The other couple I got to know were Fred and Sheryl. Sheryl and I spent regular time together, even before I discussed the abuse and MPD. It was a relationship I enjoyed. One day, shortly after my revelation to her about my history, Fred asked to talk to me. We met outside and stood on the grassy lawn in front of the administration building. One look at him told me this was serious.

'Hey Fred, what's up? How can I help?' I had assumed he wanted to talk about a work matter. The pastoral staff would regularly ask for my assistance planning events and using Music Department equipment.

'Well, this is more of a personal thing,' his face was sombre.

'Okay. Shoot.'

'I'm really glad you and Sheryl have become friends. She has enjoyed mentoring and reading the Bible with you.'

'Feeling's mutual.'

He looked at me and then said thoughtfully, 'She told me about the conversation you had the other week about your abuse. I'm so sorry.'

'Thanks.' Silence. I was waiting for the other foot to drop.

'And then she told me about your working with a therapist and you had been diagnosed with Multiple Personality Disorder.'

'Yep.'

He looked down, and then looked back at me. 'Well, we prayed about it, and Sheryl isn't comfortable.' He corrected himself. '*We* aren't comfortable with her spending time alone with you. Sheryl wouldn't know how to handle it if something happened. Like, if an *alter* came out or something.'

Now I was really confused. 'Oh.'

'I hope you understand. But it's a safety issue.'

My defensive wall went up. 'Whatever. It's your choice.' I started to walk away and spun around. 'I don't understand. You've known me for a while, and suddenly I'm not safe? It's not like I've changed, it's just letting you know more about me. How can that suddenly make everything different?'

He shrugged his broad shoulders, looked down and then back at me. 'It just does.'

'Well, that's that, I guess. Nice of you to have prayed about it and got God's permission to blow me off.' I stormed away.

We had no relationship after that. I already thought I was weird being MPD, but I wanted to believe that others didn't think the same thing. I vacillated between self-pity and anger, but still managed to control it. I still had to work with him on a regular basis and needed to remain civil. Maybe I was learning. I felt like a lioness with her cubs. I needed to protect *The Girls* from anyone who might harm them or hurl horrible insults their way.

One of the notable aspects of living in North Dallas and working in this church was the wealth of its members. It was everywhere, from the huge homes to the BMWs and Porsches. Women dressed well and men wore designer suits. There was an unspoken expectation to wear your wealth, look the part. Due to the generosity of many members, the church had some great ministries which made a real difference in the community. A by-product of this was that how you looked mattered. I was trying to dress the part, but I knew I was still fat and ugly. I decided to go on a health kick, and dieting and exercise became my new norm. I was desperate to believe being healthy was my goal, but underneath, I knew my aspiration was to be thin and pretty. Bubbling below the surface was *Pretty Girl's* hope to be accepted by Mother. I participated in diet programs, ran three or four times a week, and took up social activities such as hiking. It felt good to be in control of my eating habits and doing something positive, hoping this would make me acceptable. I told myself this wasn't about a childhood longing for my mother's love, but just wanting to be healthy.

What I couldn't predict was the effect this would have on *The Girls*. With #2, I was gradually understanding that fat was their friend. Being fat had not only nurtured and comforted them but also protected them at various points from unwanted advances. Simply losing weight was seen as a threat by *The Girls*. I didn't feel it directly, instead it came out in subtle ways. I was starting to make friends with more guys my age. There was nothing romantic, although I certainly wished for more. And it was my desire for more with these men that unhinged some of *The Girls,* and created a horrible conflict for me. Eventually, I watched these guys peel away into their own romantic relationships, acknowledging me as a friend, but never more. *The Girls* calmed down. But I was left broken-hearted and triggered. I was hurt. I was lonely. So I ate. Fat was my friend again. This pattern of my life had not changed.

Confronting my parents and choosing to break off communication meant I was effectively on my own. And while it suited my need for freedom, in truth, it was lonely. Over the course of the next few years, I was fortunate to have a few families, some with young children, some who were empty nesters, who invited me into their homes. They shared their lives with me. We would have meals together and talk about my life, sharing my goals and desires – although only superficially. We would hang out and watch movies or play with kids, and even play the odd game of UNO or RISK. All the normal and ordinary things families do together. I felt welcomed and cared for.

But even these precious relationships could not replace the emptiness where most people had a functioning and present biological family. Holidays were the hardest, knowing my parents and brothers and their families were together and I was not a part of it. Most of the time I would be invited into friends' homes. But at times, I was overlooked. And it was in those moments, while others were celebrating holidays or other significant events, that I most felt the consuming depth of my solitude. I was alone. No blame, it was simply my life.

LOVE AND OTHER MONSTERS

Even though I enjoyed my church job, I was becoming jaded. I had seen the inner workings of the large church business model. Making decisions about the future of a ministry within the church based on budgetary constraints didn't sit well with me. Financially, of course, this might have been wise, but I couldn't see that. I just thought a faith-based ministry should have, well, faith. I started looking for a new job. By the time I left, I had spent five years at the church. I was appreciative of the experience, but glad to be gone.

I began working for a brokerage settlement firm. My boss was a funny, impeccably dressed, self-absorbed peacock. We got used to Phil regaling us every Monday morning with his weekend conquests, knowing it was mostly bravado. Under it all he was a softy who loved to laugh and have fun. He turned me on to wearing ties. Bright, colourful patterns with which I could make a fashion statement. There were eight of us in the office, doing varying jobs. It was relaxing and low pressure. I enjoyed the change of pace.

It was there I learned about this new-fangled thing called the World Wide Web. Our head office wanted to hook us up to it so we could share data and reports in a more efficient way. I was proficient on the computer, so new technology was straightforward for me. The tech department at Head Office was very helpful, discussing the ins and outs and walked me through a program called CompuServe. This was the software they used for the bulk of their work communication. A chat space in essence, where I could send them files and we could discuss tech problems.

There were other features in this thing called CompuServe. There were all sorts of spaces called 'rooms' which you could access, although this was outside work hours, of course. I was fascinated. Looking around, I came across something called the Christian Interactive Network and decided to check it out. It turned out to be a space where people from around the world who claimed to be Christian could have discussions about topics which interested them. You could participate, or just watch. I was a voyeur, and it felt safe. If I was really curious, I would look at the profiles of people in these threads to learn about their backgrounds.

On December 23rd, 1995, I came across an interesting conversation about the Jehovah's Witnesses, a cult-like organisation whose doctrine was very divisive, especially for Christians. As per normal, I started looking at the profiles of the people in this thread. This was where I found Tom. His profile indicated he was from Brisbane, Australia, and he loved movies, especially science fiction. An Australian! The place Americans thought was paradise! The land down under with quirky animals like koalas and kangaroos. How cool! In a spontaneous gesture, I sent a private message, and simply said *What part of the Jehovah's Witness doctrine do you struggle with?* That was the beginning of a 3-hour text conversation and the start of my online dating life.

The next day, I went to have a Christmas Eve breakfast with a girlfriend. On the way, hopeful and giddy, I went by the office to see if Tom had sent me an email. He had! A lengthy discussion of all things geeky, faith-based and sci-fi. Mostly though, he wrote about how much he enjoyed getting to know me. I printed it out and showed it to my friend at breakfast, pronouncing I was going to marry this guy. We both laughed and blew it off. It was an easy, safe thing to say because he was on the other side of the world.

Tom and I corresponded by email and after a week, exchanged snail-mail addresses. We sent each other pictures and cards and over the ensuing months, things started to get romantic. The distance felt safe, but I started to feel rumblings from *The Girls*. Their fear of men was something I carried with me everywhere. But they seemed to acknowledge that at this point, I was in control.

Within weeks Tom and I were talking on the phone, which sent both our phone bills skyrocketing. Neither of us ever wanted to hang up and it didn't matter. We talked about things we could do together if I came to Australia. We could go to Uluru or climb the Sydney Harbour Bridge. We schooled each other in the fine art of linguistics: he taught me how to say *g'day* and I explained that *howdy ya'll* was the universal way Texans greeted each other.

One night Tom sprung on me the possibility he might be coming to North America on business. He worked for an IT company in Brisbane with a client in Toronto, Canada. 'It might give us a chance to meet and spend some time together.'

I laughed. 'Toronto is a long way from Texas.'

'Yeah. But would it be possible to meet up?'

It wasn't confirmed, he told me. This was a big client and they needed long-term support. Tom's boss was still weighing up the value of having someone there on the ground, rather than remotely, to do the necessary modifications to the program.

This was something completely different. I hadn't told him about my past – the abuse, let alone being MPD. The geographical distance between us had made it easy for me to keep this part of my history to myself. But with this, our budding relationship suddenly got more serious – and, for me, dangerous.

We decided not to push things and see how it panned out with his work. But the possibility of meeting Tom face-to-face set off a chain reaction, internally and externally. *The Girls* grew agitated. This became an important point of discussion with #2. He patiently directed me back to a simple question: what did I want? I needed to think about this. If I wanted to pursue a relationship with Tom, #2 would help my system cope. I wanted a relationship, and knew it had to be built around honesty and truth. I would need to begin the discussion of an abusive history. If we became serious, the MPD would need to be discussed. I took comfort in having #2 to walk me through this.

I wanted a relationship, but had given up thinking it might be possible for me. I was damaged goods. Could someone ever love fat, ugly me? And the fear nagged at me – what if the truth of my life was something Tom was not able to handle? Would he find this aspect of my life repulsive?

The Girls did not have questions, but rather convictions: men were horrible and would use them. They begged me to not pursue this relationship. To put it aside and move back to what was safe, hidden, protected - no matter how lonely it was.

I put my own needs before those of *The Girls*. I would tell Tom the truth, be brutally honest about who I was. It would be my litmus test. If he didn't back away, then I would take further risks. It gave me the control I needed, in a quasi-safe way. I could have hope that someone, a real person, could actually love me.

I waited until I knew Tom would be coming to Canada before I said anything. I wanted to email instead of phone, giving him time to digest what I could only assume would be uncomfortable news. I started by reminding him how distant I was from my family and didn't talk about them much. I wanted him to know the reason. I was abused as a child. Violently, over an extended period of time. And I survived because I had something called Multiple Personality Disorder.

I looked at the words on the screen. It was unnerving – okay, terrifying – to see this information about my life in front of me. It made it real. I continued writing. I was determined to be honest. Tom needed to understand this about me if there was any hope we could have more than an online relationship. I encouraged him to do some research and read books, to understand better who I was. Noting the time difference, I sent the email when I knew it was the middle of the night in Australia. I needed my own space to wrestle with his potential response. Within 30 minutes I had an email waiting. *Tell me more. Can you recommend books to read?*

I was shocked. And excited. Could this be it, I wondered. Really? I shared the titles of a few books with him. We talked about it more, but we both agreed it was the sort of thing better left for a face-to-face conversation.

Tom arrived Stateside a few weeks later, getting settled in Canada before taking a long weekend to come and visit me. I had several friends tell me this was too fast. They were concerned about me allowing a strange man to stay in my apartment. He would be in a separate room, I told them. But it wouldn't stop him from taking advantage of you, they said. I reassured them I could take care of myself. But could I? And if he tried something, how would *The Girls* handle it? I think I was so infatuated by the romance of the whole thing I didn't care. This was a mistake, putting what I wanted before the needs of *The Girls*.

We were tentative when we met at the airport. I was terribly nervous and barely able to breathe as I watched everyone get off his flight. When I saw him, I immediately relaxed. He was exactly as I thought he would be – a tall teddy bear, with dark curls, broad shoulders and a big smile. He gave me a toy koala. It was a sweet gesture, winning me over instantly.

I showed him around Dallas. We talked about his work and dreams, about things I wanted to do. We even began a brief conversation about MPD, but didn't delve deep, as he was still wrapping his head around the topic. I was relieved and happy to let it slide, still unsure how to talk about it. He made no advances and seemed to have no sexual expectations. This really was just an opportunity to get to know each other. Before I knew it, I was seeing him off at the airport as he headed back to Toronto. He said he would see me again soon.

He came back two weeks later. Things were different this time. He gave me a hug at the airport, and I took him to the Dallas Arboretum. A public, but easy place to find nooks and crannies to have quiet conversations. We were sitting in some tall grass, and he put his hand over mine.

'I'd like to kiss you.'

A kiss. I was a 34-year-old who had never had a kiss that was mine alone. Not *The Girls'*, no sexual inuendo or agenda, but mine. I looked at him and smiled. It was light, it was brief, and he pulled me closer to him. We barely touched as we sat and enjoyed each other's company.

Things escalated quickly. I hadn't anticipated how triggering this relationship with Tom would be. I was trying desperately to contain *The Girls'* anxiety and fear but was walking a dangerously fine line. I was fearful it would blow up. I might have liked Tom's gentle touch and how kissing him made me feel. But *The Girls* did not. They wanted to be as far away from him as possible and I ignored their cries and pleas for safety. I was coming alive in the feelings of fun and romance in the relationship. I was not fat and ugly. Someone liked how I looked, making my heart jump, and we kept pushing the boundaries, both physically and emotionally. What I kept ignoring was that every time Tom touched me, *The Girls* assumed abuse was around the corner.

While Tom and I would occasionally discuss abuse and MPD, it was never at the centre of our relationship. We wanted it to be about *us*, not about *that*. I found this refreshing. He accepted this about me, and didn't feel the need to go deeper. I took this as a good sign. In hindsight, I should have seen it as a red flag.

Physically, Tom was keen to deepen the relationship. (Another sign he didn't understand *The Girls*.) We were out for dinner one night when he said he expected to sleep with the girl he wanted to be with before they got married.

'It's not my values. I won't. It's not right.' I looked at him, almost daring him to disagree. I knew this was a deal breaker.

'Yeah. I get it. But don't you want to know if we fit together physically? That we can work?'

'If we are meant to be together, we'll work.'

He looked at me for a minute and then we moved on to something else.

It didn't stop us from playing with fire. Nor did it stop my unwillingness to pay attention to what was going on with my system. *Slut Girl*, the only alter with any interest in sex, was a significant part of ratcheting up the relationship. I was an early riser, Tom was not. I would get up and go into his room and crawl into bed with him; cuddle and feel the closeness of his body next to mine. No words. He would reach out, pull me next to him and we would quietly spoon, clothes would slip down, and we would be skin against skin. I let the desire and passion of *Slut Girl* stream louder through my head than the fears of any of the others.

I would extricate myself from his arms before it went too far, telling him I was off to make breakfast. He was confused and as I left the room would say I was teasing him. It wouldn't take long for him to come out and kiss me on the cheek while I made breakfast. We were playing house. All forgiven.

This happened often.

I was lost in hopes and emotions, overwhelmed that someone found me desirable and that I might have some sort of normal future where I was loved. I chose to ignore *The Girls*. Their fears were not logical I told myself. What they needed to see was a good relationship. I would set the example and make everything okay for them.

FAREWELL

The end for me came on one of our quick getaway weekends when I took Tom sightseeing through the Texas Hill Country. We walked hand in hand through endless fields of Blue Bonnets and red and yellow laced Indian Paintbrush. After a picnic lunch, we ventured south along the Texas Coastline to Houston. Tom was excited to visit NASA and see the moon rovers and space rockets. It was a bucket list experience for him.

Then it was off to Galveston, an island just south of Houston. It was connected to the mainland by a causeway which stretched as far as I could see. We rocked up to a seafood shack, where I convinced Tom he would not die if he ate crab. We ordered a platter of the red crustaceans, laughing as we cracked shells, juice dribbling down our chins and across the table. Tom survived and the meal was as delicious as I'd told him it would be.

Tom wanted to see more of the Texas coastline and compare it to Australian beaches, which he said were the best in the world. I told him the long white beaches of the Texas coast could most definitely compete with whatever Oz had to offer. The next day we continued our trek on Galveston Island, hunting out sandy beaches where we could sink our feet into the famous Texas sand.

As we held hands and stole the occasional kiss, we dared to talk about a future together. He wanted to show me his home in Australia. I would love the culture and eclecticism of Sydney, he said. We got back to my car, and I leaned back against a door, facing him – an invitation. He moved in to kiss me, pinning me against the car in a passionate embrace. We stopped briefly and looked at each other. No words were necessary, we slid into the back seat. Tom was determined. I was flying blind, following his lead.

Our hands were all over each other. Kissing, lips locked. It felt wonderful – unnervingly so. In my head the reactions were ballistic. *The Girls* were scattering in fear. They knew what was coming. Sex would be horrible, it would hurt – I was betraying them. I kept trying to push their fears to the back of my mind as I experienced these amazing, intense sensations.

With every caress, there were screams and terror from *The Girls*, who it was my responsibility to protect. With every kiss, I was destroying their trust. But I kept kissing, allowing myself to be touched in ways that hurtled my senses off the charts. *Slut Girl* was with me, pushing and probing, using my hands to stimulate and create as much erotic pleasure as she could.

How could I do this? How could I betray *them* like this? I was as confused and ashamed as I was excited. I wanted to run away. Leave. Hide. Whatever I could do to get out of this situation.

So I left. Giving no thought to the ramifications for *The Girls,* I went and hid away. It was my turn to go inside, to leave this world I had tried to navigate for so long. I didn't know what would be left behind, but I had to go. I had started from nothing all those years ago when Maggie was just three, and now I chose to go back to nothing. I looked in my head, to the secret places *The Girls* inhabited, and went further, to darker spaces where I could sleep in peace and forget about the failure of a life I had once inhabited. I barely felt my shoulder touch Maggie's as she was forced out to deal with the life I had left behind.

PART TWO: MAGGIE'S STORY

APRIL 1996

I, Maggie, became – *returned* – on a late Spring Day on a beach on the Gulf of Mexico, just outside of Galveston, Texas, in the back seat of a dark blue Toyota Corolla.

I was coming up for air, bursting through the surface of a rough sea. I had gone to sleep at the age of three with a blow across my face, and was waking up as an adult, wrestling with who I was and this strange new world I had been dropped into.

I was aroused. Touch, excitement. Hands were exploring my body and kissing me. I was confused, scared, and stimulated in ways I did not understand, thrust into a reality not of my choosing and which made no sense.

In the midst of this clearing fog, I felt the presence of someone else. Instinct told me her name was *Slut Girl*, with an innate ability to navigate this complicated situation. She ran her fingers through this man's curly dark hair, offering her body for his exploration, giving the promise of intimacy, limbs locked, a warm glow rising from my gut that was both electrifying and awful.

As I surfaced, *Slut Girl* relinquished her control. I became embarrassed, physically pulling away. I looked at this man who seemed to know me intimately, grateful he too was confused at the ferocity and physicality we were sharing. It gave me an opportunity to pause, collect myself and acclimatise to my surroundings.

I was with Tom, the man Annie thought she would marry. This much I knew.

Instantaneously, I integrated the vestiges of Annie's last moments. I knew she found the physical and emotional intimacy of this relationship too difficult and, with shame and regret, had vacated. Tom and I were now sitting side-by-side in the back seat, excited, confused, and breathing hard. Our passion subsided and we sat close, holding hands. In this quiet moment, I began the process of coming to terms with Annie's life, knowing I was alive because of her strength and ability to control a system of alters (I even knew her term for them was *The Girls*). They lived the abuse while I was hidden away.

Tom and I talked as we drove back to Dallas, reflecting on the weekend and how much he had enjoyed seeing this part of Texas and making plans for our next trip - Niagara Falls, another place to tick off his bucket list. He would be flying out the next day, headed back to Canada to continue his work.

I was grateful I wouldn't see Tom for a few weeks. I had so much I needed to work through regarding this life I had stepped into. A storage system of postcard images and stories filed away in my (or was it our?) brain, immediately became available to me. The job Annie did to earn a living, the way she met Tom, her interests, therapy with #2 (someone who had apparently been a great resource for Annie as she dealt with the truth of who she was), her love of music, friends, and church – they were all there. These were important snippets of information I gradually began to access so I could paint a picture of the life I now inhabited.

I could barely see the edges of her relationship with the Parents.

YES!

Back alone in Dallas, instinct told me I needed to adapt quickly to the life Annie had lived. In a sense, I became her replica. I reproduced as much as I could, including her values and beliefs, so I could live her life, stepping delicately in her footsteps.

It was the relationship with Tom that required the most attention. I went through each of the emails we shared in detail. I contemplated phone calls and looked at photos we had taken to make sure I was the person he was expecting.

Years later, as my life unravelled, I would come to understand this was the job Annie had left me with – to exist as a shell of her. Do nothing out of the ordinary, have no dreams or wishes of my own. Nothing to make me a unique individual – all I had to do was exist. She had been, and for all I knew, still was, the system administrator and she was giving me a job to do like all the others.

Later, on our romantic trip to Niagara Falls, I was sitting on Tom's lap, chatting about the events of the day and the majesty of the Falls. He asked, 'Any more deep, dark secrets you need to share?'

I laughed quietly. We had talked about my history; he knew it all. Annie had made sure of that. With this question, I chose to believe he understood the implications of my life and the potential issues a history of abuse might raise in an intimate relationship. My head wanted to believe he understood. My heart wanted to believe in our fairy tale relationship.

I wrapped my arms around his neck and said, 'No. No more dark secrets.'

'Well, how about we make it official then. Will you marry me?'

I had hope, a vision that something could be made of this replica life I had vicariously walked into.

'Of course, yes.'

It was official.

We spent the next two months travelling to see each other. He would come to my home in Dallas or I would meet him in Toronto. This was our version of a courtship; fun, exciting and certainly not how couples typically came together.

He met and was grilled by several of my friends. These were people who cared about Annie, so cared about me. They were protective, and this was a comfortable, safe feeling. I liked it immensely. They wanted to know Tom's background, how serious he was about his faith, what he did for a living. Would we be living in Australia or Texas? How would the immigration process go? All this demonstrated to me that the friends I had inherited from Annie were genuine and caring. Satisfied for the most part, one by one they accepted his place in my life and saw we could work, despite the unusual way we met. Our relationship had their tick of approval.

WEDDED BLISS

I made sure I learned everything I could about Annie's expectations of marriage. She became a Christian in a stereotypical southern Baptist church in Central Texas and upheld their conservative values. This included the belief that a wife should be a submissive and subservient partner to her husband, and as we went through marriage counselling with my pastor, those values were reinforced. Central to a harmonious and blissful marriage, would be my role as Tom's helper, nurturing and caring for him. I accepted this as my obligation to help build a lasting and loving marriage.

Shrink #2 called me Annie, knew me as Annie, and I had no desire to change that. While Annie would never admit it, she depended on him to provide stability in her life. Every week, like clockwork, he was there for her. I respected this, but it wasn't for me. And I couldn't bring myself to tell #2 that I wasn't Annie. Maybe I assumed he would figure it out (which I can see was an unfair expectation on my part). Maybe, and I think this is more likely the heart of it, I wasn't sure myself what had happened between Annie and me. At the age of three, after being hit across the face, I disappeared and became this wacky thing called MPD. I was scrambling to hang on myself. Talking to #2, who was a complete stranger to me, seemed a bridge too far. I was struggling to come to terms with who I was. Maybe I hoped somehow by maintaining the status quo, it might make me normal.

Tom and I both agreed it would be important for him to have a professional perspective on the implications of MPD in our marriage, so I organised an appointment for him with #2 during one of his trips. I was grateful to have a trained professional's perspective on our situation.

#2 started. 'Are there things you wanted to ask me?'

Tom looked at me. We'd already discussed how we would proceed. I wanted him to ask whatever he needed, no matter how uncomfortable. He turned to #2. 'I guess, well, we've spent a bit of time together, but Annie's never become another, uh, well – person. What am I supposed to do when that happens?'

'I think there are a few things you need to consider.' This was the start of #2's explanation about what MPD might look like. 'Annie is high functioning. Essentially as an adult, she doesn't flip. She is influenced by alters, absolutely. There could be a sudden change in demeanour, something out of character. Chances are that unless part of the system feels highly vulnerable, it'll be okay. Alters tend to take over if they think they feel threatened.'

'And when could that happen? Feel threatened?'

'It depends. Arguments, loud voices. Situations where Annie might feel vulnerable or unsafe. Have you two talked about sex?' #2 looked at me this time.

'Not really. We've gotten physical, but nothing happened.'

That was the moment I should have come clean, been honest about this dramatic shift in my brain. Would things have been different if I had admitted I wasn't Annie anymore, but Maggie? And was it because things had gotten so physical between Tom and Annie that *The Girls* were terrified? Instead, I kept quiet. I still wasn't able to admit to myself, Tom, or #2 what had happened on Galveston beach.

'So yeah, sex.' Tom dove straight in. 'Could something happen, like when we are having sex?'

'It might. You just need to be aware of your circumstances and follow Annie's lead. Ask questions, make sure she feels safe. If she feels okay, let her be your guide. Make sense?'

'Yeah.'

I expected more. I wanted Shrink #2 to give a blow-by-blow of – I'm not sure what – but to somehow make everything clear. (To me or to Tom?) I wanted Tom to ask more questions, to show me he understood. But I let it go, hiding behind the facade of a love-struck, dutiful, doting fiancé. Tom had a romantic notion that somehow it would just all work out and I trusted in that.

I knew one thing for certain, I did not trust #2. He had glossed over things, important information which could have helped Tom and I carve a way forward that was stable and secure. Instead I felt unsafe. The exact opposite of how I should have felt.

It was a June wedding. We couldn't afford much so it was a small gathering in a friend's backyard. After we exchanged vows, we sat around tables enjoying the company of these dear friends. Everyone brought a dish to share, and we had a small Italian Cream wedding cake. Kate came down from Canada and Jane flew in from Denver. I wore a tea-length lace dress and carried a small heirloom family Bible Tom's mother had sent across from Australia. The florist had added delicate lace and a single purple iris bud.

We booked a B&B for our honeymoon weekend. When we arrived, there was a special present waiting. Friends from work had put together a picnic basket full of goodies, along with a bottle of champagne and two goblets with our names engraved on them. The attached note simply said, *now you don't have to leave your room.* We both laughed nervously.

I was determined to make this a special time and had purchased a sexy bit of honeymoon lingerie. I was no fool, newly married couples only occasionally left their bedroom - the honeymoon was all about the sex, especially for those couples that had refrained until marriage. Sex was something Tom was keen for, and I was desperate to enjoy. When *The Girls* had to perform their duties, I remember that Annie's Mother used to say, 'Just lie back and think of England'. (I was still adjusting to the fact this was my mother as well.) I suppose in her own way, Mother was trying to make the act of sex more bearable. Spread your legs, do your duty, and it will all be over soon. I feigned delight, Tom was happy.

I liked the physical cuddles and closeness of sleeping next to Tom (although his snoring kept me awake most nights). But the physical act of sex was tortuous. This became the pattern I got used to for most of our active sex life. There were the occasional almost pleasant moments, but the intense orgasms and sexual abandon you see in movies were never a part of my life.

I went back to work after a few days before we embarked on a two-week trip to Australia. In the meantime, my waterbed made sure sex was kept to a minimum. (They never tell you sex can be difficult in a waterbed, but I was grateful for it.) In all this I never felt or sensed Annie or *The Girls*. I simply did not like sex, and put it down to my inability to let go and have fun.

Tom constantly reassured me his family would accept me. I had already talked to his mum on the phone and as I was part of the family now, she insisted I call them Mum and Dad. I was nervous but quietly hopeful these people would replace the family I never had.

Tom's family lived on the NSW/QLD border near Murwillumbah. I fell in love with the landscape, the long white beaches and the endless fields of sugar cane. Apart from a few days in a caravan park, we stayed with Tom's family. I got used to a pot of tea and biscuits on the table every time we sat down. Tom introduced me to his family and despite my nerves, I could sense they were good people. We had yet to figure out where we would live. They didn't press us for an answer but simply said they hoped we would move to Australia.

Tom's dad was a bit gruff, old-fashioned and opinionated. He jokingly said I had stolen Tom from the Aussie marriage market. (I doubted it was a joke, and actually more of a jibe.) His mother seemed to feel she had to do everything for everyone. I saw her as a doormat, always making sure her husband had what he needed, serving him and others while sacrificing her own needs. I cringed, fearful Tom would expect me to be the same. It wasn't until years later, after she died, that I came to appreciate how her gentle kindness was a bedrock for the family, and under his tough veneer, Tom's dad regretted he did not show his love for his wife more openly.

I left Tom at the Gold Coast Airport. We hugged and kissed and cried. The US immigration system was making our lives difficult. I was not an American citizen. I had a permanent residency visa. (The official description was Resident Alien. Go figure.) This meant that even with Tom's professional credentials, he was not eligible to live in the US. On the other hand, Australia was keen on welcoming immigrants, and it would be no issue for me to move to Australia. This was something we had to address but were putting off.

I made the long trip home on my own. Gold Coast to Sydney, Sydney to Los Angeles, then on to Dallas. I was grateful to be home in my apartment. It felt empty but familiar. While I missed Tom, the space and time to process what my future looked like was important.

We talked constantly on the phone, discussing options for where we could live. It became clear I would be the one moving. I found this overwhelming. In Tom's ever-optimistic style, he saw this move as an adventure. Why wouldn't I want to go?

My answer was simple. He was asking me to uproot myself from everything I was starting to know and find stable and safe. Why did I have to move? It was our first real argument. I remember getting off the phone, pulling my wedding ring off, and throwing it across the room. Anger. What an unusual sensation. Liberating, to be honest. I threw myself on my couch and lay in silence. Anger gave way to a sense of grief over losing a life I was just beginning to know. Anger because Tom, in his ever-naïve romantic way, had no concept of how much he was asking me to give up. I began wondering if I had made the worst decision in my life. Doing what Annie might have wanted didn't mean it was the right thing for me.

In the end, I made a commitment to a man who Annie (and I?) believed she could spend her life with. Through sickness and in health, good and bad, the vows carved on my heart. I knew I had to go. US immigration made it so. We took it as direction from God to make our life in Australia.

LETTING GO

Tom found a new job in Sydney and I began the process of applying for a visa to immigrate to Australia. We talked about all the interesting places we would go once I arrived. From the Opera House to the Outback, we would see it all. We also had steamy conversations about a love life I was assured would be an important part of our daily routine. I couldn't bring myself to tell him that in the few weeks we'd had together, sex worked – but I didn't like it. I reminded myself Tom seemed happy, and that was more important. Of course, I knew there was abuse in my history, but I told myself, yet again, that was Annie's life, not mine. I decided I was being silly and pushed my fears aside, convinced it would work out. We were newlyweds after all, still adjusting to each other. I didn't discuss any of this with Tom, instead assuring myself that once I was in Australia, things would be easier, life would make more sense.

Accepting that I had to leave became a pragmatic decision. I believed I was leaving Annie's life behind, not mine. She had walked away, so what did it really matter? I began ticking things off, cutting ties to a life in North Texas, divesting myself of her history.

Giving notice at work was easy. They expected it and were excited for me. I would be living the dream in the *Land Down Under*. It was the personal relationships I would miss, those people I was just getting to know and was saying goodbye to. I could rattle them off. Sharon, someone Annie could call in the middle of the night when she was having anxiety attacks. Harry and Beth – Harry had performed our wedding and neither of them ever flinched at accepting Annie for who she was. Tina had helped Annie put the failed overseas work behind her and look forward. These were Annie's friends and network of support who I would now carry with me as memories, not part of a new life I would build in Australia.

Kate was a different matter. The bond with her transcended the constraints of MPD. Annie loved Kate, and I loved Kate. They had lived with physical distance between them since college, but they had still made it work. She assured me she would make trips to Australia. And we had this thing called the Internet which meant we could communicate easily and often.

As soon as my visa was approved by the Australian Government, I began selling off my furniture, trying to clear everything out. Then it was down to those things I would keep, which I carefully boxed up for transit, making a detailed list for the movers so it could all be accounted for. I packed all the delicate wedding presents to ensure they reached Australia unbroken. Then there were all Annie's books, trinkets from the Philippines and shells from her adventures with Kate. I respected that all these things were the stuff of Annie's life. Practically speaking, it was important to have these references for continuity in my new life in Australia. But Annie's life was my history also, and I felt a sense of obligation to hold on to her memories as an acknowledgment of her past. I also kept a box full of her old journals. Reams of paper, a chronicle of her life journey I was responsible to care for.

I remember watching the movers put box after box on a pallet in their truck. As they shrink-wrapped the contents with a duplicate of my packing list clearly displayed, I filled out the final paperwork. These relics of the life I had only started to get to know would travel from my apartment in North Dallas to Los Angeles and finally on a ship, destination Sydney.

This was just the beginning of my journey coming to terms with who Annie had been. Her life was a counterpoint to the life I wanted to build. And in all this was an unspoken truth: *Tom had fallen in love with Annie, not me.* I was not prepared to consider or fathom the toll this unacknowledged reality would eventually take on my life.

IMMIGRANT STATUS

September 1996. From my window seat on Qantas flight QF8, I watched the sun rise over Sydney. Even before we touched down, I was ready to step into my new life in Australia. I wanted permanence, to make a home with Tom, a place where we could grow old together. I was excited to be making a fresh start. I accepted that I would feel lonely, and that culture shock might be a challenge, just as it would be challenging to leave behind everything familiar to me, even if that was Annie's life, not mine.

In one way or another, I would struggle with this for years to come.

But I embraced it still, believing the adventure ahead of me would be far easier to navigate than the vestiges of the life Annie had lived in Texas. She was gone – and had hung me out to dry, frankly. (Okay, slight exaggeration, but certainly how I felt.) Why shouldn't I do what I wanted? I was ready to put distance between myself and this thing called MPD. That was Annie's life; why should it be mine? I believed this new land, with its exotic animals, endless beaches, and strange way of speaking, would be the place where I could build my own life and put the darkness of a foggy history to rest. Most importantly, *the system* at the heart of Annie's existence was not the life I would live.

I was determined. Annie's history would be a reference as I moved forward, not a foundation. Often in the early years of my return as Maggie, as I re-established my identity, I felt as if I would flick through Annie's memories (what I called her 'postcard memories') to give me a sense of who I had been, to help me build the story of *my* new life. They were my starting point, but I also believed the longer I lived in Australia, the more Tom and I built a life together, I would be able to shed her history and create memories and a life story of my own. I would pick and choose which bits to claim and which to ignore. It felt straightforward. I would enjoy the pleasant memories and ignore the pain.

I look back now and wonder, did I really think it would be this easy?

SYDNEYSIDER

In one of our numerous conversations before I arrived, Tom had asked what sort of area I wanted to live in. 'Just something multicultural and reflective of what Sydney is like,' I'd said. 'Surprise me.' He was up for the task. Our newlywed abode was a quaint two-bedroom cottage in the heart of Auburn, in the western suburbs of Sydney.

Our landlord, who conveniently lived behind us with a door in the back fence, announced his presence one day with a pot of Turkish coffee. He was a kind and gracious Lebanese man, with a twinkle in his eye and enough English to spin tales of his homeland, and he watched with humour as I drank his rich dark concoction, full of sugar, that put hair on my chest. Small moments such as these were highlights of those early days in Sydney.

In our little house, there was a big empty space where a table and chairs should have been. Being newlyweds, we hadn't the money or inclination to buy necessities such as a table and chairs. Instead, we ate dinner on the couch. As we watched the TV news, I asked copious questions about this fascinating country that was becoming my home, and Tom was my willing teacher. When it came to politics, I learnt that the Labor Party was actually left-leaning, and the Liberal Party was right-wing conservative (in spite of the name). Paul Keating (Labor) had just lost the federal election and John Howard (Liberal) was about to be sworn in as the new Prime Minister. Voting was compulsory, and when you did vote, you voted for a party, not a person. It was only when the winning party was announced that the Prime Minister (the leader of that Party) was confirmed. And there was someone else, an Independent called Pauline Hanson, who claimed to represent true-blue Aussies, but seemed to do nothing but rant and rave in a way that I could only describe as racist and closed-minded.

I learned that Australia and the US are roughly the same size, and that adapting to the metric system was going to be important, especially when it came to weather. I became adept at converting Fahrenheit to Celsius, understanding quickly that 32 degrees was hot, not the freezing point for snow.

There were, of course, straightforward language translations. Jelly was jam and cookies were biscuits, while biscuits were scones. Ketchup was tomato sauce. It was easy to get lost in the food because it's just so bloody interesting. ('Bloody,' I learnt, was casual Aussie slang to emphasize almost anything.) Tom's favourite cake was a lamington, which was a small, square sponge cake covered in chocolate and coconut. (If you were lucky you'd find one filled with whipped cream.) And when I was introduced to something called a caramel slice, with a cookie base (oops, *biscuit* base), a thick sludge of caramel in the middle and a hard layer of dark chocolate on top, I could feel the *kilos* layering on my hips.

Tom introduced me to the fascinating history of Sydney. Each weekend, we would take trips on the ever-efficient, but always confusing train system into the city, or to explore another suburb. When we got off the train at Circular Quay and I saw the Opera House for the first time, it was breathtaking. Its famous white sails were known throughout the world as an icon of the place that was now my home. We would walk hand in hand around the foreshore at the Opera House, and steal the occasional kiss as we wandered through the Botanical Gardens and then through the historic Rocks. It was fun, we were in love. I was convinced we would be happy.

As with any new marriage, the longer I lived with Tom, the more I learned about him. We had seen quite a bit of Sydney, but I wanted to meet his friends, those people he considered important in his life.

'When are we going to meet your friends?' I asked one night over dinner.

'What friends?' He looked confused.

'You know, your friends, the people you do things with outside of work.'

'Oh. Yeah.' Nothing.

'What about Carl? You mentioned him a few times back in Dallas. You said he was your best mate.'

'Oh, Carl. Yeah. Well. I dunno where he is now. We haven't seen each other in years.'

I was perplexed. 'What about other friends?'

'What other friends?'

'People you do things with? Like go out to dinner or have a beer or something.'

'There are no other friends,' he smiled. 'But there is you and me now.'

And that was the end of the conversation. I began to realise what a solitary life Tom lived. It left me at a loss. I was wary of being isolated, scared that Tom was my only lifeline in this huge country on the other side of the world.

DANGEROUS CREATURES

A host of dangerous and deadly creatures call Australia home. From great white sharks and box jellyfish patrolling the coastline, to land-based snakes and spiders that could fell a grown man with a single bite. And spare a thought for the poor maligned huntsman spider, whose only fault was growing exceedingly large. Aussies learn to co-exist, if somewhat uncomfortably, with huntsman the size of baseballs.

My weakness was the slug. This small slimy creature would make my skin crawl. I had only ever known them as inhabitants of snail shells, and as a child, I knew that Annie had eaten one or two as escargot. But I had never seen any the size of slugs in Australia. These were snails on steroids. Without a home.

In my first few weeks in Australia, I was taking a shower, getting ready to start my day. I had been washing my hair and as I wiped the water away, I saw something out of the corner of my eye. On the inside of the shower screen was a creature at least fifteen centimetres long, a brown-patched grey body squirming its way up the glass, leaving a thick slimy trail behind. I screamed and threw myself into the corner of the shower cubicle. Tom came running.

'What happened?'

'What in God's name is that?' I waved my finger, careful to keep at least a metre away, lest it sprout legs and somehow leap on my naked flesh, leaving an acid trail I was sure would lead to an early death.

Tom laughed. 'Oh, that's just a leopard slug.'

'Get rid of it!'

'Okay, okay! Hang on.' He left the room in search of something to put it in, I heard banging in the kitchen and couldn't fathom what was taking so long.

'Hurry up!'

'I'm coming,' he said, sauntering into the bathroom. 'It's just a slug. It's not like it's gonna kill you.'

'I wouldn't be so sure!'

I watched him scoop it into a pot and take it outside.

I would never look at slugs the same way again. If I saw one, large or small, I would I give it a wide berth, sure it could smell my fear and then attack me.

SHRINK WRAPPED

My pallet of goods arrived in Australia roughly two months after I did, unceremoniously deposited in our still-empty dining room by two large men who said little, asked for a signature and moved on. This shrink-wrapped pallet of belongings was all that remained of the life I'd left behind. (Or more accurately, *our* life, Annie's and mine.) But for them it was just another drop to tick off their long list of deliveries for the day.

I stared at the pallet, remembering the day it left Dallas. I felt like a kid on Christmas morning. It was a wooden crate full of memories, not just of my life as a single person, but of the life built before, by Annie. Reminders of people, places, and experiences indelibly woven into my existence. This crate represented everything Annie and I were. It had travelled halfway across the globe and held important relics of my life; a signpost of who I (she?) was and had been, and a promise of who I could be.

I started unpacking, breathing in the lingering woody scent of Texas cedar as I went, wondering which treasure I would rediscover first. I'd stacked the pallet according to the importance of each item, or how I'd thought I could use them to recreate and remember those important parts of my history. Our wedding plates and gifts were put straight to use in the kitchen. But then there were photos of holidays with Kate, seashells from every country Annie had ever visited, stuffed animals, books and clothing and even a boxed set of *The Chronicles of Narnia*, a gift from Mother when Annie had been ill as a child and confined to bed for a few weeks.

It was an ending with a history. Annie had a nomadic heart and believed that ultimately she would live overseas. She never questioned this. For her, it was the Philippines. But this journey was mine, and I chose Australia. My move to Australia was, in its own way, fulfilment of Annie's dream, just not the way she would have orchestrated it.

It was also a beginning – for me. A clean slate, a new chapter full of stories and experiences I could create as I go. Yes, there would be struggles. I was a newlywed in a new culture with no one to rely on. But this was now my life. I had chosen this and left Annie's dreams behind.

I stared at the label wedged under the shrink wrap. Port clearances where this pallet had travelled. I had a vague memory of another time. Another cargo boat, a child traveling with her family to a new life in a new land. It wasn't clear, but it was a memory I could almost touch at the edge of my mind. I had an inkling then, as I stood looking at this crate, of a life that was hidden. Of something left behind. But I turned away, my instinct telling me this was something I did not want to know. It was too hard, too complicated, something I couldn't wrestle with. I chose to focus on this new life and new marriage and a new home woven into the fabric of this exotic land called Australia.

AN AUSSIE CHRISTMAS CAROL

Each summer, cognitive dissonance would arrive right on schedule. Warm weather and Christmas – together? This always bewildered my North American brain. It didn't matter how long I lived in Australia, this reversal of seasons confounded me. I had memories of living in Denver where Annie would curl up – alone – with a good book and a hot chocolate. She would watch the falling blanket of white and dream of crackling fires and making snow angels. On the other hand, this festive holiday season I was in a t-shirt, shorts and thongs, making plans with Tom for the beaches we would explore together.

I had only been in Australia a few months when Tom and I made our first trek to the far north coast of NSW to spend Christmas with his family. I packed bags full of trinkets and presents, hoping to curry favour with a family whose son had married a foreigner. I was full of the typical new in-law jitters, having only spent a short time with them when I'd come over for our honeymoon.

I unpacked my jeans, reminding myself they were not necessary. It would be a strictly shorts and t-shirt affair as we ventured north to the NSW/QLD border, where it was warmer and more humid than Sydney, minus air conditioning. This lack of comfort, as well as using a clothesline rather than a dryer, were also things I found I had to adjust to.

We stayed with Tom's parents. (A bit cramped for newlyweds, but it was a budgetary thing.) We would use their place as a base and plan our adventures from there. Tom acquainted me with the area, from the beaches of Fingal Head up to Currumbin, to the streets of Murwillumbah and Tweed Heads. I watched in wonder as people gathered along foreshores and dangled legs off jetties or dropped in a line on this fine summer day. I reminded myself that it wasn't as if there was snow in Texas at Christmas, but winter winds could still be bitter and frigid if you weren't rugged up properly.

We went to a mall in Coolangatta to do some last-minute Christmas shopping. I was relieved to be inside on this sweltering 35^C day. The air conditioning was working overtime and *I'm Dreaming of a White Christmas* and *Jingle Bells* were heralding in the festive season. I stopped in my tracks. Hanging from the ceiling in the middle of this multi-story arcade was Santa. It was no Santa I'd seen before. There was the requisite chubby man with a white beard in a sleigh. But in this truly Australian version, Santa was decked out in a Hawaiian shirt, shorts, and sunglasses. And the sleigh was not being pulled by eight sleek reindeer, but kangaroos (called boomers), hopping through the sky for Santa's all-important Christmas deliveries.

'Welcome to an Aussie Christmas,' Tom whispered as he leaned in and kissed me.

It was a family tradition for Tom's brother, Larry, and his wife Sharon, to host our Christmas lunch. I was reminded how warm and friendly they were. Larry and Sharon and their two kids lived in a large home outside of the town of Murwillumbah, hidden down country roads, through endless acres of sugar cane fields. (Tom told me stories of cane toad hunting in these fields, sending shivers up my spine.) Our Christmas meal would include platters of cold meats and salads, topped off by Tom's mum's trifle dessert. It was not the traditional trifle, full of ladyfingers painted with jam and soaked in sherry and jelly (I reminded myself jelly was jell-o and jam was jelly), instead it was full of red, green, orange and yellow jelly cube treats mixed with chunks of Madeira cake and slathered with custard and cream. It was his mum's Aussie take on an English classic. The family loved it. After lunch, everyone relaxed outside, beer in hand as kids swam in the pool or played with their new toys while dogs ran around the big backyard.

These treks for Christmas were an institution. I began to adjust, accepting a warm Christmas was the new normal.

The holidays were also a time when I was forced to reflect on my connection with Annie. Snow and hot chocolate, the Christmas parties Mother threw – these memories were all Annie's and I had vicariously absconded with them.

As I leafed through the *postcard memories* from Annie's life, I could see her as an excited young child unwrapping a book from under the carefully decorated Christmas tree, with all its glass baubles and tinsel. It was Christmas Eve and Annie clutched this book of fairy tales to her chest, eagerly taking it to bed. She read into the wee hours, listening for Santa to come down the chimney and scoff the milk and cookies she had laid out for him. The crumbs and a few drops of milk were all that was left the next morning, making Annie giggle with glee. The family had Christmas traditions, from the Twelfth Night Party to inviting international students to our home so they wouldn't be alone on such a family day. These Christmas memories were small flickers of joy in the dark mist hiding so much of my history.

I did the calculations. Annie met Tom online in December 1995. He came to the US in February of 1996. Then came the day when Annie left and I returned, which was sometime in April. We were married in June and I was on a plane to Australia by October. I, Maggie, never actually had a North American winter with hot chocolate and cold noses. When Annie lived in Denver, her Christmases were about snow angels and snowball fights. Or frozen windshields needing to be de-iced before going to work. I never had that. Everything I cherished about Christmas came from Annie, her experiences and memories, not mine.

It made the things I thought I knew seem hollow, built on the pretence that I had lived a life which I knew I hadn't. I would eventually refer to these memories, and many others, as me/she/we times – acknowledging they weren't mine, but somehow, because of this shared body, I could claim them. We were connected, and while there were things hidden away, these simple things, these happy moments were experiences I could draw on to make my life that bit more whole.

I wondered at times if marrying Tom and moving to Australia was another form of running away. By moving to the other side of the world, I thought I had left Annie and her history of abuse behind. It was a ludicrous hope on my part. Annie was with me. Even though she was hidden away, I couldn't get away from her feelings. I carried them with me, including the way she missed the few things she cherished about her life. One year of hot Christmas Days with cold food platters and trifle was nice, but as the years passed, I missed a cold northern hemisphere Christmas.

This became the way it would often happen. I would live Annie's feelings for something which was, in fact, hers and could not truly claim as my own. It was part of the complicated entanglement which, as time went on, I realised I would never be able to undo.

GO WEST

One weekend we took a day trip to the Blue Mountains on a City Rail Country Train. This area west of Sydney is full of quaint tourist towns with elegant settler-style B&Bs and clifftop lookouts with stunning views into deep green valleys. In the same way Denver sat at the base of the Colorado Rockies, the Blue Mountains called to me from the flat lands of Sydney, rising above the urban sprawl below.

Our country train had large picture windows, allowing us to drink in the views as we left the suburbs behind and crossed the Nepean River, before meandering into the foothills. The Blue Mountains got their name from the oil of the forests of eucalyptus trees which on hot days hung over the mountains in a blue haze. This haze was visible long before we were out of Sydney, hanging over the hills in a mystical fog.

I closed my eyes as the train climbed into the mountains, feeling the repetitive tick, tick, tick of the wheels beneath me. In my mind, I could see the Colorado Rockies. This was something that happened more often than I cared to admit. I never lived in Colorado, Annie did. There were moments when her memories would bleed through me on an almost spiritual level, as if our souls were communing. I never talked to Tom about these experiences. Of course, he knew I was MPD, but it wasn't present in our daily lives. In hindsight, I should have discussed these experiences with him. It might have saved some of the fallout from our marriage in years to come. But I was fearful this knowledge would scare him.

As I wrestled with my MPD life, I had no one to support me the way Annie had Shrink #2. I was alone in this new land, with no idea how to access resources for the type of support someone like me – with MPD – would need. On this occasion, I did my standard *push it away, put it in a box and focus on your life now* routine. It worked. I hoped.

The train line meandered up through the hamlets of Springwood, Hazelbrook and Leura, and we got off at Katoomba, a town full of coffee shops, bakeries and stores selling vintage wares. We wandered the streets and made our way to Echo Point, where we could look out over the magnificent Jamison Valley and The Three Sisters, rock formations steeped in indigenous history, which stood as sentries over the stunning vista. The wind was cold and chaffing, a reminder of Annie's days in the National Parks of Colorado, or hiking in Canada with Kate. These were her memories, not mine, but I decided to just enjoy the experience for what it was.

Late, physically spent and emotionally full, I flopped into my seat on the train heading back to Sydney, my arm linked through Tom's, snuggling into his warmth. I declared I'd like to live in the Blue Mountains. I enjoyed these moments of physical contact, feeling safe and secure in Tom's intimacy. He laughed and said it was too far out of Sydney and the commute would be a killer. I was quietly determined, and already planning our next trip back up the hill.

CAREER OPTIONS

I found a long-term casual job at a national department store chain, with headquarters near the train station in Lidcombe, another Western Sydney suburb. I worked in the accounts department alongside five other women, reconciling daily sales figures from stores around Australia. It was a job I endured – plugging numbers into an Excel spreadsheet all day long was not my idea of fun. And besides, maths and numbers were not my thing. I had Annie to thank for that. She had struggled with school, maths specifically, and this was something she had passed on to me.

Being a casual position, it meant that when I slipped on a wet step in our backyard and broke my ankle, I had no job. My pay check, while not a necessity, was what we were putting away to buy a house. I tried not to worry as Tom went off to his job each day, leaving me on the couch, remote control in hand, watching far too much TV.

Tom encouraged me to look at up-skilling and training in a new area as a way to keep myself busy. He suggested thinking about IT, his field of interest, which he hoped to share with me. The age of the World Wide Web had arrived and he encouraged me to learn about this thing called HTML, which was how web pages were built. I barely knew what the Internet was, let alone knowing how to use all the lines, dots, dashes, asterisks and symbols required for the coding behind these pages. Tom said it would be fun. Everything I knew about IT I learned from him.

I knew at some point Tom wanted to go out on his own, to be his own boss and live his life the way he wanted. By me taking a course in web page building, he hoped it would give us the opportunity to one day work together.

I found a course and signed up for it. It was a month of Saturdays spent with geeks who were keen to try their hands at web page building. The class was interesting, probably in most part because of the friendliness and knowledge of the teacher, a man named Phillip Wade. Phillip and I got along well and I picked up the logic behind HTML quickly. I surprised myself. Annie's memories were of academic failure. Book learning wasn't her thing, and I wondered if this success could be mine alone.

After class one day I was talking with Phillip and told him that my husband was a software programmer. I said that Tom wanted, one day, to go out on his own and try web programming, but he was more about databases, not just pretty pictures. Phillip listened and said his day job was working for a large multinational and he managed a number of their web projects. He was always on the lookout for new programmers. Maybe he could talk to my husband? I said I would pass it on to Tom.

This began a series of coffee meetings between Tom and Phillip. Before I knew it, Tom was up late at night, working on projects for Phillip. He was happy, doing what he enjoyed and being independent. I got the odd HTML job, but it was Tom who Phillip was interested in. He had the programming skills to link databases with a web interface, which at that time was new and innovative.

At the same time, our landlord in Auburn gave us notice to move. I was quietly happy about this. I liked the landlord, but was ready to explore other areas around Sydney. Tom started to look at other rentals in Western Sydney, while I began my quiet campaign to move up the hill. He was still not keen on the idea because of the required commute. How about Penrith I asked? I figured if I could get him that far then maybe I could eventually get us up to the mountains. We looked at train timetables and it turned out to be basically the same distance for him to travel to his day job. It was also easier to find rentals in Penrith. My final argument was to remind him that the work he was doing for Phillip was remote and would not be affected. Tom acquiesced. Penrith it was. Whether he gave in to my nagging or actually agreed, I wasn't sure. I didn't care. I was getting us a step closer to the mountains.

The longer I lived with Tom, the more I realised how little I knew him when we agreed to get married. Not only had we not lived together until Australia, but the bulk of our courtship had been conducted by email and phone, which created a false sense of intimacy. It was easy for me to say things over the phone that, face-to-face, would make me blush. And I'm not referring to sexual innuendo, but sharing deep-running emotions and matters of the heart. Phone calls and emails can't reveal subtle cues and vulnerabilities, when body language makes things much more transparent. We hadn't had the benefit of slow, relaxed time together when we could get to know these small things about each other. We were forced to dive into the deep end of relationship acclimatization.

One thing I learnt quickly was that Tom was very methodical in his thinking and needed time to process information. When we had discussions, he needed to go away and work through things internally. It could take him days, if not weeks, to provide me with his thoughts about something we had discussed. We never really tossed things around, debating and considering all angles of approach. This was a process he was used to doing solo. On the other hand, I was more inclined to verbal diarrhoea. Whatever was going on in my head I would say aloud, not considering how my ill-formed thoughts might be received. I was an external communicator; Tom was an internal processor. I found this a challenging part of our relationship, but I was his partner, and this was a commitment requiring patience and openness.

When it comes to a person's behaviour, employers are not so patient and tolerant. Tom was threatened with dismissal at his day job. They found out about the after-hours work he was doing for Phillip and believed he was using proprietary company information for personal gain. Tom assured them this work was completely different, but they refused to discuss this and simply fired him. They were brazen enough to say they didn't think he would challenge this because he was such a quiet and reserved person.

Instead, Tom decided to file an unfair dismissal lawsuit. I don't remember much of it, apart from the fact it was a brutal process. The company's solicitor made accusations about Tom's intentions and attacks on his character and even put me on the stand. In the end, Tom won the case, and although solicitors' fees left us with just enough money to go out for a celebratory dinner, it was an emotional victory for his sense of value and personal worth.

The work from Phillip continued to come in and Tom was introduced to others in the company who wanted to utilise his skills. At one point, Phillip invited us over for coffee and began his hard sell on a future in the Internet industry. There were two approaches we could take. One would be for Tom to continue programming work as a sole trader. There were plenty of opportunities, but more and more, because of perceived reliability, large corporates wanted to engage with a business, not an individual. This is where option two was presented. Phillip encouraged us to hook up with some of the front-end graphic developers he knew and build a partnership. It would allow us to grow and would open up lucrative opportunities.

This was Tom's dream come true. He was a loner who liked his independence. This translated to his work as well. I was unsure, fearful even. I had no confidence and no experience in running a small business. But this was Tom's opportunity to follow his dream and I wanted to support him.

We opened a small office in western Sydney to establish professional credibility. From there Tom continued his work for Phillip and others. More importantly, we began to network with other industry professionals. My job was to nurture these relationships and seek out new work, doing the occasional HTML job when it came up. Almost immediately I found myself wading through a sea of sales and marketing, teaching clients about usability and database management. On top of this, Tom and I were both directors of our small company. And while Tom handled the tech side, management of the business was left to me. I was flying blind. But the work kept coming in so I assumed we were doing something right.

JUST KATE

I missed Kate, remembering the late-night antics and conversations she and Annie shared. So, even though it was in the middle of our crazy expanding business when she decided to come for a visit, I was thrilled.

I felt youthful with Kate, with a sense of freedom I realised I did not feel in my marriage. Kate was well, just Kate. Full of life, questioning everything, and appreciating all the opportunities life brought her way. This attitude was contagious. I knew why Annie had found a place of joyful respite with her. I did too, and it lightened my heart. We talked occasionally on the phone, but most of our communication was now by email and I missed our connection. When I picked her up at the airport, it was as if nothing had changed. We laughed often, just like she had done with Annie, and now with me. This continuity was a salve for my heart.

Kate's plan was to spend extended time in Australia. She was still young and single and wanted to explore the world, visiting as many new places as she could. How fortunate that I lived in one of these exotic places she wanted to visit! She would use our home as a base, and in typical Kate style, was intent on traversing the continent on a push bike – alone. She would do this in several different trips, and she would spend time with us in between.

I was looking forward to spending time with someone who really knew me. Every time she came back through Penrith, we made plans and did day or weekend trips together, exploring areas around Sydney that were off the beaten track. We had long discussions about politics, faith, lifestyles and everything in between. We didn't always agree, but it didn't matter because of the mutual respect and love we shared.

Kate and Tom got along well, their shared love of music and sense of humour made them easy friends. We spent numerous evenings playing card games and listening to new music Kate introduced us too.

Kate considered herself a wine aficionado and was keen to experience some Australian varieties. We went on a trip to the Hunter Valley just north of Sydney, where we could let our inner wine snobs run free, making a list of what we liked at each of the wineries we visited. We left with our car full of bottles of water and bread rolls to stay hydrated and headed home with the boot crammed with wines to taste and share later. My heart and stomach were sated with the joys of this rich, lifelong friendship.

When Kate left, life went back to normal, which was all about work. But I was left with an empty spot in my heart which only Kate could fill. And even with how dear she was, I still hadn't told her about me, my new reality. Why not? Kate knew Annie was MPD. It was something she had been completely transparent about with her. Annie knew it made no difference to her. In fact, as Kate had told her, it was one of the things that made Annie (me?) a fascinating friend. So why couldn't I tell her?

I had wondered a few times how I would say it. 'Uhm, you know the person you became such good friends with at school? Well, surprise! That was someone else. She disappeared and now you're stuck with me.'

If I was honest, I had no idea how to explain it all to Kate. It was easier to focus on my marriage and new life in Australia. At times, I would try to explain to myself the puzzle of my life. But it was built around a psychological concept, instead of the concrete person who had inhabited my (or was it our?) body for thirty-odd years. I could barely understand it myself, let alone say it out loud.

Until I could accept all the pain and confusion in my past and understand how I, Maggie, had come to be, how could I expect anyone, even Kate, to understand? I wasn't prepared for the questions. And Kate, I knew, would have questions.

One of the things I was struggling to come to terms with was God and faith. It was important to Annie, and I became intent on trying to understand how it translated to my life. We were attending a booming non-denominational church in Mt Druitt. It was huge, eclectic, and multicultural. We socialized each Sunday, enjoying the sermon and music, but not taking it to heart. Faith was peripheral, I wasn't owning it, unsure how it might look for me in this new home and culture. I continued to carry the burden of the Southern Baptist orthodoxy Annie had adhered to, the rules of which were driven home to me in our pre-marriage counselling. Be submissive, support your husband, nurture him. He is the head of the household, whatever he says goes. It was all I had to go on. This remained the foundation of my relationship with Tom. And it was easier to hide in the busyness of life and marriage than figure out who *I* really was. So, my pattern of pretend, denial, and hard work continued.

UP THE HILL

Business was booming. We were determined to increase our profile and make our first million. We'd been introduced to a few front-end web design companies that appreciated Tom's skill with computer programming. They managed the look and feel of the website, while Tom did all the back-end coding. I was managing relationships and new business, but it was Tom's brain they wanted, his deft skill with computer programming. It was my job to translate into a proposal the goals which Tom would discuss with the client. Once the work was accepted, I was the middleman, a project manager, and usability consultant. I constantly felt out of my depth, double-checking everything with Tom for fear of missing some crucial bit of information, jeopardizing the project. This worked well for the most part. Tom and I didn't get in each other's way, and anything important we didn't have time for, we discussed on the trip home to Penrith.

We allowed ourselves to dream about owning a home of our own. Nothing over the top, but something we could call ours. I continued to push for the Blue Mountains and Tom admitted he did like the area. It was more conducive to family life when the time came to have kids. So, we pulled out the train schedule and quickly learned about the Blue Mountains country trains, known by the locals as *The Fish* or *The Chips*. Both were express trains to Central Station, only stopping at the major stations, Penrith, Parramatta, and Strathfield. There was no reason not to include house hunting in the mountains in our mix. We decided to look as far up the hill as Springwood. This was a major stop and the commute to the office would be roughly forty-five minutes.

Before we knew it, we had signed on the dotted line and become the proud mortgage holders of a three-bed, one-bath house in Springwood. The garage had been converted by the previous owners into a large study, perfect for our home office. It was a small, secluded home in a quiet cul-de-sac backing onto a nature reserve, giving us nothing but green quiet space behind us. We had barely started unpacking boxes when we were greeted by the couple next door and the older woman from across the road. We felt welcomed and at home. Between work and applying a fresh coat of paint, I was happy. I became a domestic goddess, cooking and working to make this space a home.

We had decided early on that we wanted to have children, but didn't feel we should try until we were financially stable. For us, that meant owning a home and having secure jobs. We were on the way now, and it was time to get real.

I had suspicions I couldn't get pregnant, but for no real reason I could identify. I didn't want a medical exam to confirm something I didn't want to know. There was an image in my mind of a gynaecologist in Texas advising Annie she had internal scars, which would make it difficult to get pregnant. Tom and I discussed at length the ramifications of this before we were married. He understood this was part of our lives if he married me, and how adoption would be central to growing our family. Now we were finally in a place to look into what the arduous process of adopting might look like.

The best way to describe the Australian adoption process is 'hurry up and wait'. And by wait I mean months, sometimes six to nine months between contact from what was then the Department of Community Services (DoCS) and the next step. We were told this upfront. Learn to be patient, this isn't a quick process. But commit to it and you will grow your family. It's what we were told. Reams of paperwork had to be completed, medical exams done, self-histories and financials documented. This was all just to submit an expression of interest. When we were approved, we could then book into an introductory seminar. We followed the rules and waited.

While we waited, we worked. We moved our offices to Surry Hills, a vibrant district just out of the Sydney CBD. It was close to clients and the airport, allowing us to easily service our growing clientele in Melbourne. Our work lives were joined at the hip, we would take the train most days, or if we had to visit a client, we would take the car. I tried to take one day a week and work at home, giving me time to get laundry and shopping done, but the demands of a growing business meant this didn't happen often. I was the face of the business to clients and had to be available when needed. I was often taking phone calls while I was in the supermarket doing our weekly shop.

The business was becoming too much for just the two of us, so we hired additional programmers, a project manager and a front desk receptionist. This was never the path I would have chosen. I would never have imagined myself working as the manager and director of a small business trying to find its way in a burgeoning tech industry I knew very little about. We were living in a world where ridiculous amounts of money were being thrown around just to get the edge on the latest gadget and new, you-beaut application. I was never sure this was what I should be doing, but succumbed to the lure of the secure future I hoped all this hard work would give us, optimistic that one day the sacrifices would pay off.

We had been told this was the hard part about growing a business – the bottom line would steal our freedom. The need to balance the books and hopefully turn a profit would become the monster which owned us. Time was precious, and rather than prioritising our young and developing marriage, Tom and I became consumed by the demands of the business. We had a house, a mortgage, two dogs, and two cats and that was it. Our constant late hours and trips away meant our personal lives and our relationship was put on hold.

Outside of work, there wasn't much in our lives apart from our local church. The congregation was kind and gracious. Many were like us, city commuters, which meant they had no time other than weekends for socialising. Their days were consumed with rushing to trains and following timetables. We understood this all too well. Work, work, work, then occasionally see church friends on weekends. This was our routine.

We found the time to occasionally piggyback a personal getaway with a business trip. Once we flew to Perth for a pitch. We never got the job, but after the meeting, in an attempt to *be* together, rather than just doing business together, we had a few days at Margaret River, wine tasting and whale watching.

We were aiming towards a long-term payoff, a future in which the hard work we put in now would allow us to slow down, enjoy children, and be financially secure. That was the goal. But the truth was, we had unconsciously sacrificed our marriage for work.

9/11

At our peak, we had a staff of fifteen working for us. They were mostly programmers who focused on building databases to integrate with graphic design, and we were building strong relationships with some of the front-end design companies Phillip had encouraged us to work with. We even shared offices with a design group at one point, testing the waters to see if we should look at merging. We thought this would make us a force to be reckoned with in the industry. In the end, we decided the autonomy of being able to work with multiple groups would serve our goals best. But the reality of this was that we were hired by the design and front-end companies who almost always took the lead on projects. This put us at their beck and call, and came between us having our own relationships with the end clients. For the most part, this worked, and we maintained good lines of communication with clients and designers.

Then the end came.

Phillip had referred us to a tech company in Melbourne and they approached us about working with them on a complicated project with a large multinational client. This tech company, three times our size, would take the lead with the client, which was also in Melbourne. It sounded like a good plan and would be worth several million dollars. It was the sort of job to set us up the way we wanted. This was always our bottom line, doing what we could to eventually build financial independence.

It was sadly ironic that our singular focus on success meant we missed the signs of trouble. We couldn't fail at this job. It was too big, too important, failure simply wasn't possible. The first warning came when two of our senior programmers passed on their hunch from conversations with the staff in Melbourne that something wasn't right. I couldn't see it, and Tom was too neck-deep in project deliverables to notice. But the problem grew.

Pleasantries with our partner disappeared and I started getting curt emails demanding quicker turnaround on project milestones. It was only when I received a late afternoon call from my counterpart in Melbourne asking me to come down as soon as was convenient to discuss delivery and meet with the client, I began to understand the full extent of what had gone wrong.

What I discovered, as our partner and I headed off to our meeting, was the individual in charge of the project inside the multinational was in trouble. Their job was on the line if this project failed and they hoped they could save their own skin by demanding more from us, essentially laying the blame at our feet. We were at the bottom of the food chain and the tech company which had contracted us was stuck in the middle. In the end, they decided to hold us accountable the only way they knew, by withholding payment for services rendered.

The size of this project meant we had put off all other work. This was a huge mistake, as it was our sole income stream to pay our staff. In the end, I was meeting payroll from our emergency funds, already in overdraft. There were rumblings from staff that something was amiss, and when they started asking about unpaid super contributions, the full impact of our situation hit me in the face. If we didn't act quickly, we would lose everything.

Tom and I discussed the situation with our financial adviser. Pragmatically, we needed a partner, someone who could inject funds and help with direction and leadership. So we went fishing. Even the company in Melbourne which had hired our services wanted a slice of us. But everyone who saw our financial statements saw the same thing. We were a failing business with a single large client. One by one each potential investment avenue dried up.

In all the turmoil, MPD lingered in my mind but was never at the forefront. I was anxiety-ridden, a lot. I felt out of touch, often. I wondered, but only on the odd occasion when I was feeling desperate, what would happen if the MPD reared its head. How would I cope with no support? But I would push these moments aside and return to focusing on the immediate prospect of our business falling apart. This was how I was able to keep the world of MPD at bay. The beauty of MPD was being able to unconsciously segment my life into manageable experiences, keeping me safe. In my own way, I was dissociating. I was so busy trying to save the company and be the perfect partner for my husband, that I was able to successfully keep Annie and *The Girls* completely out of my mind. MPD never came up; there were never inklings or internal rumblings about another existence. I hoped it didn't matter. Maybe I was like someone in remission from cancer. There was no evidence of the disease, so I lived as if it wasn't there.

The day we finally decided to wind up the company and go into administration was devastating. We were killing our business. I felt so much shame. Somehow this was justice meted out as I thought of everything our employees lost – benefits, security gone. I was so full of self-loathing I couldn't attend the liquidation meeting. I left Tom to face the anger and confusion of our staff.

We drove home in silence, lost in our own spiralling emotions. I thought about all the things we would personally lose. There was our house and our car. That was bad enough. But the biggest loss would be our future family. We would not be allowed to go through the adoption process as bankrupts. This was the ultimate kick in the guts. It would be at least seven years, the length of a bankruptcy, before we could re-enter the process. I was thirty-seven. This would effectively age us out of the adoption program.

We walked into the house. I wondered how much more time we would have in this place. The dogs and cats greeted us, demanding food and affection. At least they needed us. We were spent. We had no more to say to each other. I made a quick pasta dinner and flopped on the couch, seeking respite in whatever was on TV.

Something was amiss. There was breaking news on every channel. We were confronted with the images, replayed over and over again, of two airplanes slamming into the World Trade Centre towers in New York City. There was footage of the aftermath of another plane hitting the Pentagon in Washington, D.C., and of a third plane which had crash-landed in a field in Pennsylvania, apparently destined for the US Capitol, but diverted off-course by brave passengers. The news anchor kept returning to the crumbling Twin Towers, where people were scattering, running for their lives through a blanket of grey ash.

Tom and I looked at each other. 'Well, I suppose there are people in this world who have it worse than us right now,' was all I could think to say. We had our lives and our health, while thousands did not. This might have provided some perspective, but by no means made me feel better.

Our lives continued to crumble. We were waiting in limbo. The shame of our failed business sucked out the core of our marriage. We never talked about our pain. We simply went through the motions, trying to figure out what the next day would hold, whether it was the bank coming to evict us or bankruptcy paperwork we needed to file. Even buying the most basic of groceries seemed too much to do. We could not comfort each other or come together in our grief. I suspect we blamed each other but would not admit it. We lived in a vacuum of silence and loss.

DEPRESSION

I was never more grateful for our church family than at this difficult time. They knew we were committed to our business and our adoption process and understood the loss we were grieving. Church friends called us in concern, asking how they could help. We didn't know what to ask for. We couldn't explain how we were feeling, or what we needed. We'd been blindsided by grief and loss. Talking to others about how we felt or what our practical needs were was more than we could do. But our church friends were ever faithful, kind and thoughtful, even bringing us groceries, in case we would be left with nothing to eat.

These relationships with accepting souls who asked for nothing in return remain a cherished memory to me. Because of them, I started looking outside my grief. I would sit with friends late into the night trying to find the words for the overwhelming loss I felt, daring to ask the question: why did God let this happen? I didn't understand, but I had to believe that somehow this would all work out. It was the point of faith, wasn't it? Trusting good can come out of bad? Was there a bigger purpose we did not yet comprehend?

Or was it simply an opportunity for Tom and I to draw closer to each other? These were all things I kept holding in my mind, sifting through them, trying to find some sort of elusive hope.

It's hard to explain how depression starts. No one deliberately goes there. It ate at me, a bit each day. The first big step into depression for both Tom and I was the letter we had to write to DoCS explaining we had to pull out of the adoption program. Explaining why was the hardest, forcing us to admit our weaknesses and fallibility. Our dream of creating a family was being taken from us.

Tom and I dealt with our pain very differently. Tom would retreat to the bedroom and sleep. I would go to a friend's house and we would talk, where I would question endlessly the fairness of life. I think in the end this is what helped me heal quicker. I reached out, looked at what was outside myself, and simply did something, no matter how feeble an effort it seemed.

Hope first came in the form of a couple in the church who had a house they wanted to rent. It was a simple, three-bed, one-bath place and still in Springwood. It was near the train station and our church. It was a roof over our heads. I saw this as a tiny glimmer, an assurance God would provide for us.

I ended up with a front desk job at a not-for-profit organisation in the Sydney CBD. It was a long commute, and the work was quite basic. But it was a job. It got me out of the house and it paid our bills. My employer quickly realized I was overqualified and started giving me more responsibility. It was nothing over the top, but she valued my contribution and I appreciated the no-stress work life.

I never wanted to run a business again – it was a burden and a responsibility I was not prepared or equipped to handle. I was sure the failure of the business was my fault. Everything was always my fault. It was a deep-seated belief I held, that I was a failure and a fraud. Where did that come from? I couldn't put a finger on it but knew it was a truth living deep in my heart. I would talk about this 'flaw' in my character, telling people there were children dying in Somalia and it was my fault. They would laugh, I would laugh. It was a joke, but not really. Everything was my fault.

It took Tom longer to find work. His self-doubt hit him hard, and he felt unqualified for the jobs he applied for. This had a direct consequence on his confidence. It was his life's dream to be financially independent, free to pursue the work he wanted. I understood this about him and gave him the space to wrestle with this loss. We were like ships passing in the night, acknowledging each other, but not really talking or communicating.

Tom began getting contract work and we were able to pay extra toward our bankruptcy debt. Under it all and despite the depression, Tom remained a romantic. I think, for a little while, he really believed somehow things would work out. We put together a plan to pay out our debt, focusing on mine first. Paying a little bit extra each payday to the Bankruptcy Trustee, in hopes of ending our sentence early. In Tom's mind, getting rid of this financial curse would somehow make everything right.

The underlying current of depression was a dark beast. The focus of those years was to get our bankruptcy paid off, but no matter how hard we tried, each day it seemed further away, swallowing any hope we dared muster. We were living in a rental we were grateful for, but it was not ours. We had an old car we tried to use as little as possible, for fear it might die on us, and could not afford another one. In every opportunity to find hope, we instead found a way to make a dark and sombre assessment of our failures, forever comparing any glimmer of achievement to what we had lost. We didn't talk. We hid our pain from each other in order to survive. I never discussed how horrible I felt about myself, instead allowing the mantle of blame and failure to settle over me. We learned the fine art of dancing around each other, our shared gloom propelling us further and further apart.

ELUSIVE HOPE

When Tom and I did manage to talk, it was about the loss of a family, and how it was affecting us. In a last-ditch effort to hang on to the dream of children, we decided to try and have a child biologically. We wanted to find something to fill the void of emptiness we lived with. For the first time, we were talking. Yes, the chances were slim, but why not? Screw it, I told Tom, let's try anyway.

I went to see an obstetrician and they confirmed, after copious tests, what my gut already told me, I probably couldn't get pregnant. I had secondary infertility – I didn't ovulate. There was no explainable reason. The doctor said he would try and help, but there was very little chance of conceiving. I was prescribed medication to help jump-start my cycle and he mapped out the most likely times of the month when I might be most fertile and could get pregnant. It became prescriptive for both of us, the fertility window each month marking the date for another bout of perfunctory sex, to be followed by the pregnancy test, always negative, the requisite weeks later. My body was refusing to come to the party and make this baby. I hated myself.

Even more than my self-hatred was an unwillingness to admit the truth that was unfolding in my mind. Every time the pregnancy test was negative, from somewhere in the dark parts of my brain, I would hear a faint voice pleading, *'Please don't be pregnant – I can't do that again.'*

This was like a slap in the face. I couldn't avoid my past. It was easy to say I was abused, but what I couldn't say was that I was MPD. The only person in Australia who knew this was Tom, and I intended to keep it that way. I was convinced if I admitted my MPD to anyone else, I would be branded psychotic. And yet I knew my inability to get pregnant was a direct consequence of this history I pretended didn't exist. My doctor called it secondary infertility, but if I scanned through Annie's memories the physical damage caused by the horrific sex she and *The Girls* survived was obvious.

I was too ashamed to talk to anyone about any of this.

The tests, the routine sex (which I tolerated for the hope of a child), these were all desperate attempts to create a family. Tom and I were trying to rebuild the semblance of a normal life. And every time the pregnancy test came back negative, hope died a little more. We quickly reverted to conversations about grocery shopping, our jobs, and what were we going to watch on TV after dinner. We steered clear of the very conversations we needed to have, deep matters of the heart in which we would push back the veil of self-protection and meet each other halfway in our fear and vulnerability. But we couldn't do it.

There is a lot of vagueness to this time of my life. For several years we relied heavily on church life and the friends it gave us. And although pregnancy eluded us, month by month, we did see our bankruptcy debt decrease. This, at least, should have given us hope.

But the unspoken damage the failure of the business had taken on us as a couple was much deeper than either of us could imagine. We worked and lived together, no more. I was desperate for communication, for someone to lean on. Tom, well, I wasn't sure. The best I could guess was that he wanted space and freedom. I craved a deep relationship with my husband, in which honest, direct truth was valued. But Tom had demonstrated over and again this was not something he could do.

I am sure in these years, because of all these factors, I descended into an utterly co-dependent relationship with Tom. My sole goal was to earn his approval, whether by making his favourite meals, ironing his clothes, tolerating sex, or torturing myself (and him) trying to guess at any time what I could do to please him. In doing all this, I believed I would be a good wife and he would love me. But the more I yearned for Tom's attention and approval, the more he emotionally disappeared. The walls went up as he protected himself against my insatiable neediness.

A few women in the church had revealed in passing their own marriage problems and I braved myself to talk to them. I realised quickly that they too seemed to crave a depth of relationship they weren't getting with their spouses. Finding out that I wasn't alone in my situation should, or could have, helped assuage my desperation. Instead, I interpreted this as symptomatic of what I had observed was a more relaxed Australian approach to faith than the hardline Southern Baptist doctrine I had inherited from Annie. In response to disappointment inside their marriages, it seemed these women created their own sense of worth independent of their spouse. They were better partners because outside of their marriage relationship they had found something that engaged and nurtured their soul. This apparent contradiction would take me decades to understand.

My anxiety was running rampant, perhaps partially due to early onset menopause. I was not aware enough of my body to read those subtle clues. I felt trapped in circumstances beyond my control. I lashed out at Tom. I was angry that he was depressed and not taking care of himself, bouncing from contract to contract, instead of finding a secure job. I was so wrapped up in my own pain I couldn't see how paying out on someone who was depressed was never going to help either of us. There was no kindness or empathy on my part. Tom and I were at an impasse.

I was becoming aware of how triggering this emotional chaos was for *The Girls*. In times of high anxiety, I realised that I was much more in tune with their fears. They were scared of Tom, hated the sex, and were afraid they would be used, again. They believed I was putting them in another abusive situation. I think this was the catalyst for even more emotionally erratic behaviour. I suspect much of this was behind my clingy neediness and fear of rejection. We had arguments over everything and anything. I remember very little behind the why of these arguments, but I do remember that my first instinct was always to run, to get in the car and drive. I spent one night in a hotel, another in a friend's house. I even spent one night parked in a dark corner of a national park, wide awake and thinking that if someone did come and attack me, would anyone really care? When I came home from these flights, Tom never said anything. We never discussed what had happened, we never returned to the cause of the fights. Nothing was said and I just got on with making dinner or whatever was the next chore to be done to try to make amends for my behaviour. This was our standard mode of operation.

Tom eventually secured a long-term contract with the State Government. It was a good job and allowed him to work from home, only occasionally going into their Parramatta office. This turned into a full-time job offer, with a boss he liked and who respected him. It was a great opportunity and I hoped the job would help him rediscover some of his self-worth. We were back to both being commuters, and both earning an income. There seemed to be some balance. And while the walls were still up between us, instead of the dreaded silence, we fell into an amiable companionship. We talked about his work, getting back into the work-a-day world. We even made vague attempts from time to time to go out and enjoy each other's company.

We dared to put together a time frame for getting out of our bankruptcy. Our mantra became diligence, persistence and determination, and within a matter of three years, our bankruptcy was discharged.

This freed us up to return to our ultimate goal – a family. This was the only real thing keeping Tom and I connected. I knew he would be a good dad. He was, after all, a kind and thoughtful person who had a lot to give. We returned to the business of adoption.

THE CALL

Small changes began to happen, emotionally helping Tom and I to put the loss of the business behind us. We saved enough money to move into a bigger house. Friends were moving to Sydney, and we rented their four-bedroom, two-bath home with a large backyard in Faulconbridge, barely five minutes from the Springwood train station. Still in the Blue Mountains. It was the perfect place for play equipment and building a tree house. Ideal for a growing family.

I started a new job as Development Officer at a local independent school, responsible for enrolling new students and promoting school events. No more city commute for me. Between us, Tom and I were earning good money, putting my entire pay aside for all the costs we would have to cover for the adoption.

Every step of the adoption journey required us to make decisions. What country? Did we have an age preference? Would we accept disabilities? In addition, each country had their own restrictions, most giving preference to those who had fertility issues, and not allowing couples over a certain age to adopt. The list was long.

In our case, we knew my age was a factor. I was forty-one and we would not be approved for a baby. But we would be considered for a toddler or older child.

Our country of choice had always been the Philippines. It made sense, even to DoCS, although they did emphasise that my age could be an issue. The Philippines was a Catholic nation, so we ticked the religion box. And Annie's (my) experience of living in country would also be seen as something positive.

It is inexplicable really, how during the lengthy process of adoption, you begin to love a child you do not know. Form by form, we filled out all the requisite paperwork, underwent the necessary tests and social worker visits, and all the while our love for a child we did not know grew in our hearts. Our own version of the love parents might feel for a baby in the womb. Whatever it was, each step, from completing DoCS paperwork to sending our file to the Philippines, gave us hope and joy. Our love grew, held motionless in time and space for a faceless, nameless child.

There comes a point, when all the paperwork is done, that there is nothing to do but wait for *the call*. As each day goes by, you get more excited, knowing you are one step closer to your child. When *the call* comes, you know the questions to expect. Are you pregnant? Have your financial circumstances changed? In the adoption community, that in-between space between being approved and getting *the call* is a sort of no man's land called the *Waiting Room*.

We were having dinner when our caseworker called. I stood there as the person on the phone went through the questions with me, I looked at Tom, waving my hand, trying to get his attention. 'No,' I said slowly and clearly. 'I am not pregnant. No, our financial circumstances are the same. We are still employed at the same jobs.' Tom stared at me, eyes wide – he got it.

The caseworker then began to give us some basic information. We had been allocated a girl. Her name was Maria. She was two and a half years old, at a small orphanage in the mountains east of Manila. We were told we couldn't call her our daughter yet. We had to read the family history; and until we signed off on the paperwork, we couldn't even begin the process to call her ours. This was DoCS's painfully honest way of reminding us there were protocols which had to be adhered to. But in our hearts, she was ours. The caseworker said he was delighted for us, and a bit surprised. Most people were waiting eighteen months to two years for an allocation and we had waited only nine months – the duration of a pregnancy. I did not see this as a coincidence. To me, it was a sign. Our daughter was already filling a hole in my heart. Tom and I hugged, shedding tears of happiness and relief. After everything we had been through, after all the heartache, our greatest desire was being realised. A family.

Later, I stood in the doorway of the room we had set aside for our child. It had dark dingy walls and was being used for storage. I began to dream about painting and decorating – for Maria. My girl, my baby.

PLUS ONE

Within days we were sitting with our social worker looking at the allocation photo of Maria. She had long dark hair, big eyes, brown skin and a lopsided grin. She was wearing a striped shirt and cream pants, and she held her hands in fists in front of her. She was beautiful, adorable, *ours*. We raced through the final paperwork and put together a package to send to her. It included a white spaghetti strapped dress with butterflies all over it, a book called *My Family*, where we could insert pictures of each of us, and a scrapbook full of photos about us and her new home. There were photos of me cooking in the kitchen, Tom building a cubby house, her bedroom and our pets. These things would be forwarded to the orphanage. I dreamt of the carers showing Maria the scrapbook full of pictures of us, telling her about her new home and all the wonderful things waiting for her when her mummy and daddy came to pick her up.

The money in our savings account quickly disappeared as we sent fees to cover her immigration health checks, donation to the orphanage and processing fees for ICAB (the Intercountry Adoption Board of the Philippines). Flights and hotel accommodation were not included. This was the hard wait. Up till now, we had been waiting for a child. Now, we were waiting to be with Maria. She was real. She was tangible. She was our daughter. It was this knowledge which made the continued waiting bearable. Each step completed was a step closer to her. In the meantime, we kept ourselves busy. IKEA was a must-stop for all things cool, funky and practical for a child's bedroom. I bought adorable outfits for her, hoping they would fit and wondering if she would like them. We didn't have a clear idea of sizing, so tended to opt for clothes marked as 24 months. Through this time, I remember a vague emptiness at the back of my mind of about not having had beautiful clothes as a child and felt somehow this was making up for it. But I didn't want to linger on those memories, I had happier things to think about.

The bedroom Maria would have was currently dark blue. That had to go. I painted it lilac with lime green trim, going for the lady bugs and butterfly motif. I even found a canopy leaf at IKEA to sit over the top of her bed. Her toy box began filling, and the little shelf was full of books for those late-night cuddles and reads I was looking forward to. Family and friends gave us gifts, celebrating this joyous occasion with us. I would think about Maria all the time. What was she doing? What games and routines filled her days? Did she have many friends? The case report said she had a big personality and was a natural leader. What did that even mean? And would it affect how she reacted to us?

I was both terrified and excited at the prospect of being a mother. Would I cope, or be uptight? Would I teach her to cook? The growing list of books we had was evidence of my desire to read to her. Stories to inspire and nurture all the possibilities of who she could be. I knew Tom would be a good dad, and he planned on taking two months off when we came home. We felt completely in sync. We were even beginning to talk about parenting jobs, who would do what, bedtime routines and what we would let her watch on TV.

Once in a very rare while I would feel a strange, confusing familiarity with unfamiliar situations. I realised quickly that this related to Annie's life. I had felt a similar thing when unpacking my crate from the States, a sort of co-ownership of her experiences. But this time, instead of memories, they were feelings. Our adoption was the fulfillment of Annie's dream. I knew this was something she wanted, to adopt a child from the Philippines and keep her love of that country close to her heart. I was glad I was part of this for her. From that dark place where she had gone to heal and hide, would she know her dream was becoming a reality?

The next exciting news was something called *Authority to Travel*. It meant Maria's paperwork was in order with both the Australian and Filipino governments and Tom and I could fly to the Philippines and bring her home. We left Sydney on December 30, 2005, and watched the fireworks on New Year's Eve from our room in the Novotel in Quezon City, as if they too were celebrating our new family and the promise it held. In two days time we would meet Maria.

The Philippines was familiar to me on an instinctual level. From the humidity which wrapped me in a blanket of wet as soon as I got off the plane, to the ubiquitous fog of exhaust fumes and the homeless living in cardboard lean-tos on every corner. The sights, sounds and surroundings had been dear to Annie, and I drank them in. Traveling up into the hills to the province, the concrete jungle gave way to the freshness and beauty of the lush green mountainsides. It was as if

Annie's experience in the Philippines was coming full circle, as I too became emotionally attached to this place.

We had been told it would help Maria's adjustment to us if we stayed at the orphanage for a few days. Maria let it be known immediately she was not inclined to any sort of bonding. Instead, when the Mama (the name for the carers at the orphanage) called her over to meet us, she took off to continue laughing and playing with other kids, wanting nothing to do with these white strangers. We waited patiently, sitting and taking in our surroundings. The orphanage consisted of three large cement buildings with green tile roofs safely tucked away behind a tall green security gate. I watched people with groceries come and go through the small door in the gate, Mamas hanging out laundry while the babies napped and grounds staff were cleaning up and making the odd repair. It was a hive of activity.

Eventually, we were invited to wait in the guest house, a small apartment situated above the kitchen, a quiet place set aside for family bonding time. Within minutes Maria was brought up, but she still refused to come to us. We were left alone and I tried to think through what would allow us to get near her. Maria had no English, only Tagalog. Then I had an idea. I asked Tom to put on a *Barney the Dinosaur* video. She was quickly glued to the screen, which allowed Tom and I to get close, tolerated as part of the surroundings. Gradually, between dinner, games, more videos and looking through some books, Maria grew to accept our presence. The next day she allowed me to hold her hand and brush her hair, even walking around the orphanage with us. Success!

There were so many first moments, but the one I remember clearly was back in our hotel after we left the orphanage. We had a rough night settling Maria in. She was living up to her 'full of energy' description from her case report, but what we hadn't expected was her fear of water. All she'd ever had was bucket showers. So when I picked her up to put her in the bathtub with a few toys, she went ballistic, screaming at the top of her lungs, clamouring over my shoulders to get out. I persisted for about ten seconds, and then decided it wasn't worth it. She instantly transformed back to her bubbly self as I stood her on the bathmat and used a sponge to bath her. Tom and I were relieved, and I'm sure whoever was in the next room was grateful as well.

The next morning we went down for a buffet breakfast. No big deal, right? I hadn't considered how this vast array of western food might overwhelm Maria. I offered her several different, bland items – toast, eggs, bacon – to help me figure out what she liked (besides rice). I buttered a piece of toast, holding it out for her to take it. She was tentative, but reached out, staring at this offering like some strange new toy. Coming from a diet of rice, leafy greens and occasional eggs, this was a startlingly new experience. Instead of putting it in her mouth, she licked it. Her eyes turned into saucers, and she put it down, grabbing instead the small bowl of butter I had used for the toast, dipping her finger in and shoving a big glob in her mouth, licking her finger as she went. Tom and I both laughed. This was what I had imagined life as a family would be.

The plane trip home was another event. She attached herself to me and would barely let go of my hand as we made our way through Manila Airport. She smiled and laughed at everyone around us, all the while clutching the Elmo toy we had brought over for her. On board, everything went smoothly – until we began our descent into Sydney. Maria began crying and tugging her ears, the change in cabin pressure was getting to her. The *put on your seat belt* sign had yet to go on, so I pulled her into my lap and let her rest her head on my shoulder. In a split second I felt the warmth and nurturing of being a mother with a little child who was my responsibility. In the next moment, I felt the totality of said commitment as she threw up all over my shoulder. The steward was a gem and took Maria and I to the back of the plane where I sat down with reams of damp paper trying to clean up. He smiled gently at Maria, wrinkled his nose, and grabbed something out of a drawer. It was cologne. He apologised that it was all he had to help with the smell, then suggested we buckle in there, and once the plane was on the ground we could disembark.

Those early years held many ups and downs. Tom was a big white guy; Maria was little and only used to women caring for her. Bonding with Daddy was not an easy task. One day, exhausted and needing a break, I went to lie down for a brief nap. I left Tom on the couch and Maria on the floor in the living room, watching *Dora*. My head had barely touched the pillow when I heard a bellowing scream. I rocketed out of bed and ran to the living room. Blood was oozing from Tom's arm. Maria ran to me and grabbed my leg, sobbing. He looked at me confused. 'All I did was try to pick her up and she bit me!' We laugh about it now, but there were plenty of little hurdles like that to overcome.

THEN THERE WAS FIVE

DoCS required us to wait a year after bringing Maria home before we could begin our second adoption. This time, we were adamant that we wanted to add a sibling group to our family. DoCS tried to convince us otherwise. We were too old, they said, and the length of time we would wait could easily be three to five years. But we were convinced this was the right path for us, we had prayed about it, we were sure. DoCS begrudgingly sent our file to the Philippines, and again we were approved and entered the *Waiting Room*.

It was twenty months later when the call came. We were vacationing in Western Australia with a group of friends who had all adopted from the same orphanage which Maria had come from. It was a reunion and opportunity for these kids to remember their roots. For some of the kids it was a chance to reconnect with friends they hadn't seen since they'd lived at the orphanage together. We were in our hotel room when my phone rang. The familiar questions started. My heart was racing and Tom had the same stunned look as I said, 'No, I'm not pregnant. No, our financial position hasn't changed.'

The difference this time was that our six-year-old daughter was in the room with us, excitedly chirping around, happy to see her friends, oblivious to the fact that she had just become a big sister.

And there was more good news. Our *allocation* was for two brothers, aged two and four. It was what we wanted – a sibling group. We hugged and cried. Maria didn't understand until we sat her down and told her she was an *Ate*, the Filipino word for big sister. We reminded her of all those times we talked about and prayed for growing our family. She was going to have two little brothers, Kyle and Danny. She became as excited as we were – this was her journey too. I was nervous, but our dream was becoming a reality, again. My head began spinning with all the things we had to do when we got home – meeting with the social worker, the copious amounts of paperwork and preparing a home for our boys. Our afternoon became a celebration with friends. Our family was growing and we were sharing this with other adoptive parents who understood our journey.

When dealing with the public service, some things are predictable. We met with the social worker as soon as we got back home. She showed us the file and a beautiful picture of our boys – happy, healthy and full of life. Kyle was the big brother, a bit sombre and reserved, while Danny was outgoing and cheeky. And they were in the same orphanage where Maria had spent the first years of her life.

It was much the same paperwork and time frames. But it was now times two, including costs. We weren't as financially set up as our first time through the system, so the bulk of our costs to get to the Philippines and make those last-minute arrangements went on a credit card. We knew most families in the adoption process did this, took out personal loans or maxed out credit cards. It was part of the cost of creating a family and we had no regrets.

Finally, everything was organised, and we had our *Travel Authority*. We flew via Hong Kong and spent two days at Disneyland with Maria – a last hurrah as a family of three. Then, August 2009, we were back in the Philippines. As we landed in Manila I reflected on when we had picked up Maria. It was January 2006, Maria was almost three then, and Kyle would have already been born. I felt a touch of sadness thinking about the years we missed with him.

And then there was Kate. She had been with Annie in the Philippines and had a love for all things Filipino. We asked her to come along and help out. She arrived the same day we did, and we spent the night in a hotel in Manila before being picked up in the orphanage van and taken back up the mountain. She would spend a week with us, and then travel further up the island to Bagiou City to see some friends. We asked her to come along with a specific job: to keep Maria occupied so we could have quality time with our boys. Maria was very excited to see Kate. When we had arrived home with Maria, her Ninang Kate (Tagalog for Godmother) had come to visit from Canada. Both Tom and I were grateful to have her with us.

Because the boys came from the same orphanage as Maria, we knew many of the staff and were familiar with the area. The orphanage was a complex on the outskirts of the small town of Sampaloc. We loved the place and were looking forward to going back. The orphanage director collected us from the hotel and spent the entire trip up the mountain talking about our boys and Maria. As we drove through the orphanage's green gates, the children ran up to greet us, laughing and waving. Maria rushed out of the van, the familiarity of this place still in her bones. She began hugging the carers and generally being the carefree spirit she was.

We had barely taken our luggage out of the van when two little bodies were unceremoniously dropped into our arms. Our boys, Kyle, and Danny. They didn't pull away. I held Danny and his beautiful eyes stared straight into my soul. I was in love. I glanced over at Tom and could see that Kyle was having the same effect on him. We held them close and proceeded up the stairs to the guest apartment. Kate joined us for a while and then went off to the separate apartment the staff had prepared for her. It wasn't long before Maria was holding Kate's hand and showing her around the grounds.

Our brief orphanage stay was lovely, with none of the challenges we had with Maria. We made a point of walking around the grounds, talking to the Mamas and sharing meals with them. But we were keen to keep moving and begin bonding as a family, and only spent one night at the orphanage and then made our way to Batangas, a seaside community protected by a bay just off the South China Sea. We stayed at a simple resort with nepa huts, each with beds and a bathroom around an open eating area where we could cook our own food. Boats brought in fresh seafood and vendors walked the beach selling all sorts of goods. It was idyllic, apart from the hot and humid nights. Even with fans on high we were dripping in sweat.

We went down to the beach each day. Kate and Maria would head off on their own adventure, meandering along the seashore while we played in the surf with our boys. They had never seen a beach before. Kyle was curious, splashing in the water, Tom swung him through the air and into the surf. Danny was a different matter. I had to sit in the shallows with him clinging to my neck, swishing water gently over his feet, assuring him water could be fun.

Our beach adventure over, we headed back to Manila. We booked into the Fernandina 88 hotel. It was less westernized than the Novotel, and served an array of traditional food in the dining room each day. It was time for Kate to continue her own holiday. With her typical tear-less goodbye, she hugged us and hopped on a bus to Baguio. It was our time now to begin the serious work of learning to be a family of five. In the contained safety of our hotel suite we played games, danced and wrestled. On several occasions Tom had all three children piling on top of him, laughing. Maria enjoyed the big sister role, leading the boys around playing games, already teaching them some of the basics of English. I knew this was the idyllic part of building our family, so I soaked it in. I was prepared. Difficulties waited for us at home, for sure, but there was no need to go there yet – we just wanted to enjoy these moments together.

We had official duties with ICAB before heading home, signing papers, and saying thank you. We also did the tourist gig and explored a bit of Manila, heading down to Intramuros, the old historic district, and to Rizal Park, named after the national hero, Jose Rizal. We managed to fit in a shopping trip, buying clothes and souvenirs. We were much more comfortable in the Philippines this time, and not afraid to go slightly native, enjoyed the chaos of our family in the hustle and bustle of Metro Manila.

An indelible image of our time in the Philippines was crossing Tuazon Blvd near our hotel. A chaotically busy six lane street with jeepneys, trucks, and buses travelling at breakneck speed. The lines on the road gave an illusion of order, but in reality, they made no difference. Drivers seemed to ignore them. Tom and I stood at the edge of this mayhem, determined to cross the street. We needed to be as fierce as the oncoming traffic. Tom held Maria and Kyle's hands, while I carried Danny in my arms. At a brief break in the traffic, we made a mad dash, speeding through the pandemonium. Danny decided it was all too much, wiggled out of my arms, and with a thump, sat down, crying on the road. Cars were careening towards us and I swooped him up in my arms, running to the other side. I should have been in shock, overwhelmed by the insanity of what had just happened. But instead Tom and I both laughed. If we could survive Manila traffic, we could certainly face the challenges life would throw our way as we raised our family.

The boys were full of amazement as we boarded the plane to head home. Flying was a whole new experience, and they were drinking it in as I clicked them safely into their seats. I sat in a middle row with the boys, while Tom and Maria were across the aisle, watching what was going on outside their window. As soon as the plane moved away from the terminal, the boys were in awe. But it was when the plane took off and headed straight up with all the g-force it could muster, that I watched their eyes light up. Their hands clutched their armrests in a few seconds of fear, then wonder began to creep across their faces and they burst out laughing.

THE RHYTHM OF LIFE

We hit our groove as a family. Maria was in Year One at school, Kyle in preschool and I had Danny at home. We were a beautifully multicultural family. We went to great lengths to remind our kids that they may call Australia home, but their roots were firmly in the Philippines and they should be proud of their heritage. I was learning to make Filipino dishes like adobo, lumpia and puto and to build our kids' relationships with other adopted children, we went to Filipino adoption camps, normalizing the fact that they were not the only kids who didn't look like their parents. We would tease Tom, telling him he was the minority, lost in a family of Filipinos and a Texan.

Tom continued in his public service job, where he felt valued and appreciated for what he did. I was home with the kids, leaving my job to put family first. It was a deliberate choice to stay at home. I didn't give a thought to the long-term implications this might have for my future employment options. Instead, I put effort into cooking healthy, tasty meals and caring for my family, although what this meant in practice was doing a lot of laundry, grocery shopping and any other number of necessary errands. I went to school programs and helped in the classroom. I told myself that it didn't matter I wasn't earning an income, what I was doing around the house was about giving our family a better quality of life and investing in the kids' future. Tom's job was providing for us, and we had saved enough to buy the rental property we lived in. We were ordinary, normal citizens again, with a secure, simple life.

With three children, life was not quiet. Between school activities, church and cultural playgroups, I felt stretched in every direction. I was at our church one day talking to a mum who had five kids. She was calm and chilled, even as some small altercation had her child screaming in her ear.

I asked her how she did it.

'Do what?'

'How do you seem so at peace with the chaos of so many kids?'

She smiled. 'Once you have more than two, it's all just chaos. It doesn't matter if it's three or thirteen, once you go past two, life is crazy. With two, you can hold both their hands and convince yourself you're still in control.'

She laughed. 'But as soon as you have more, you have to start looking at things differently. Kinda just have to adjust and deal with it. I wouldn't have it any other way.'

Her words became my mantra on the days where I felt totally run off my feet and unable to cope with the lively and fun-loving kids we had.

Before kids, I didn't understand playgroups. They seemed to be these organized events where mothers would go each week and do something magical, giving them superhuman powers to get through their week. It made no sense to me. But as soon as Maria came home, I started attending a playgroup attached to our church. Suddenly, it all made sense. Playgroups were all about our kids engaging in affirming, educational activities while mothers could stop and communicate in an adult way with other mums. Actual adult conversation. It was astounding how such a little thing could make such a big difference. And of course, Maria was making friends and learning her place in a social setting. But there was one thing missing: kids of colour. She was the lone chocolate child. There were no other kids to help her not feel like the odd one out.

Through word of mouth, I discovered there were a few families in the Blue Mountains with children from the Philippines. We decided to start our own playgroup. Initially, it was just two or three families. We would gather at a home in Katoomba and let the kids run rampant. In comparison to the other playgroup, where activities were organized, this was a mums' playgroup. We would talk about the ups and downs of parenting an adopted child, of language acquisition and bonding challenges. Nothing was off limits. We understood the specific struggles we had as adoptive parents. Those years with these mothers were so important to me, when Maria started and then the boys came along. We even had a go at learning a few phrases in Tagalog, and often ate pancit or rice for lunch. It was a cocooned environment, instilling Pinoy Pride in our kids' hearts.

Maria lived up to her huge personality and the boys were picking up English quickly, making friends at preschool and church. There were of course night terrors, temper tantrums, and not wanting to sleep in their own beds. These were expected. Life became about bonding. At a DoCS seminar we had been told that the older a child is when they are adopted, the longer it takes to attach. And by attached, I mean that they stop being fearful you are going to abandon them. This is a theme which runs deep for adoptive children. This, above everything else, was why I chose to stay home with them rather than go back to work. Even when they started going off to school, I ushered them onto the bus each morning and was there at the door waiting for them when they got off in the afternoon, asking about their day, their friends and what they learned. It was my presence which provided stability and reassurance that Tom and I weren't going anywhere.

One day, I was at the local newsagent and I picked up the latest copy of Better Homes & Garden. I was always looking for the next cool house reno to drool over. This issue came with a book. I don't remember the name, but it was about a middle-aged couple who had left the city and moved to the far north coast of NSW to buy a small property and live a sustainable life, growing produce to feed themselves. I was entranced by the idea and devoured the book. I couldn't stop talking to Tom about it, about the possibility of a country life where we grew our own food and were doing the right thing by the environment with room for the kids to run and play. I found a course on the basics of permaculture and it transformed my thinking. I could actually feed our entire family from a backyard garden! I came away from the course determined to change our backyard into something of abundance. We built garden beds and grew beans, potatoes, and tomatoes, along with an array of herbs, basil, parsley, thyme, and marigolds. All fresh and fabulous. We even got chickens. Tom and the boys built 'The Chook Hilton.' The kids helped feed our hens and collect the eggs, as well as picking fresh food from the garden. Danny was particularly fond of cherry tomatoes and it was rare for them to make it to the house. I had plans for a few fruit trees as well.

Family life was good. Tom was a fantastic dad, kind and gentle and I was doing my bit to be a reliable mum.

I couldn't have asked for a better start to parenting life than those years in the Blue Mountains, watching our kids settle and grow in their new culture. I accepted that the kids would be the focus of our family. And Tom and I seemed to have come to an unspoken agreement about our inability to have a close relationship. This seemed to be an acceptable, even half-fulfilling way to live, although I still craved deep and meaningful communication, when what we had felt a bit shallow. My anxiety seemed to be under control, which was saying something. I would think about Annie every now and then, but sensed nothing. Maybe I had this MPD thing licked and put to bed after all.

ROAD TRIPPING

Prior to having kids, we would try to visit Tom's family on the Far North Coast of NSW a few times each year, but especially at Christmas. With kids, it became a long, but important trip. We made an adventure out of it, always finding a beach on the way for a kick around in the surf. The kids loved their Nana and Poppy and Tom's extended family. These trips helped cement the kids' identity as our family. They had lost so much in their short lives, bonding with all the family was important. Tom's parents were ageing and had some health concerns, and we wanted the kids to know them before it was too late.

After the kids had gone to bed one night, we started talking. 'I'm worried about Mum and Dad,' Tom said. 'What if something happens to them? It's a full day's trip up to Tweed. What do you think of moving up the coast in the next few years to be closer to them? Maybe I could start seeing what jobs are out there now, to get an idea.'

This began a conversation about security for the kids. There was a lot to consider. The boys had been with us just over a year. Uprooting them too quickly could be destabilising. On the other hand, kids are resilient, and as long as they had us, they had security. I liked the idea of finding a small property where I could put into practice on a bigger scale the sustainable principles I had been learning in our backyard. There was nothing wrong with seeing what opportunities were out there.

By the middle of 2011 Tom found a job in the Northern Rivers, as Technical Department Head at a large company in Lismore. It was less than two hours from his folks. Close enough to get to them in the event of an emergency, but far enough away to live our own lives. We made a mad dash up the coast with the kids to look around and see where we might live. There were several small towns around Lismore. Our choices seemed limitless, but our finances were not. A quick look at the prices on the coast confirmed that a beach lifestyle was out of our reach. We went the other direction, checking out property prices and schools at Casino, thirty minutes west of Lismore.

Casino was a sleepy country town. A world away from Sydney with its bright lights and bumper-to-bumper traffic. There were no traffic lights. The number of petrol stations could be counted on one hand, and there were three grocery stores. We found places in a local independent school for Maria and Kyle and enrolled Danny in an area preschool.

I made a solo return trip a few weeks later to find a rental home until we could buy our own property. I found a lovely old home on the Richmond River in the heart of Casino, with high ceilings and a large yard for the kids. There were garden beds where we were given permission to grow beans and tomatoes. I put up a small portable greenhouse to keep the trees we would eventually plant on our dream property. Tom even had a go at a small aquaponics setup, something we could add to our sustainable life once we bought somewhere.

By October we were on the road, moving again. I loved the Blue Mountains and the friends we'd made in our decade living there. They would remain in my heart, but I was equally excited about this next chapter of our lives. And I was quietly hopeful that this new environment might rekindle our marriage. The kids had been given farewell parties by their classmates and we moved between school terms, giving us time to get settled before the kids started at their new school. I felt a sense of satisfaction as I watched the kids make friends and settle into their new classrooms. Maria was in Year 2 and Kyle in Kindergarten. Even Danny was enjoying his new preschool, taking to it with great gusto.

I missed the familiarity of the Blue Mountains but found the warmth of this country town charming. We were quickly ensconced in a local church and had new friends, keen to get to know us. Having three adorable children didn't hurt. I found my calendar quickly filling with play dates and the kids barraging me with comments about this friend or another. They were settling in well.

I was concerned about our kids' connections to their Filipino legacy. Besides the playgroup in Katoomba I had come to cherish, we had been involved with ASIAC, an organization providing cultural camps and workshops to keep kids attached to their birth cultures. Little did I know that Casino was home to a large contingent of Filipinos. Our children quickly found new friends with the same skin colour and heritage. I learned quickly that this connection didn't rely on skin colour.

Maria came home one day, not long after we had moved, and couldn't stop telling me about this girl in her class, Mandy. They got along like a house on fire and loved playing together. But then, out of the blue, Maria said, 'And she and I are alike.'

'How are you alike?' I asked, expecting something to do with loving creativity or music.

'She lost her birth mother, just like me.'

I barely held back the tears. 'That's really special sweetie. I'm so glad for you.' I gave her a hug. Maria and Mandy were best of friends for years to come, with sleepovers and quiet girl gossip along the way.

We found a small five-acre block of land ten minutes south of town. It had long stands of paspalum grass, excellent feed for a house cow, a spring-fed dam, and a small stand of trees, the perfect place to build our sustainable home. We decided to take the leap and move out to the property and live a simple life, which in the end were two caravans, cooking on a gas camp grill, composting toilets, and mostly cold showers. It was an adventure! This was what we told ourselves and the kids every time we brought in compost, built beds and put chickens in domes to make mandala garden beds. With the help of friends from our new church, we had a water tank installed and brought power in from the street so we could at least run a refrigerator and washing machine. This was our simple life. It was hard work, and not very comfortable, but we kept telling ourselves it was worth it.

There were many things to be grateful for about the way we were living. I was becoming enmeshed in the lives of friends in Casino, the kids were thriving, and Tom was happily settled in his job. Or so we thought.

Within months it became evident Tom and his new boss were not getting along. There were threats of disciplinary action for unspecified breaches of who knows what. Tom would be told he was an idiot. The bullying became so difficult Tom took stress leave. During this time off he began looking in earnest for a new position. It would be impossible to find something local and match the pay and seniority Tom's skills could draw. Something had to change. He began looking for work and resigned himself to having to travel, maybe to the Gold Coast, or even Brisbane. If this were the case, the farm would be left to me while Tom stayed up the coast during the week. This idea terrified me. Fortunately, he was trolling through the job placement websites and came across an IT manager's job for a local council, fifteen minutes from where we lived.

This began a dance for Tom, between managing the hell of his current role, and waiting for interviews and hopeful callbacks for this new position. The interview process was positive, and he loved the security that working for local government could provide. Tom and I collectively held our breath and exhaled in joy when the offer was made. Then things ramped up. With this new job secure, he requested a meeting between his current boss and the head of HR. Tom didn't have a chance to discuss anything, his supervisor began berating and belittling him. The HR manager stepped in, asking Tom to wait outside. After a few minutes she came out and asked Tom what he wanted as an exit package in order not to make waves. Dance done. Tom came out the winner.

For almost a year we lived on our small five-acre block in caravans, saving for our dream of a sustainable house, doing our bit for the environment. Our neighbours were not so impressed and reported our meagre existence as being in breach of council regulations (which it was). We had to move. This led us to the farm. It was a property much further out of town than we had imagined living, but it was a hundred acres with a modest home, a large shed and a granny flat which with a little refurbishing could be a warm and inviting place for friends to come and visit. There was even a bus stop right across the road. We would put our stamp on this little patch of earth. It wasn't perfect, but it was a footprint of something we could work with.

In all of this, there were no rumblings, no inklings of Annie and *The Girls*. There was no anxiety, no wondering about Annie. Dead silence. I took this as a positive sign. Perhaps, just perhaps, things had resolved themselves and this move with its new environment had provided some sort of settling change. I began to hope this thing called MPD might no longer be part of my life.

OUR VERSION OF SUSTAINABILITY

Tom and I talked about big dreams, things on the farm we could do together as a family. Tom wanted to do men's shed stuff with the boys, building chook houses and fixing things – they would have fun doing blokey stuff. I knew exactly where I wanted to put our veggie patch and mini-orchard. We would move the chooks we had onto this area to start ripping up the soil and getting it fertile for planting. The kids could learn to drive a ride-on mower and play in the bush. All this was part of the sustainable dream we had wanted right from the start.

The reality of those dreams was hard won. Farm life was not easy, and as a novice going in blind, all those romantic notions of fresh produce and living off the land came crashing down. The dream collapsed for Tom long before it did for me. He was working full-time and finally loving what he did after the catastrophe of his previous job. He had nothing left to give at the end of the day and needed a break. I managed my days, growing food as best I could. Tom was a tech head so building things was not first nature to him. With a limited budget and minimal skills, he did the best he could. Unfortunately, these efforts were often not thought through and didn't last and he was sick of trying to stay ahead of the ever-growing list of things needing to be done. His interest and love for a sustainable life gave way to exhaustion and defeat. In retrospect, I can't blame him. He was fighting an uphill battle.

We weren't prepared for the financial impact and were overwhelmed by the cost of farm life. We did everything with a pay-it-forward mentality, investing now for what it would give us later. We knew there would be a payoff. I think we both doggedly believed this at the start. I just held on to the dream longer than Tom did.

With chooks alone, it wasn't too bad. We would let them free range and supplement their food scraps with feed. But then we added pigs, and they were always hungry, demanding more scraps and more feed. Then we added a house cow. This is where our inexperience really got the better of us. We did not realize the grass on the farm was not as nutrient-dense as it had been at the other property. It would be a very long haul, years of sowing and fertilizing, to fix it. So having a house cow (which would give us lots of milk, cheese, and all sorts of other delightful dairy products), meant supplementing, again. But this time with not only grain but hay as well. Our bottom line was taking a thumping.

We were barely breaking even each month, and more often going backwards. I kept having to tighten the purse strings. I tried to do it in subtle ways so it didn't really affect the running of the house. What hit hard were doctor's visits, school excursions and replacing the kids' school uniforms. We kept paying anyway, keeping up the pretence that we were excited about what we were doing. We talked about the possibilities and not the pragmatics.

This meant that when an emergency came and we had to put it on the credit card, arguments would start. Normally it was Tom who hit the roof first because he wasn't over the finer details of the family budget as I was. I should have shared more of what was going on but I was fearful there would be no easy solution. Instead, we lived with a constant undercurrent of tension and anxiety. Every time one of the kids brought home an excursion form or some other opportunity presented itself, I sighed, wondering how we were going to pay for these additional expenses that seemed unending.

I learned to live in the moment. After getting the kids on the school bus and Tom off to work, I would walk the paddocks or work in the veggie patch, taking great pride in the seedlings I was sure had grown at least two centimetres overnight. I loved the space, the way the seasons changed. I became attuned to these shifts. The red-tailed black cockatoos came early every spring, chattering and eating the new growth at the top of the trees. I learned to keep the chooks locked in their fencing when the wedge-tail eagles, as beautiful as they were, started circling. Invariably, within a day, a small or sick chook would simply disappear. It was the way of nature. The Wedgies were top of the aerial food chain.

The trees didn't change much, but the water levels did. We were on the edge of drought conditions and fortunate to have a very large spring-fed dam. Daily I would tap our tanks to see how low they were getting and watch water levels in the dam rise and fall with the weather conditions. I always noted if our tanks were below half full. This was my reminder to tell everyone to watch their shower times – and we lived by the mantra, *if it's yellow let it mellow, if it's brown, send it down*. It certainly made the kids laugh.

We had a rescue dog named Bella. She looked like a Lab but had the energy of a working dog. She loved the farm and would happily roam around for hours, hunting up some new scent. While she wasn't trained to be a livestock guardian dog, herding and protecting the chooks was second nature to her. She was adept at chasing the goannas which were always after our chicks and eggs. More often than not, the goannas would make it up a tree. But on the odd occasion when they didn't, they met the wrath of Bella, who clamped her teeth onto their tails and gave them a good thumping.

What I loved more than growing vegetables was tending our livestock. It brought the landscape alive for me. I could watch the cows chewing their cud, or the calves suckling their mothers, for hours on end. Our inexperience showed when our first house cow, Rosie, gave birth. It was exciting, and I couldn't wait to tell the kids all about it when they got home from school. They eagerly ran down to see this gorgeous grey four-legged fluff ball, arguing about what they would name it (we had a strict rule on the farm – if you were going to name an animal, it had to be named what its purpose was, e.g., rump, or rib-eye, which meant it was destined for the freezer).

The next morning, I went down to find our little calf. Rosie was mooing her head off. I tried to calm her, but the reason for her fretting became obvious. Our new calf had disappeared. It was Saturday, so everyone went into panic mode as we wandered the property, looking for the lost calf. While the others were wandering the bush, I combed the paddocks in our old X-Trail. I thumped over a rock near the cows' overnight paddock and stopped. As I got out, the kids were running up the dam road, with Tom behind carrying the calf. I waved at them excitedly and then looked a few metres behind the car and saw another little grey ball of fluff. I was terrified I had run over it, but as soon as I approached, it got up, Rosie called out and it went running to her. The kids and Tom stopped in their tracks. Twins! We happily reunited both calves with their mamma.

Making friends with folks on adjoining properties was a delightful necessity. There was Bill who grew mandarins and traded a box for whatever fresh veg I had on hand. Terry never brought anything but always loved to walk the property and see what we were growing and doing with our animals, staying for a cup of tea and a gab. And then there was Phil. Phil lived alone in a shipping container on the adjacent property, with portable solar panels as his only source of power. A bit of a recluse and a gentle soul, we would have him over for meals and even shared Christmas holidays with him. One day he came to say hi and handed me a noisy box with six keets in it. I must have mentioned at Christmas dinner I wanted to get guinea fowl at some point because they kept the snakes and ticks at bay. While his generosity knew no limits, my knowledge of how to raise keets was less than adequate. We had a big old crate we had used for dog transport at one point, and this became short-term housing for the keets on our back porch. They grew, eventually went free range (but still stayed around the house and knew exactly when feeding time was), multiplied in droves and were safe from just about everything. Kyle called them bumpy bums because when they ran, their backsides would bounce up and down. I would watch in awe as they flew effortlessly to the highest branches in the trees to roost at night, safe from all possible predators. I thank Phil for the fun of owning these amazing creatures who kept our property safe from ticks and snakes.

These were all the good times. Challenging, but good. As time went on, challenging became frustrating. Frustrating because there were never enough hours in the day to get jobs done, and because Tom and I were arguing regularly about all the equipment breaking down and the jobs we needed to do. Any time I would bring these things up, he would get angry or sulky and tell me I was being mean and bitchy. Little things became wedges between us. We were financially strapped and barely making enough to make ends meet. We both felt trapped.

The beast of anxiety returned. Alone on the farm each day, I felt physically and emotionally isolated, fretting about how we would make things work. Where would I find the money needed to fix a fence or buy new star pickets? Alone with my thoughts, I convinced myself I was a failure as a wife and a mother. But worst of all, I was a fraud because I refused to acknowledge my unspoken fear, that somehow, this thing called MPD was going to swallow me whole.

MPD was the hidden noose around my neck. I had told myself for so long being MPD wasn't relevant because Annie and *The Girls* were asleep and weren't affecting me. In the end, it didn't matter that they might have been asleep. What I didn't understand was that I was playing my role in the big picture of how the system worked. I thought the dissociation and fragmentation was something I held at a distance. But instead, it was my day-to-day life, tending animals, working in the veggie patch that was helping me dissociate from the truth of my childhood. It was how I survived. I wasn't creating alters to get me through difficult times, but I was living in a busy dissociative fog to avoid my past.

RE-ENTRY

Weekends on the farm were hard. Big trips into town limited by our ever-tightening budget; only going when we had a long, planned list so as not to waste petrol. Weekends also meant Saturday farm chore time, when those big things I couldn't handle by myself were taken on as a family. The kids grunted and groaned as chickens were moved, fences repaired, or some sort of water shortage issue was addressed. Tom and I tried to reward these efforts and at the end of a hard day's yakka, we would sit around a big campfire (often more a bonfire) with sausages and damper, followed by gooey roasted marshmallows. The kids chased each other with sticks of red glowing embers. Tom and I stared at the stars, identifying constellations, and making valiant attempts at talking about little things that were safe territory, which always ended up being the kids and their needs, or his work.

As the kids grew older, weekends changed. They became about soccer games and sleepovers. The dream of a happy farm family was moving out of reach. Weekends became an unending list of chores and a time of resentment and frustration. I came to expect the list

I had made would either be carried out with grumpy resentment or ignored completely. We lived with short tempers and a lack of empathy on all fronts.

I found it impossible to be objective. I was sure I was the problem and that somehow everything we were doing wrong was my fault. What I couldn't see, but learned in hindsight, was this was the farmer's life, a constant list of problems to tackle. Never reaching an end, just more jobs needing to be done.

Tom and I had been impatient with each other for months and circulated through the same old issues. We were standing in the lounge room when I snapped.

'Do you think this is fun for me?' I barked. 'Things are falling apart!' The kids instinctively scattered from their comfortable spots on the sofa.

'Don't you understand I'm tired and just don't have the energy?' he bellowed.

'How is anything supposed to get done? We agreed to do this together!'

I was desperate to be heard but this was lost in my anger.

'I didn't agree to this! It's so hard. What the fuck are we doing?' He paused, and for a brief moment his pain was transparent and unequivocal. 'I hate it here, I feel like an idiot all the time. When I fix things, they fall apart within days. I don't know what I'm doing.'

For the first time, he was being honest about how he felt and I should have listened to him and tried to understand. Instead, I was furious. I didn't care he was baring his truth in a way he hadn't before. I was angry. I wanted to be heard, I was desperate for us to be in this together, to figure it out, together.

'It's because you don't do it properly or ask for help. You won't even look online for the right solution.'

'We don't have the money to do things properly. You spend it all. There's never anything left.'

'Oh, there you go again. It's always about money. And it's always my fault. If you don't want me to manage the bills, then why don't you fuckin' do it yourself!'

I stormed through the kitchen and went out the side door, slamming it behind me as I stomped down the hill. My head was pounding, I was breathing hard, my chest was tight. Anxiety was pumping through my veins at breakneck speed. My mind was in a fog. I knew I wasn't being rational or holding my temper. I knew I needed space to calm down. But Tom had followed me out and we stood across the small paddock from each other, like gunfighters getting ready for a shootout. Our bullets were words, hurtful and accusatory. If I even heard what was said, I don't remember it now. But it was a spiteful barrage, each of us intent on inflicting pain.

From deep inside my brain, the words let rip. 'If you hate it so much then leave!' Instant regret. But I meant it, didn't I? I had never used those words before. I didn't want him to leave. I would be alone. I had spent years learning how to walk on eggshells with Tom. He went on the offensive at the slightest criticism or challenge. I had learned to be careful. It was self-preservation. This pepper spray of nastiness was way out of character for me.

I watched as Tom stormed off towards the shed and felt a bomb go off in my head. This was more than a headache, it was as if my brain split open and was screaming at the sky. I could feel everything inside me shift slightly, finding a new balance in a new place in my brain.

And then I heard – her.

'Why am I here?' Clear as a bell, in my head.

I was stunned. It took me a few minutes to understand what was going on. Any hope I had of pretending I could carve out a normal life with kids and a somewhat broken marriage was impossible. I knew the voice, I felt the presence. Annie was back, yet I was meeting her for the first time. She was the person I had almost touched in passing as she left me to deal with a life she couldn't handle. She was reconfiguring my brain, making space to accommodate us both, establishing her own new normal. And now, instead of sensing her history from postcard memories and flushes of emotion, I was confronted by her presence as she talked directly to me.

She asked again, *'Why am I here?'*

PART THREE:
CO-EXISTENCE

CO-CONSCIOUSNESS

(the art of being multiple)

After Annie returned, I continued to go through the motions of everyday life. Perhaps I was in denial, but more likely I couldn't cope with the truth. I was overwhelmed, confronted by the very thing which I had been trying to hide from for years, so I did what came naturally. I dissociated.

In those early days of Annie's return, I would get the kids on the bus, do shopping, gardening, or feed the animals. Routine was my salvation, day to day chores which required my body but not too much of my brain. I had long since given up trying to get Tom to do anything on the farm, and now he and I barely talked. Instead, it was about the kids; they remained the focus, from music lessons to soccer or homework.

When I had time to stop, my new reality overwhelmed me. I was sharing my brain with another person. I read somewhere that what I was living with was something called co-consciousness. (Maybe it was Annie who came across that in the days when she was learning about being MPD.) While I could clearly see in my mind *The Girls* and the house where they lived, Annie was the familiar presence for me. She was a tangible, dare I say, more *real alter* than the others, simply because of her proximity to my life.

All the years I had been with Tom, Annie had slept, and with that *The Girls* had been cocooned away. Now the curtain had been drawn back. But I continued to push *The Girls* and their lives away. When I did stop and dare to look, I felt as if I was watching a horror show. The familiarity made me squirm but still, their lives weren't my life. All those years ago, I had unconsciously chosen anxiety over abuse, without understanding that there was really no way I could escape either. And that Saturday afternoon when Tom and I had our huge argument, the anxiety gave way and I could no longer hide from the reality of being MPD.

I found out very quickly Annie would rather not be there with me. I got it that she would rather be asleep; she would have preferred to stay hiding rather than be part of my life. But since she couldn't, she shared freely her condemnation of how I was living, compounding my own feelings of failure.

What I couldn't see at the time (how could I?) was all the self-talk I had believed over the years about my relationship with Tom – our business failure, our inability to get pregnant – all the things I took on as my fault were an expression of being MPD. Even before Annie came back, I could see that all this self-talk was a consequence of having *The Girls* in my life. They were in the far corners of my brain the whole time, contemplating the dangers they perceived day after day as I walked through my life. It was no wonder I was overwhelmed by anxiety most of the time. I was standing amid my chaotic past and couldn't understand what was going on because I had pushed it all away.

I was reminded of these shortcomings with Annie's return. She was determined that if she was going to be awake, then she would speak her mind – and it was a very negative, judgemental mind, ready to give voice at any time.

She picked on my parenting skills. *'You don't know how to discipline. Aren't they simply the rudest creatures in the world? Why would you want to be a parent in the first place?'* It was in absolute contrast to the love and care I strived to show my kids daily, imperfect though it might be.

And there was Tom. Our relationship was the very reason she had retreated in the first place. I would try and discuss it with her in an attempt to make her understand. These conversations would always come about after some sort of uncomfortable situation with Tom.

'Why did you marry him?' Annie would ask.

'Because I thought you loved him. I thought I was supposed to be you.'

'Humph.' She would turn her back on me, receding into the dark regions of my brain. This was how we talked to each other; jibes back and forth as each of us tried to justify ourselves.

To the outside world, I kept the truth of my life completely secret. No one else in Australia knew about this embarrassing psychotic part of my life. Friends from church would ask how I was doing. 'Life's been better, but I'll survive,' was my flippant response. I could not imagine anyone in this quiet country town being able to cope with me saying, 'The voices in my head are driving me crazy.' Even Tom was not aware of how my internal world was all over the place. He knew about my MPD of course, but we never discussed it. I was convinced he wouldn't understand, and as our relationship imploded, all his little stings and jabs confirmed it.

Tom and I were in a regular pattern now – we fought or we avoided each other. I had no mental space or patience for parenting children who needed a calm and thoughtful figure in their lives. Tom and I were not on the same page and the kids were getting mixed signals. I tried to be kind to myself, acknowledging the huge change I had to adjust to. So I would seek relief in my familiar self-imposed busyness to find some sort of equilibrium. Blaming myself for the lack of intimacy with Tom was painful, but reliable; blaming myself for not being a good parent was comfortable. Anxiety remained an intimate companion, which in turn fuelled my erratic outbursts.

So instead, I played the game, pretending life was normal. I cherished the necessity of milking cows, making cheese, working in the garden, and cooking. These things grounded me and gave me a purpose. Everything I needed to do for the kids, going to church each Sunday, even ironing Tom's work shirts, made my life bearable. It was when I slowed down that I couldn't hide from Annie. I could see this internal construct she had described decades before to Shrink #2. Our mind was like a house where everyone lived, all *The Girls* and Annie and me – and now it was as if she had come home, found everything in disarray, and was giving the place a vigorous spring clean.

If I was coming to terms with Annie, she was also adjusting to me. She was trying to put her internal world back in order, trying to work out where I would fit. Annie needed to provide for *The Girls*. I needed to provide for my family. The problem was that almost everything which defined my existence threatened her ability to control her world. The choices I was making were, in her eyes, completely contradictory to her definition of safety. Children were an annoyance, but they were not a threat. Tom, for no other reason than being a person with a penis, was a huge threat. Sleeping in the same bed, the arguments, his mere physical presence, were enough to create conflict between Annie and me. She would harp at me about our non-relationship, and then retreat as soon as I reminded her she was the one who hooked up with him in the first place.

Trying to look at things objectively I could see that Annie and I needed to find a way to co-exist. Whether I liked it or not, we had a symbiotic relationship. Her job was to protect, and by maintaining the status quo, to keep her house in order. She required my acquiescence to this new way of being and my refusal caused conflict. Her life had been formed by traumatic experiences in which people couldn't be trusted and change was dangerous. Even if my life seemed now to be only about survival, my aim had always been to understand who I was and to grow as a person. This difference in our perspectives and the inevitable way it seeped into my life meant anxiety and hyper-vigilance lived with me like a well-worn shirt.

ANNIE'S INTERJECTION

In truth, now that Annie had returned, my life became *our* story. Whether I could emotionally accept it or not, Annie was an inextricable part of my existence, and had her own perspective on what had gone wrong and how she had to cope with me.

***

When I left, all I wanted to do was sleep. I tried. The Girls were asleep, but I was far too aware of what Maggie was doing. I could not escape her, no matter how much I tried. I had given her one job when I left: exist. It's all she had to do. No emotions, no feelings, just take steps each day to eke out an existence. Go through the motions, do the necessary things to stay alive, be small and unnoticed. I needed her to do that because I knew it would keep The Girls safe. It's how we survived before, just do what you must to stay alive. I didn't think I was asking too much. I was sure it would work.

But she didn't get it and I didn't explain. I wanted her to understand so we could live in peace. I should have understood the challenge of our complex life, but I didn't. And I didn't care. I was angry that I had to deal with her life. It was a mess, a barely manageable struggle of unresolved problems which, because it was my job, were mine too.

When I came back, it was fifteen years after I'd left. I was in a foreign country on the other side of the world, far away from anything familiar, stuck with her struggling marriage, and the children I had hoped for decades before, but never really imagined would exist. Co-existing with her and the anxiety about the life she was wrestling with was too loud for me to ignore.

SHRINK #3

Back on the Couch

Somewhere in the middle of this mayhem, early onset puberty caused Maria's hormones to begin raging. (Early onset puberty was not uncommon for Asian girls who move to a Western diet.) Yelling, crying, demanding cuddles one moment and two seconds later pushing me away saying she hated me – it all took a toll on me. I lost my calm parental veneer, succumbing to my own inability to handle stress.

All of this could be easily explained away as a consequence of her deep-seated adoption issues, or the struggles Tom and I were having. But in my gut, I knew it was more.

I began trawling the net for information about difficult mother daughter relationships. Article after article said women with historical abuse could be triggered when their daughters entered puberty, whether their trauma had been dealt with or not. Could it be that something as natural as my daughter growing up was causing me to re-experience the childhood abuse Annie and *The Girls* had coped with? I had, somewhat successfully I thought, kept it all at a distance.

But often, uncomfortable feelings would rampage through me unpredictably, leaving me numb and out of touch as I tried to deal with my daughter growing into a young woman.

I stood in the parking lot of the little country church we attended one Sunday, talking to Janice. She was someone I knew as compassionate and caring, with a family full of struggles which she was, at times, brutally honest about. I made the leap and thought if I could be open with anyone, it would be her. I told Janice I was struggling. (I didn't share the MPD; that was a road too far.) Did she know of anyone I might see? She immediately tore off the corner of the church bulletin and wrote down the name of someone in the nearby regional centre of Lismore. My heart relaxed ever so slightly. Now at least I had some sort of direction.

The challenge I faced was how to include Annie, and I suspected *The Girls*, in therapy. We had such different perspectives. For me, I knew therapy had to be about my life now and how I was going to work through my circumstances with the added layer of MPD. For Annie, it was completely different. She had done therapy and wasn't keen to go, even as a remote bystander. I needed a therapist because of the here and now. Annie's life was trauma-based and I naively assumed the system's trauma was not mine. The postcard flashes I would see in my head held no emotional attachment for me. I was sure both Annie and my perspectives would be required if therapy was going to succeed.

And so it was I found myself in the office of Shrink #3. When I first met him, I thought he was straight out of the Aquarius generation. I was warmly greeted by a tall willowy man, a definite hippie with a ponytail of long grey hair.

'What can I do for you?' He sat down and his chair creaked as he leaned back to listen and take the occasional note.

He was gracious and receptive as I told him about my marriage, parenting stresses, depression, and of course the MPD – how my system was affecting me. I was nervous but felt assured by his gentle demeanour. I told him I was depressed, diving into a detailed explanation about what I was learning (or re-learning?) about my system and how I was on edge all the time. He leaned forward and with big bright eyes said, 'For someone who is depressed, you have an amazing energy about you.'

I might see this as a red flag now, but I ignored it then because I needed to be there, in that place, in that room. But I couldn't help wonder, with his years of experience, that surely, at least, he had heard of MPD? And that this is how it works, that the internal chaos of my system was what brought on the abundance of energy he was sensing?

He started talking about once going to an art show of someone who was multiple and said it was fascinating. Then we talked about how he worked. He was about the here and now as the focus of therapy, helping me to cope each day, not focusing on my history, which could cloud the waters. He wanted me to see this as a fresh start. I took a deep breath, hoping he was right.

So each week I would talk about my marriage, about being an emotional wreck and about how my system – Annie and *The Girls* – was affecting how I coped with my daily life. And each week he would stop me and say he didn't want to think about my history as this would distract us from looking at my current issues. And with that, he would gently steer me back to struggles with my marriage and parenting and general lack of joy. These were all important, but I knew they were the presenting issues, not the core problem, which was of course MPD and my relationship with Annie. Every time I talked about *The Girls*, he would talk about my life now, giving no credit to how being MPD affected my life. But I went back each week because I thought I had nowhere else to turn. I saw it at least as a safe place where I could try and let my guard down and talk honestly with someone about my life.

THE MOTHER OF ALL JOURNALS

It is worth stopping to reflect on Annie's journals – the copious notebooks she had used to communicate her soul to Shrink #2. These were where Annie took refuge, in *her* words, as she told *her* story. Those journals travelled with me from the States and were now packed away in our farm shed in a pile of taped-up boxes marked 'Journals'. Even then, I saw them as the vestige of a life which no longer existed, so I don't know why I didn't leave them behind. But as I packed them, I remember thinking this was Annie telling the story of her life and I needed to respect that. I never had to open the box, but just by keeping them, I was acknowledging her life experience.

At some point while she was seeing #2, Annie had also taken the time to laboriously edit and transcribe the journals onto a computer file. All those evenings, she would spend at work after everyone else had left, poring over her words, making a record of this aspect of her life. I had a copy of this as well, in a large brown envelope, hidden away in a box marked 'collectables.' It was in the back of a closet in the house, easily accessible should I want to read it – although I was sure that day would never come.

I had been seeing #3 for nine months and I felt like therapy was going in circles. At times this was gruelling for me because of the way *The Girls* reacted. They were full of anxiety because they assumed he was denying their viability. Annie? Well, she was not impressed by him at all.

I tried to appreciate the insights #3 offered regarding my present-day life, but it was a stop-gap measure at best. The images of Annie's history ran rampant in my brain. I was desperate for someone to understand my truth. It was time to put it all out there. I did the only thing I could think of: I found the box at the back of the closet and pulled out the transcript of Annie's journals. I decided to share this with #3 and hoped, rather desperately, he would finally understand the complexity of my situation. I desperately wished that by reading Annie's own words about her life, he would understand the role she played in my world today.

I sat on his couch holding this envelope in my lap as if it was a precious treasure, anxious to impress upon #3 the importance of this document. I may have even been excited, certain this would be a turning point in our therapeutic relationship. #3 spun his chair around to face me.

'How was your week?'

Fidgeting with the edges of this envelope, I began by saying I had something I wanted to share with him, to help him understand me better. How my past was impacting my life. I barely had time to get the words out of my mouth when he held up his hand and said he didn't want to see it. Simply – no. Anything about my history was the past, and he was about dealing with the present. I was desperate for #3 to 'get me,' the importance of MPD and how it affected every aspect of my life. But this refusal confirmed my fears that therapy with #3 was not going to work.

Terrified of not having support, of being alone and forced to figure all this out on my own, I began searching for a new therapist. I talked to a few people, trawled the internet, and a few swings and roundabouts later I discovered someone in Lismore who might have some experience with MPD. I had a brief phone conversation with him – I was up to #4 now – about taking me on as a client. The only hurdle #4 could see was that he was being supervised by #3, but he didn't think it would be a problem. I just needed to discuss it with #3 first. I felt empowered. I was taking control, trying to make sure I was seeing the right therapist. This meant that leaving #3 didn't feel so earth-shattering, in spite of how misunderstood I felt.

I sat down in #3's office, prepared to tell him this was my last session. He sat down in his seat, pulled out his customary sheet of paper, and swivelled towards me. 'How was your week?'

'It was okay. Same stuff with the kids and still struggling with Tom and my depression. But I'm trying.'

'Okay.' His head bent over his notepad as he jotted notes.

'Actually, I've been doing some work myself.' He pulled out a thick stack of paper. 'This is a copy of the DSM-5 Manual. Have you heard of it?'

I certainly had. The Diagnostic and Statistics Manual was the psychologist's bible for diagnosing and working with mental disorders. Why in the world was he bringing this up?

'Yes, I'm familiar with it.'

'Well, I've been looking at the information on MPD – or DID, as you know it's called now.' Then he looked at me. 'I've been a therapist for a long time, but never had a client with DID. I realise this is very important to you, and a big part of your life. Looking at what the DSM says, well, I feel a bit out of my depth.' He continued with a tale of living in regional Australia where there wasn't any real support, and finding anyone to work with could be difficult. 'But…' He flipped through the pages of the DSM again. 'I'm willing to give it a try. I'd need your help though. In some ways, you would really need to teach me.'

I was stunned. My first coherent thought was, *I've been seeing him for over nine months and he's only just believing me? Great, just great.* But I stopped, remembering he'd done his best.

'Well actually,' I chimed in, 'I think I'm going to see someone else.'

'Oh?'

'Yeah. I really appreciate all you've done. But I need to see someone who at least has had some exposure to MPD and already understands how it works and the implications for my life.'

I saw a sense of relief on his face. 'Okay. I'm curious. Who is it?'

'Well, you supervise him. I wanted to discuss that with you.'

The next fifteen minutes were taken up with amiable conversation. #3 understood my need to see someone who had the right background. He felt #4 could be a positive step in my healing and coping process. He even smiled and had a twinkle in his eye when he said, 'Well, since I supervise him, I'll be able to keep in touch with how you are doing.'

We stood up together. I smiled, 'Thank you.' And then uncharacteristically, I hugged him. He wished me well. I never looked back.

SHRINK #4

I went to my first appointment with #4 full of hope and purpose. Here was someone who had an understanding of abuse, PTSD and most importantly, Multiple Personality Disorder. But it didn't stop the nerves. My first impression of #4 was that he was little more than a kid himself, comfortable in jeans and a t-shirt, a barely visible tattoo on his upper right arm. We sat down and he launched right in. Thoughtful and considered, ready to take notes about my history.

'Including the MPD?' I asked. I shouldn't have been uneasy, but my experience with #3 made me wary he would brush it aside.

'Absolutely the MPD.' He must have sensed my nerves as he reminded me he had seen a few clients with MPD before and understood the central role it played in my life. And then with a pad of paper and pen next to him, he took copious notes as I told him about my life.

I painted a picture of my current home life, my marriage, our children. I talked about Annie and her return, and how the internal system was more than I could handle. I didn't know what to do. And then I told him I had a timeframe. It was May now and I wanted to be done by Christmas. My goal was to be able to function, and not be overwhelmed by my system. I didn't need to integrate, I knew Annie and I were not compatible, but we needed to be able to get along. Annie had been in therapy for almost ten years with #2; I wanted to be done much quicker. #4 listened, keen to hear me out, asking thoughtful questions about my system and how it functioned, sidestepping my time-frame requirements.

Annie's voice was with me constantly in this process. Nothing new there. I wanted to believe I was getting used to her incessant condemnations of my life, but I wasn't. I found myself putting up clear boundaries with Annie. She could come and watch, I reminded her, but unless she wanted to talk to #4, she had to remain quiet. And by quiet, I meant no nattering on while we were in his office. I was desperate to believe I was taking control of our internal relationship.

I wanted to explain my system to #4, so on a big piece of butcher paper I drew the house and its surrounds. #4 carefully laid this out on his desk and invited me to look at it with him. He gestured at the rudimentary drawing.

'So this is the house?'

'Yeah.'

'What are the important things I need to know?'

'I'm pretty sure this is the construct of how the system is put together. As far as I know, each alter has a room built around their existence.'

'Can you describe what it looks like?'

'Honestly, all I can think of is a Monet painting. It's impressionistic, like the style of painting. A bit blurred and almost hidden away on a hillside by the tall grass around it.'

#4 nodded. 'The nature of MPD means that systems are put together in whatever way works for the person.' He looked at me, 'Why do you think yours is a house?'

I said the only thing that made sense. 'I think because a home is supposed to represent a place of safety or security. And maybe because they didn't have this at home, they built it for themselves?' I said it as a question because I felt like I was grasping at straws, admitting my own doubts.

He continued to stare at the drawing. 'What's this?'

I laughed. 'It's supposed to be play equipment, but I didn't draw it very well. Just a swing set and sand box.'

'Any of the alters use it?'

'Sometimes. Two alters seem to spend a fair bit of time there. They're snarky and nasty. Hate everyone really. They are two versions of the same person, one older and one younger.' This began a lengthy conversation about the names and responsibilities of the alters, and how their lives were based around a function, rather than a linear life. There were at least three pairs like these two — a younger and older version of the same alter, connected, having similar names.

He thought for a minute and then pointed to a set of overlapping circles. 'What's that?'

'I was trying to draw how Annie's and my life intersect. Her life includes all the alters. So I think I'm trying to show what I know about her life. The overlapping part contains the alters I'm aware of. And that's kind of where our lives overlap.'

'Do you think there are other alters you might not know about?'

I shrugged. 'I have no idea.'

We came back to this drawing over the next few weeks. #4 would ask questions about how things interrelated in and around the house and about my relationship with Annie. I would share what I could, but this was Annie's domain, where she retreated and cared for *The Girls*. It was a fluid place changing all the time, with no foundation in the external world. I felt a sense of freedom as we talked. I got the sense #4 really began to understand how the past was a critical part of my present and how MPD was interfering with my life.

#4 encouraged me to get to know their home and engage with it as part of my healing process. I needed to find my place in this house. Did I fit in? Was this a place where I was welcome or forbidden? I could see it in my head from a distance, and there was a sense of unsettling familiarity. #4 was right. If I was going to understand how my history affected my present circumstances, I had to be willing to look inside their home.

HOME IS WHERE WE BEGIN

In a far-away land, in the recesses of my brain, there is a house, nestled at the edge of a field surrounded by a carpet of yellow daisies which seems to go on without end. It is a large old European cottage, with cracked plaster and a thatched roof dark with age; unmistakably impressionistic, with muted tones of blue and purple. It's shrouded and misty, as if trying to hide from view. This house has known the intimate stories of many lives.

Even at a distance, I see someone sitting on the window seat of the house. It's Annie. I wonder if she will try to influence my visit to this sacred place. Our relationship is full of conflict, I expect this visit to be no different.

Standing on the front porch is a six-year-old girl dressed in a pink floral paisley pinafore and bare feet. She waves at me with excitement.

I follow the trail through the lush carpet of flowers and pass another girl, lying on her stomach in the field, barely visible. She is studying the petals of the bright daisy she has plucked. Butterflies and bees swarm nearby, unnoticed. Her head is bent to the flower.

Our eyes meet briefly as she acknowledges my presence before returning to her task. I follow the well-worn path through the lingering scent of the blooms towards the house.

Annie talks to me, even from this distance. She is circumspect.

I can see everything from here. I wish you could understand what I really do. This house is how things stay in control. It's where I hide our secrets. That's my job.

You stand between wonder and fear. I wish you would stop lingering on the edges and engage with us. But you won't – I know why. You represent everything I've screwed up. It's not fair to hate you, it's just the easy thing to do. You don't connect with us, you just watch.

Her arms gesture around the house. *This home makes sense of everything we went through. I don't know how it all got made, but it did. I keep things in order. I used to have an external life, before, while you were asleep, safe and hidden.*

Is this Annie's challenge to me? I feel she is trying to see if I am up for the work of understanding the life hidden away in my brain. I continue down the trail, my unspoken answer to Annie's challenge.

The girl in the paisley pinafore greets me warmly, like an old friend. She reaches for my hand, drawing me onto the porch. She stops and turns, holding me with her gaze.

Remember, home is where our story begins.

As soon as we cross the threshold, she smiles.

'I will show you the artwork later.'

Then she is gone. I am on my own.

There is nothing normal about this house. It feels and functions differently from any I've ever known. Walls are transparent, I can clearly see girls through them. Some girls live in everyday bedrooms. When I look closer, there are other girls, their bedrooms encasing them in the circumstances they were created for. In the front hallway, girls come and go. This is where Annie sits, in the window seat. From here she can look back up the path I took to get here. The young girl lying in the flowers is still there. Annie decides she will tell me about this place.

The field is where Flower Child lives now, it's her home. She can't see anything else. The pain she knew was too much, so she was sent to live in the gentleness of flowers, butterflies and bees. She'll never come back. The real world is too hard for her.

From the window, there is another path leading to a play area with a swing set. Two figures sit perched on the edge of the sand pit, facing away from the house. The older one has her arm draped protectively around the smaller child, a younger version of herself.

Annie continues, *They might come back. But they are hurt and angry, and happy to be that way. I suppose they could come back. The older one sometimes interacts with the world, but only to make trouble really. They like being pissed off and will probably never change.*

I turn and look back, inside the house. The rooms seem stacked on top of each other, and yet they are still visible. Rooms have shut doors, yet seem wide open to the world. Some rooms aren't rooms at all, but experiences which *The Girls* keep revisiting. They seem comfortable, even content with these arrangements.

The walls are covered with faded, yellow striped wallpaper dotted with tiny flowers, reminiscent of an old 1950s farmhouse. If I stretch out my hand, I can put my fingers through the wallpaper and into a room, where an electric spark sends shivers to my bones. The girl in this room becomes aware of my presence, I retreat, feeling like an intruder.

In one bedroom, there is a girl in a vivid ocean-blue dress with a delicate lace collar. She has big blue eyes and Shirley Temple blonde curls tied up in a matching blue ribbon. She sits on a bench in the middle of a vast empty park, swinging her legs. When she senses my presence, she looks directly at me and asks, *'Is Mommy coming soon? Do you think she will like my dress?'* She pats her dress to make sure it is in pristine condition. *'I hope Mommy comes soon. I think she will love how pretty I am in this dress.'* She quickly forgets about me, her eyes scanning the park, waiting for her mother.

Annie continues to interpret what I see, telling me about the girl I just saw. *Her job is simply to look for her mother. She embodies everything we hoped would make Mother love us. She will always be like this. Never able to feel secure in who she is, because she wasn't good enough for her mother.*

I sense this house is in a constant state of flux. There is a corner at the front of the house, bare, apart from an attractive middle-aged Mexican woman who sits in a rocker. *Mamacita*. She doesn't speak, but has an all-knowing look on her face. She has long straight black hair, milk chocolate skin, and piercing dark brown eyes. She wears a bright yellow peasant dress, with beautiful multi-colored embroidery. In the real world, she would be a sight to behold. Here, I am uncomfortable with her presence.

Annie pipes up. *Don't bother with her. She controls this place like a prison matron. Once, she put locks on all the doors. It didn't make a difference to The Girls, but it made sure absolutely nothing got in or out. She comes and she goes when she sees fit, or when the security of the house is threatened.*

The number of rooms and girls is overwhelming. This sight leaves the reality of my own heart quite broken. In a detached way, I know them, but I don't. I know these girls lived a fragmented painful existence, protecting me. I am keenly aware of this uncomfortable truth.

Hallways curve this way and that, but also remain absolutely straight. I can see a bright white kitchen at the back of the house. It is stark and empty. I see through a door to a girl who is disturbingly familiar, she is *The Girl in the Cage*. She stares directly at me, unafraid. She understands the fragmented world in which she exists is different to mine. She wants to understand and communicate her story. Am I ready to hear it?

I could lose myself in this place; I am quite certain it would swallow me whole.

I look at the long wall in the corridor. There is a place where the floral wallpaper is peeling back, exposing something underneath. Out of curiosity I look closely, peeling back the paper just enough to expose a bit of the hidden treasure behind it. I look at Annie.

I have been trying to hide this from you. But you just can't stop trying to figure things out, can you? You were not meant to see this; you will never understand the truth of the artwork underneath.

Annie sighs and then continues, *Next time you come back, look for the Curator, the one who greeted you when you arrived. She will show you the complete artwork.*

A small child zooms between my legs. She is a small pudgy thing who intermittently crawls and then runs. The child is filthy, wearing only rags. She races around my legs a few times, as if trying to trip me up. And as quickly as she came, she disappears around a dark corner.

Don't bother. Annie's last words on the house. *I gave up on them a long time ago. It's hopeless to try and communicate with the really little ones. They have a reality which adults will never get, and they can't explain.*

There are more rooms, more girls, and more pain than I care to comprehend. This is the inexplicable art of dissociation. It is why I am alive. It is hard for me not to wonder at the way this place has been put together. Piecemeal. One explosive experience after another built this monument to a destroyed life.

Someday I may stand in awe of the creativity required to build this home, this system built to allow a body to function, finding the will to live in spite of what happened. But for now, it's simply overwhelming.

LOSING IT

I started seeing #4 in May of 2016. By November I was stretched to breaking point. I tried to live my life, raise kids, be a vague semblance of a dutiful wife, all the while coming to terms with my identity as someone living with MPD. It was one thing to accept I was multiple, but another to understand how to live my life. I was apparently high functioning. What did that really mean? When it came to the *The Girls'* reactions to what seemed normal in my life, I often felt like I was being jerked about on a string. Things that were innocuous to me could cause extreme responses in them.

    I knew the clock was ticking on my goal to have finished therapy by the end of the year and I was impatient to be done. I had imagined #4 would hand me a set of coping mechanisms I could apply to situations in my life and move on. It was a ludicrous expectation.

Coffee: the aroma, the taste, the buzz, I loved everything about coffee. I would often stop at my favourite cafe for my takeaway latte. I was a familiar face and the staff knew my order as soon as I walked in.

'The regular?'

'You bet. How's it going this morning?'

'Great,' would be the chipper response. I paid and waited outside, resting my arm on the long, polished stretch of wood, giving me a ringside view of the baristas' dance as they churned out cup after cup of caffeine goodness.

A man stood next to me. I noticed his particularly tight bum and muscle-bound torso.

Wow, a voice said in my head. *He looks good. His tight ass is a real turn-on and those muscles.* (I was pretty sure it was *Slut Girl*; her sexually obsessive chatter was unmistakable.) Uncomfortable, I could feel the colour rising on my face. Why was my coffee taking so long?

I wonder, this voice continued, *what it would be like to screw him? Are his legs as thick as his arms? I bet his prick is huge. Would love to have a taste of him inside me.* I gazed down, fidgeting. As I glanced up, I caught this man's eye. He looked at me briefly, did I imagine a horrified look? Oh crap. Did *Slut Girl* actually say that, out loud? Not just in my head? While I wasn't aware?

My coffee arrived. I smiled, said thank you, kept my eyes down and left. This sort of thing was happening more often. I felt an increasing lack of control over my circumstances and what *The Girls* were saying in my head, or even out loud. Often I just wasn't sure.

I get that neurotypical people have thoughts running in their minds, things they would never be caught saying out loud. The fundamental difference were the voices in my head had names and histories. They had a function and purpose when I was a child. They were as real to me as my own kids. They had opinions and thoughts on just about everything I did and everyone I knew. Some were more intrusive than others, driven by intense fear, anxiety, or as in the café situation, heightened sexual awareness. From time to time, all these things invariably spilled over into my life.

When I was aware of who was thinking what, I found it easier to come to terms with what was going on. (In this case, when it was *Slut Girl* acting out the role for which she had become.) It didn't necessarily make it easier, but at least I understood why they said what they did. I worked with #4 to try to understand this dynamic in the hope this would diminish its effect on me.

Other alters were blatantly terrified of sex – and any expectations Tom might have about it. Our sexual relationship had ended years before, but this didn't stop *The Girls* from thinking he might demand it. My nightly routine revolved around me surfing the net or watching Netflix until very late so I would fall into bed exhausted, long after Tom had gone to sleep. Even then, I would curl up into a ball at the top corner of the bed hugging a pillow, because alters were terrified the man I shared a bed with would demand sex.

One day, we went to a friend's property where one of our heifers was to be slaughtered. We had taken the heifer there sometime earlier to fatten alongside our friend's steer because when the time came, it would cost less to have them processed together. Today was the day.

The butcher came out and we wandered down to where the cows were being grazed. My friend mentioned that one day their bull had gotten into the paddock, but played it down. She didn't think it was a big deal. I took her at her word and to avoid watching the butcher at his work, we stood chatting on the far side of the truck. A few minutes later when the butcher had the carcass strung up, he cut it open and I heard him say, 'Oh, that's too bad, your heifer was in calf.'

I collapsed against the truck in sensory overload, gripping my stomach in agony, my vagina on fire. This was confirmation of something I had never wanted to know. I saw an alter in my head who had had an abortion and lived ever since in ongoing grief and loss. I went into a fog. This was my fallback position, detaching enough to be able to go through the motions until I felt safe enough to engage with reality again.

Annie's voice remained the loudest, especially when it came to my friends. She had nothing nice to say. They felt sorry for me, they thought I was boring. The stream of derisive commentary was endless. She would remind me that worse still, all these people I was coming to know and love would at some point betray me. This was her belief and she insisted that I own it too. This could happen while I was having coffee or walking along the street. I was unable to keep her voice at bay so I became adept at putting up a front, pretending nothing was going on.

But the voices would become overwhelming. The sexual innuendo, the anxiety, the fears all grew louder in my head and no matter how hard I tried not to listen, I would eventually lash out at whoever was nearby. I would get angry with the kids because, yet again, they hadn't fed the animals, or with Tom because I felt he wasn't listening to me. It was always irrational. They were volcanic outbursts I couldn't control.

It was not until the emotion had passed and I was able to have a coherent conversation with #4, that he would point out the pattern behind these outbursts. It was *The Girls* and their fear of being abused that was causing my reactiveness – so many of the feelings regularly overtaking me were actually feelings belonging to *The Girls*.

I was a high-functioning multiple. This meant I rarely lost time. I worked hard with #4 to stay centred and in control when I could feel my life reeling out of balance. I would do deep breathing exercises or curl my fists and toes up tight in an effort to ground myself in *my* reality, *my* body. This helped – to a point. Doing things I enjoyed was my best grounding though, giving me my own identity and purpose separate to the system. Cheese-making, walking through the veggie patch, collecting eggs and making bread all helped. Cooking nourishing food for my family gave me a huge sense of accomplishment, whether sweet treats for afternoon tea or homemade soup, I loved feeding my family well. These things reminded me I was Maggie, a person with my own interests, not merely a shell for *The Girls* to live through.

All of this was happening because I was trying to heal, but instead, I felt like I was falling apart. I wished I wasn't MPD, that my abuse was ordinary. (How ludicrous was that?) I regularly talked with #4 about a simple question: was I losing my mind? Or was I beginning to understand the truth of my life?

THE GIRLS

I talked to *The Girls* often. I told myself that getting to know them was a part of my therapy; it would heal and care for a lost part of my psyche. This process consumed me.

Once the morning farm chores were done and the family was gone, I had nothing requiring my attention. I became inventive, working these deliberate exchanges with *The Girls* into my daily routine. I would be standing in the kitchen stirring the cheese curd while my mind would walk through their house. If I saw an alter in their room, I would engage with them if I was inclined. I often talked to Annie while I was weeding the veggie patch, trying to find some middle ground in our relationship.

After a morning's work and shower, I would sit down at my computer, sometimes for hours, and journal about my observations, or create conversations with the alters.

Journaling was easy, I wrote about how an alter felt or what they looked like, their function and the pain they held. It was a way for me to understand who they were, making their presence more tangible. Putting these thoughts in my journal allowed me to capture them on the page and go back to them later. There were times when coming to terms with the truth of what *The Girls* represented was overwhelming. It was good to be able to walk away from the computer, knowing I could come back when I was ready. This process gave me more control and it also gave #4 valuable insight into the inner workings of my system.

The conversations were another matter altogether. It was something I came up with to try and get to know each alter, one-on-one, and transcribe these conversations while we spoke. (Yes, it was all in my head.) This was another way for me to understand each alter and their jobs and roles in the system, but significantly more personal. It also gave me insight into how Annie lived and how she managed the system. In retrospect, this was foolish. It sent me headlong into the life going on in my mind, forgetting the reality of my own life. I would come out of these conversations a bit dissociative. Understandable, but it meant I sometimes spent hours in a fog and it could take ages for me to get back in the swing of my day-to-day grind.

The way I approached these conversations was to talk to an alter based on revelations from a therapy session or some other event. *Little Girl*, for instance, was someone I needed to understand more about. I would sit at the computer and visualise her where she would be in the house.

What follows is one of the conversations I transcribed on the computer. I would always start with an overview of what I was seeing. Every time I did one of these, it felt like necessary self-torture.

***

Little Girl, who as far as I can tell is almost four, sits on the ground in the Parents' bedroom, banging the back of her head on the dresser by the bed. Wedged into this space, her feet are tucked under the bed, hands on the floor. Her head, thump, thump against the dresser. Where do I even begin? She speaks as a child and she is in pain. A very specific pain in the back of her head.

I know you're there. Leave me 'lone. I ain't gonna talk. You mean, mean, mean. It was quiet before ... but now ... it's all bad with things in my head.

I'm sorry this is making you so upset. Must hurt your head, huh?

It's fine. It hurts and that's better than the other kind of hurt. It's okay dohkay.

Would you like it not to hurt?

NO!!!!!

Oh, why is that?

Coz when it hurts, I don't have to think about things. She stares at me. *If I hit my head hard enough and long enough, maybe I will mess up my head and die. That would be even better!*

I wonder if hitting your head all the time is why my head hurts a lot? Do you think it might be?

Her eyes become the size of saucers. *I don't know! Not my fault!*

I'm not saying it is, I'm just wondering if somehow, well, maybe they are related to each other.

I don't get you.

How can I explain this? Okay, the other day *Middle Girl*, she said that you and her and I were connected. What do you think of that?

She stops in her tracks and looks at me. *Yes.*

Yes, you know?

Yes, I get it. I know.

Okay. Well, I wonder if maybe because we are connected, I can feel some of your pain.

She looks down. *Sorry.*

I know you don't mean to hurt me. It's okay. It gives me a really bad headache at times, I can't imagine how it feels for you.

Shrug of the shoulders. *My life. Dragged in here, hurt and then want to die. My life.*

Does it happen a lot?

It happens always. Every moment, every day.

That must get tiring.

I hit my head to try and die. He's going to catch you soon and hurt you too if you ain't careful.

He? You mean Dad? I'm not too worried. I don't think he can hurt me.

Oh he can!

Why?

Because he hurts everyone. She leans forward. *I even know he hurt mommy.*

Yeah?

I had to watch... sometimes.

That must've been hard.

It's what it was.

And this still happens. He hurts your mommy?

No. He comes in like a dark shadow now... and just makes me put his thingy in my mouth. It keeps happening all the time... all the time.

So no. Not mommy. She's dead now. You know, yeah?

Yeah, I know. Can I tell you something else?

What?

Dad is dead now too. He can't hurt you.

She goes quiet and just stares at me. *I don't think so.*

My brother called me from the other side of the world and said he had died.

But he makes me do things. Even now! No ... Not right. No! No ....

She turns her attention away from me and goes back to thumping her head against the dresser. Time for me to leave too, gotta take some aspirin.

***

I was emotionally spent after these encounters.

In this conversation with *Little Girl*, I learned new things. First, Father had been abusive to Mother in some way. I also learned that *Little Girl*, like a number of the others, was stuck in a time loop, staying the same age, holding the same fears - day in and day out.

I thought back to when my brother had called to tell me Father had died. It left me cold and emotionless. I was unaffected by the news. This was incomprehensible to *Little Girl*. The alters had no ability to understand the world had changed, that the Parents were dead, we were on the other side of the world and they could be safe.

#4 read this conversation and talked to *Little Girl* in our next session. She spent her time curled up on the floor of his office, hitting her head against a chair. #4 coaxed her in his best gentle parent voice to stop. She did, but quickly left, embarrassed.

I felt like I should have found a way to comfort her, but I was too afraid. The truth was, *Little Girl* was a part of my life who I was unable to completely accept as me. I could write about it, even acknowledge this had happened, but not to me, never to me.

It was my body, but used by someone else.

ANIMAL BASHER

I discovered at times, farm life could be a trigger, especially when it came to animals. Tom and I would talk with the kids about death on the farm, trying to take the edge off it, using euphemisms such as 'processing' or 'dispatching' instead of killing, as if somehow this would made the experience less confronting. Butchering cows, pigs and chooks was a grim necessity. It's how we lived sustainably. I adapted, telling myself at least these animals had good lives.

We had a yearling heifer to process and brought in a mobile butcher to handle the job. With my best hay, I led her through a narrow alleyway we constructed with two strings of electric fencing. I was leading her to her death. At the top of the paddock, the butcher stood casually, rifle in hand. When I put the hay down, she went in lowering her head, munching. I walked a few metres and turned my back. I could never watch this. A single pop: a bullet in her brain and it was done, transformed in an instant into a carcass of beef. The butcher went about his business, creating something that would feed our family for the next six months.

It was different with sick animals. Those lives wouldn't become food for our family. Instead, they were cast aside, a useless death, buried deep in our long-term compost bin. Killing these animals was almost always my job, done when the kids and Tom had gone for the day. Those sick chicks which had problems hatching, or whose legs were splayed, or with something else which would leave them with a short and painful life. I watched videos on humane methods of killing, but they all required me to touch the animal and I couldn't cope with that. Instead, I would put the chick in a plastic bag, push it gently to one end, then put the bag on a hard surface and slam a brick down hard on its head. It was an instant death, gruesome, but merciful. I felt like a murderer.

Occasions such as this could bring on a rumbling deep in the recesses of my mind, a clue that some unknown history was triggered by this event. In this case, I understood that one of *The Girls* had killed animals. But such revelations terrified me, and I would generally shelve them. If I felt courageous, I would talk to #4 about them, but rarely. The simple truth was that the unknown often terrified me.

As we grew our farm, we kept several flocks of different breeds of chickens. Plymouth Rocks were our meat birds. We had a mix of other birds for eggs, some were Australorp or Rhode Island Reds. All known as good layers. In each of these flocks, we had a rooster to protect the hens and fertilize eggs. There were always surplus roosters being grown out for a new flock, replacements for an old or underperforming rooster, or for the plate. We had one such rooster, a Plymouth Rock we named Rocky, with beautiful plumage and great conformation. He was destined for his own flock. One problem, he was aggressive. I taught the kids how to manage him when they would go out to feed. Use a loud voice to make him back off. This was difficult for Danny, our youngest. Rocky was a big rooster, and I watched as he charged, feathers splayed. I told Danny to stand up to Rocky, use a big voice, and wave his arms around to scare him. Inevitably, the bucket of feed dropped as Danny ran to safety.

I decided to give Danny a lesson in how to manage this rooster. I grabbed a large piece of wood and carried it with authority as we went out to feed the flock. Danny stood behind me with the food bucket as the flock of twenty birds began running up the hill for their dinner. Rocky charged and I yelled at him, swinging the wood through the air to scare him. It worked momentarily, but he came straight back. My son was crying, I was upset. I swung again. This time hard, hitting Rocky squarely on his back as I yelled at him. His neck bent to the side. He stumbled and wandered off. I was satisfied, successfully showing my son how to deal with an aggressive bird. Quietly, I was worried at how much satisfaction I took in hitting this animal.

After the kids left for school the next morning, I went to check on Rocky. Something was wrong. His head hung slightly to the side, and he stumbled, barely able to walk. I had seriously injured him and was angry at myself. It was out of character for me – I loved all our animals. I quietly ignored him, hoping he would get better. By mid-afternoon, he was laying down in the orchard, wings and legs thrashing around, trying to get up. There was nothing I could do, I dispatched him.

I say dispatched. What I actually did was follow through on a death sentence I started the day before. Even worse, I had tortured him, leaving him for more than twenty-four hours in pain. As with all other diseased or hurt birds, he went into the long-term compost away from the house. I walked back, angry at myself. The guilt was overwhelming. And then, out of nowhere, in my head I saw an alter I had not been aware of. *Animal Basher*.

I saw a five-year-old child, sitting on a cement floor in underwear, laughing and hitting small animals with hammers and rocks as people watched, applauding her efforts. It started with insects or rodents and moved to birds, then tying up puppies and kittens. As *Animal Basher* became competent, the animals became larger. She was praised for doing her job well and given sweet treats as a reward. She loved killing things but craved chocolate more.

Killing this rooster, along with the other animals, opened a crack into my past, allowing this alter to bleed through into my life. Annie would stand back, watching how I would handle these revelations. On this occasion, I fell apart. I cried while I showered and then lay on the couch, exhausted and numb, the noise of the TV failing to keep the onslaught of my past at bay.

Too Many Eyes

Too many eyes look back at me in the mirror.
Depths of misery more than my heart can bear.
All-consuming.
Darkness stares into my own soul, seeking answers.
Who are you?
Why do you haunt me this way?
What do you want?
Their own questions reflect back to me.
Why are you hurting us?
Why won't you understand?
Why can't we trust you?
And the most desperate of all,
　will we ever be safe?
Questions asked by children craving security.
How can a terror like that exist?
I stare at my reflection.
Eyes of blue, brown, green and grey echo back at me.
So many questions.
So many things they want me to hear.
Too many eyes,
With questions I cannot answer.

PARA-SUICIDALITY

[*Trigger Warning. This chapter contains descriptions of suicidal ideation.*]

There have been more times than I care to admit when coming to terms with being MPD, I felt so overwhelmed that I wanted to give up on life. I walked the paddocks, collecting eggs and making cheese, contemplating the idea of simply not being. The idea seemed logical and inevitable, to make a deliberate and considered choice to move away from the pain that engulfed me and stop fighting. I wouldn't write about it in my journal because I was afraid #4 would try to intervene – it was his job after all. I certainly didn't talk about it, for fear people would think I was weak. If I was honest with myself, I was drawn to the chaos and fear of everything going on. This dark place held a bizarre comfort for me. It was in the familiarity of self-loathing where I seemed to feel in control.

When I did find the strength to discuss this in therapy, #4 and I started talking around the edges of suicidality. The idea that I was suicidal or could be prone to suicidal thoughts did not sit well with me. Bouts of depression, sure. An incessant struggle with relationships and an inability to keep my 'world' functional, you bet. I could own that. But not suicidal. I was sure I was stronger than that. My life was about the fight – that was my journey. It was a bumpy ride, but I had always managed to continue, believing there would be a new day, another opportunity to fight and get through. Most of the time.

Between our farm and town, there was a railway crossing. A freight train ran through there at the same time every day. When I was in this dark place, I would think about what it would be like to simply wait for the train and just as it was approaching, drive onto the crossing and let the mass of metal bolting down the track obliterate me. Messy, but it would work.

Beaches had the same effect. I gravitated to them when I was feeling blue. I watched the rhythm of the waves, mesmerized by the rise and fall of the tides. I thought about the surfers and swimmers who seemed so at one with the expansive ocean and wondered on those days when my life just felt too much, what it would be like to walk into the crashing surf and let the waves carry me down. I never considered these thoughts to be suicidal, as I had never acted on them. I simply wished for my life to end and for the pain to stop.

I eventually dared to write about this in my journal. #4 and I discussed these dark thoughts and how coming to terms with *The Girls* was affecting me. There were also odd times, when I was simply unable to cope, that #4 received bizarre text messages from *the system.* Alters would message him, talking about leaving or dying. (I have no idea how they knew his number, or knew how to text-perhaps they were keen observers.) Then #4 taught me a new term: para-suicidality. An in-between place, where you don't have a plan to commit suicide but are certainly happy to consider it as an option for ending the pain. It seemed that what I experienced were bouts of almost, but not quite there, para-suicidality.

One of the things I did not recognize immediately was the impact Annie's own internal battles were having on my desire to not be. When I would discuss struggles with #4, Annie would sit like a parrot on my shoulder and speak her counter arguments into my ear. When #4 would talk to Annie, I went into a sort of fog, my shoulders would slump and I would feel heavy and leaden. Annie would discuss with #4 everything he and I had done wrong, how we simply didn't get what it was like to be her. I often felt the weight of Annie's presence long after our sessions ended. Annie's ability to interject herself into any progress I was making was crippling. My journal entries recorded the debilitating effect she was having on me.

***

November 2016

My head is a mess. Nothing is making sense and Annie's constant verbal beatings are winning. I need to write this down, because somehow it gives me more control. But I don't even know if I can. She has zapped all my energy. I can't fight her. How could I? Falling asleep constantly… don't care. No focus. In my head she drones over and over:

Bitch. Just Die. It's what you deserve.
Everything you touch turns black ...
you are a terrible person.
You go and see #4 and try to talk and I will destroy you.
I don't care if it kills me too ... I will destroy you at least.
Don't you dare think anything will ever get better.
Anything you try and do, I will destroy.
I will kill you.
There is nothing you can challenge me with I can't spew back at you.
God is dead in your life. He left you high and dry ...
you have no one and nothing to cling to.
Give up.
You are a dumb stupid bitch.
You are an ass for marrying an ass.
You have no ability to be a parent –
you were stupid to get those children.
They deserve better.
You cannot be a friend.
You do stupid things all the time.
You should just die.
Put us all out of your misery ... you idiot. Just get over yourself.
You don't matter ... to anyone.
Just kill yourself and get on with it.

***

This sort of talk was debilitating. The only control I seemed to have was to write about it in my journal – this got it out of me and on the page, enabling me to hold it at arm's length. Neurotypical people learn to cajole and manage their self-berating attitude, sometimes even turning it into a tool for growth and change. But how was I supposed to manage the attitudes and feelings of another person? This was when MPD made me flounder and I felt absolutely at the whim of *The Girls*, and especially Annie. They were the voices of adults and children consumed by their own concerns and I felt no ability to change or control them. Instead, I would hear their constant droning. *The Girls'* words were often not directed at me, but I could not escape the truth of the pain they held – and this drove me to darker places as I came to terms with having to co-exist with this cacophony. Annie's hatred of me – of my life – was obvious. It felt like there was no ability to have a rational conversation with her. #4 would try to talk to her and establish a relationship in which he could provide her with a safe place to talk. But of course she resisted, as was the norm.

Did all of this make me suicidal? In the end, I had to admit, probably yes, it did. All I know is that life went dark for a few years. I often thought about how much easier it would be if I simply didn't exist. I gave no thought to the ramifications on my kids or my friends. I just wanted peace.

Anti-Hope

To begin with ...
    Anti-hope acknowledges the dark, bottomless pit is,
    in fact, real.
    Where you touch despair, intimately,
    Where nothing is worth striving for,
    nothing worth achieving.

Anti-hope is, logically, the absence of hope.
    A void that consumes everything.
    It makes sense to those of us who understand it,
    An embodiment of sublime, serene beauty.
    A view into the abyss that in its own way
    is familiar, comfortable,
    in an anti-hope sort of way.

So, own it as your own.
    Appreciate the clarity it brings to your life.
    The flavour it gives to everything your senses touch.
    Acknowledge its ability to refine your perspective.

Sit with it, feel the companionship of empty resignation,
    trust it is the one thing that will be true to you in the end.
    With this mindset you can understand
    what hope actually is.
    The irony being you must embrace the oblivion
    of anti-hope to know hope.

And above all, remember and recognise
this place will not kill you.
    And then, when the warmth and familiarity of what
    your darkness means to you
      is worn like a warm winter coat,
        then, you will start to understand what hope is.

BRICK WALLS

Another day, another weekend. I was curled up on the couch, watching TV, trying to ignore the world and my inner turmoil. I was irritated with Tom – my ever-present anxiety ensured I was always irritated with him. We had reached a point where I couldn't discuss anything in a direct manner without being called a bitch, so I started keeping my mouth shut.

And we had the familiar old problem: Tom needed to take his time to process his thoughts, while I liked to put it all out there. This created the ideal environment for my volcanic anxiety to erupt.

I don't remember the exact circumstances, but on this occasion he walked by, made a comment, and I snapped.

'Why are you always so bitchy and mean?' he said.

'Because I'm depressed and suicidal!' I threw back.

He stood at the end of the couch and swung around to face me.

'Oh fine!' he said. 'Let's just make it all about you then!' And stormed off.

You see the best and worst parts of someone when you live with them. Tom and I were no different. Except the worst parts seemed to be all we had left. We were either constantly critical, or silent. This was how we survived.

I am sure I was not an easy person to live with and that I was overwhelming for Tom. Because he processed things very internally, I convinced myself that I was more than he could handle. I knew that when Tom and Annie were just getting to know each other, she had sent him books to help him understand MPD and even took him to see #2, trying to make sure he understood what it meant to get involved with her. Because of this, I wrongly assumed that he understood me.

Tom had a romantic, if not naïve belief, that love would be enough. The first years in Australia didn't help, as I grew increasingly co-dependent, wanting to be the perfect wife, cooking meals he loved, trying to make sure he was always happy. Things had changed a lot since then, of course, but I still felt the need to make him happy, even if my demeanour might not reflect it.

When I think back on those co-dependent years, I know it was not a healthy way to live. By being so wound up in Tom, I was instead pushing him away. Our inability to actually be present for each other was obvious. The farm was not working, we couldn't keep up with the work required and ended up resenting each other because of it. We rarely talked. If we did talk, our tempers would invariably flair, and nothing would be resolved. Instead of working together to solve problems, we blamed each other and nothing changed. We were building a wall between us. Every issue, big and small, became a brick in that wall. At the cost of our relationship, we were reduced to blindly needing to protect ourselves.

My stress levels continued to rise, not only because of what Tom and I weren't dealing with, but I because I knew *The Girls* were being affected as well. I had to find a way to manage their reactions. Given Tom's quiet nature and because I never discussed my MPD with him, I think he assumed my history was no longer an issue. And because for years I had avoided facing my history, it gave him the perfect excuse to ignore it. I made this another tick in the box of my failure as a wife and partner.

We were in the middle of nowhere and, apart from #4, I had no one I trusted. Talking to him helped. But, as he told me, if you don't feel emotionally supported and safe at home, it makes wrestling with complicated issues such as *The Girls* almost impossible. #4 was my lone confidant, listening and helping me survive, with the aim that at some point I would have the strength and clarity to take care of myself. Tom was fatigued, always tired. He was facing problems at work, and I suspected he was depressed as well. I remember the relief I felt when, at some point, Tom told me he was seeing a therapist. I hoped it would help make things better, and dared to believe that with greater self-awareness we might be able to work through our issues.

But in the meantime, every weekend seemed to involve yet another argument about time, money, tiredness and not enjoying life. One weekend we were sitting across from each other at the dinner table. I had my list of things to be done. I always had a list.

'I'm worried about how we're going to cover the costs of the kids' excursions and everything we need to get done on the property. We need a plan,' I said.

He shook his head. 'I don't know. I just don't know.'

'Can we try and make some sort of plan? Something we can both agree on?'

He sighed, 'Maybe, but work is taking a lot out of me right now. Can we talk about this later?'

I watched him get up to leave. I had to pay for the excursions in the next few days. Choices couldn't wait. Things were falling apart. I desperately needed to talk and he was walking away again.

'We need to find some way to talk about these things,' I said. 'But you keep putting it off. You're always too tired, or too worn out, or work is doing your head in.'

He spun around. 'What do you want from me?'

I stopped dead in my tracks. 'I just want us to be able to communicate.'

I watched his shoulders slump as he stared at the floor. Then he lifted his head and looked at me.

'You're asking me for the one thing I can't give you.'

He walked to the bedroom and closed the door.

And again I was left there, feeling utterly lost. Why would someone be married if they didn't want to communicate? Later I would come to understand it wasn't that Tom didn't want to talk, but because he put out so much energy at his job, talking to and managing staff, he simply had nothing left to give at home, to us, his family.

Why did I stay in the marriage? It was fear. I certainly had a fear of losing the kids. (I was convinced Tom would bring in some sort of medical professional and have me declared mentally incompetent.) I had the fear of not being able to support myself. And as much as I didn't like where our relationship was, at least I wasn't alone. Being alone, I was sure, would have been the hardest thing of all.

Another night, we were having a heated argument in our bedroom. He pulled out a sheet of paper with a matrix of sorts on it.

'My therapist said I should try and identify the issues in my life.' He pushed the paper towards me. 'There is the bubble with your name on it, and how the things you do cause me stress.'

I held the piece of paper and stared at it, dumbfounded. The first thing I saw were the words, *Maggie is psychotic*. Well, how was I supposed to argue with that? I often had the same fear. Then he wrote, *Maggie is too much of a deep thinker*. True, but I liked being a deep thinker even if I did resent it was probably the MPD that made me that way. The last point was *Maggie is reckless with money*. The others I begrudgingly accepted. They were all about the MPD. But this one made me livid. He had no idea how I scrimped to make ends meet. It was my responsibility to figure out how we would pay for things. He avoided it all and then got angry when I told him things were tight. If I dared to approach him with some sort of a plan to get the fencing done, or better yet to go on a day trip with the kids to have some fun, he would either rip the idea to shreds or insist he had a better idea and declared he would 'look at it' when he had time, which was never.

By the time he was finished, I felt thoroughly put in my place. My co-dependent history reared its ugly head. If he said it, it must be true. Under all the paranoia, fear and trust issues, I still wanted to please him. I wanted to try and fix problems. Tom had pointed out that I was the problem. I was a failure, and whether it was right or wrong, I believed it. But I had no way of fixing it.

The icing on the cake was when I decided to tell him I wasn't Annie anymore, but that I was now Maggie. I can't even remember why I decided to tell him. Had #4 suggested it? No, that wasn't his style. It was more likely I was overloaded with anxiety because of all the images I was seeing of *The Girls,* and went into my usual verbal diarrhoea. Things came out and it was a mess. We were in the kitchen, another argument starting to ratchet up. What were we talking about? Maybe he didn't understand and was accusing me of being erratic, triggering me to spew.

I wasn't Annie, I was Maggie, I told him. As part of my therapy, I said, I had come to understand she had gone away. She found life far too difficult and had shoved me back out. (I didn't tell him the details of when and why, it would have been too much.) I told him my world was upside down and I was trying to figure out how to be who I was. Therapy was helping me keep a lid on my life.

He stared at me, then walked away.

A few days later when the kids had gone to bed, he asked if we could talk. I naively hoped he was reaching out so we could find some sort of connection. We sat at the dinner table, he looked at me, notes in hand. After a few fidgets and false starts, he said he respected I saw a therapist and was glad I found it helpful. However, he couldn't handle me talking to him about therapy, and he didn't want to know what went on in my sessions. I think what he meant was that he wasn't sure how to handle this revelation about my identity and its possible ramifications on our lives. From our non-existent sex life to my values and beliefs around church, any myriad of things, he simply couldn't handle it. For me, therapy was about my life – my *entire* life – and I couldn't carve off bits and pieces and only share what made him comfortable. I felt rejected, convinced that this meant he didn't want to know me.

(We have talked about this incident a few times since then and Tom has said he believes I was overreacting and took it all the wrong way. But he has never explained what he really meant.)

I understand that at times, being MPD makes me a difficult person to live with. But these types of discussions were the mortar in our brick wall. We learned the dance of disconnect. The children and our love for them became the only relief, and protection from the pain we caused each other.

GREEN EYED MONSTER

'I seriously don't get it. It makes no sense.' This is what I often heard myself say as I talked with #4 about the latest memory, or image at least, which had rummaged its way out of the shadows of my psyche. These were usually triggered by some sort of inciting incident which I would journal about and then bring them to therapy.

The hardest part was admitting that these images were in my head. I knew it was true, but I didn't want to believe there was always more of my history to be uncovered. Every time a new postcard image would surface, I would invariably fight it. After all this time, I still wanted to pretend my childhood didn't happen the way it did. I wanted to believe that denial would make my life easier. Much of my history was jumbled and confused already. Wrestling with the truth of these images made this a doubly painful process.

With Mother, it was emotional abuse. Annie craved Mother's love more than anything else. But Annie (and *The Girls*) never measured up to Mother's exacting standards, which left them with the belief that they could never be good enough – for anything or anybody. There may have been times when *The Girls* suffered physical or sexual abuse from Mother, but those moments are hazy. This is part of being multiple. Successfully holding those darker images at bay becomes self-protection. It would not be implausible for there to be other alters who kept secrets from Annie and me about their relationship with Mother. There was a certain logic to this. It was Mother's love that Annie had craved in our childhood, and it left an emptiness in me, knowing I did not have a mother who loved me.

On this day, I was discussing with #4 images from the alter named *Middle Girl*, of an incident when she accidentally walked in on the Parents having sex. This evoked a flash forward to a memory where Mother was having a serious conversation with *Middle Girl* about the fact she and Father were attending sex therapy. Mother embarked on a series of lectures about the importance of sex and what *Middle Girl* needed to know to make men happy.

Grooming. Mother was part of the grooming process.

The images I would see in my head were never the worst of it. Finding the right words and owning their truth seemed near impossible. #4 was asking me how I felt, and what I thought Mother was thinking. I hunted around in my mind, trying to find a word to fit. I was confused. The only thing I came up with for Mother was jealous. But it made no sense to me.

So I said it again, 'It makes no sense. Why would she be jealous?'

'How does it not make sense?' #4 asked patiently.

Spinning around in my head was the question: why would she be jealous of a child? And so began a discussion about Mother's role in the abuse. Putting a framework around Annie's memories of grooming, Mother's excessive drinking and misdirected anger for having sex with her husband, and therefore, jealousy.

Hauntings

You haunted me last night.
Jarred awake by a dream of all I lost with you.
Romantic notions of a childhood that should have been
    and never was.
But real still.
I thought I was finished with you,
    wrestling with your memory done.
More fool I.
As a child you scared me.
I loved you but was never good enough.
The things I did to make you happy.
Always a failure, craving approval.

Years passed. I forgot / dissociated / suppressed.
Call it what you want. Somehow I survived,
    called it good enough.
Unexpectedly blindsided by memories of you.
Feelings rush at me.
Nothing makes sense, but it affects me still.
It is logical then, why you haunt me
I wrestle with my failings as a parent.
I see you, at times,
    in how I try to love my children.
I am jealous of them.
Of what I never had.
Of a strength of character they own.

SPLIT

Of what I am scared to give them
    for fear of rejection.
I am tired.
I fight with them, but really, I am fighting me.

I am older now, some would say wiser.
I would say I am simply weary,
    with nothing to give at the end of each day.
How can I ever be for them what you never were for me,
especially when they need me the most?

DAMN YOU.

I am failing them because you failed me.
I visit the sins of my life on them (no, not my youth, my life –
    and that's not fair)
I said once to someone, somewhere I forgive you.
May I take it back please? I want to hate you.
But still, I ache to love you … even if it is only the image
    of what I needed you to be.

I'm too old for this shit.
May I find the way to love my children,
    in spite of how you treated me.
Each step, each day, I wonder as I look in my children's eyes,
    did I get it right today?

A DEATH OF SORTS

Annie and I had a moment in our relationship when things shifted, irrevocably. Or perhaps what happened was more about how I created a hurdle which, chances were, we could never get over. And because of my short-sightedness, this hurdle would become another roadblock as we tried to learn to live with each other.

Annie's journals were *her life.* Everything she was, contained in the lines of those notebooks. From time to time, I would make the journey out to the shed and open the box of journals which held that life, now starting to be eaten around the edges by rats making a nest. I would look at this history with the knowledge that here in black and white was evidence of the life we shared, and from which I could not escape. It was as if the pages were shouting at me, *Hey you! Don't forget you're screwed in the head!*

I opened these spiral-bound notebooks with the start and finish dates scribbled on the outside, wondering how they were relevant to my life now. I would crack one open and look at it. Not really reading, rather just turning the yellowing pages, noting dates, changes in handwriting, hoping to find something which might resonate in my head or heart. If I did dare to read an entry or two, after a few minutes I would slam the notebook shut and put the box away, angry at myself for succumbing to the lure of the unknown. It was her life, not mine. Why the hell did I have to look at it? But I had a morbid interest in the scribbles in those books, wanting to see if they would fit into what I called my life. Why? I fought that curiosity with everything I had, I wanted no part of her history.

Then I decided it was time to tidy up, to get rid of as many vestiges of a life having any reference to Annie as I could. I hoped that getting rid of her journals, and our shared history, might help me heal. The fact was, I already had too much information. I barely held at bay the images which haunted me. They were like a horror movie I could watch, but walk out on if I wanted. Reading Annie's journals, accepting her as part of my reality, forced me to step into her horror show and accept that I was part of it. And not just as a supporting cast member, but a lead actor in the thick of it. Why in the world would I want to go there?

So I did what any terrified person might do. I dumped the journals and a number of books about MPD into a box and put it in the boot of my car. The next time I went to see #4, I dropped the large box in his arms.

'These are all her journals. I don't want them anymore.' I waved my hand dismissively. 'Do what you want with them. I don't care. Burn them if you like. Maybe you'll find some use for them.'

'Okay.' Calm, ever steadfast and non-reactive. 'Are you sure?'

'Yes.' I moved to my normal seat and flopped down. 'I just need them out of my life. Seriously, burn them, I don't care.'

'Alright.' He opened a cupboard door and put them in the bottom. 'I'll leave them here for now, in case you change your mind.'

And I did change my mind, and then I changed it back again. The journals became the topic of conversation for numerous therapy sessions. I vacillated, but each time I came back to my original decision. No, I didn't want them back.

And then one fine therapy day, #4 said he was going out to his dad's property to burn a bunch of old paperwork. He would take the journals, if I wanted him to.

I quavered momentarily but was then resolute. 'Yep. Burn them.'

The following week he reported back. The journals were now ash.

From deep inside, like a banshee, I could feel Annie's wails of betrayal long before I heard them. In my desperation to ease my pain I had betrayed the one part of me more significant than any other. I had belittled Annie's significance in my life, brushed her aside, unable to accept the truth of my life. What I didn't realise, until that moment, was that I was forever changing our relationship. We had an uneasy co-existence already, but this was a slap in the face for her and I knew there would be little chance of me ever being trusted by her now. I tried to tell myself it didn't matter and it wasn't like we had a comfortable relationship anyway. But I knew I had made a mistake – and my act of betrayal would redefine our relationship in ways I could not yet understand.

TOWNIES

It was another ordinary day. I was alone – with my thoughts, with *their* thoughts – free to mull over the immensity of the failure I felt. I saw it in every corner of my life, from *The Girls* to our farm – it was all a failure and all my fault. This dream of a sustainable farm life was slipping through my fingers. The meagre amount we saved on growing our own food was far outweighed by the cost of feeding the animals. We were going backwards, never forwards. I walked around the property each day, watching the chickens forage or the guinea fowl charging through the bush. There was a time when I was in awe and wonder at such sights, thankful for the open space, wandering through my veggie patch happily weeding and watching crops grow. Instead, my vision was reduced to seeing everything that was wrong with how we were ruining the farm, reducing it to a derelict heap.

There was no fault or blame to be placed. I wish there were. We were simply not built for, nor had the budget, to sustain a farm life. I had a mental list of all the things needing to be done. Installing a reserve water tank, clearing out the feed area, repairing a chicken coop, mending a broken fence, the list went on and on. This was the normal farmer's life, but not one our family, with pre-teen children, could adequately handle.

At the same time, we had started attending a new church almost an hour away in Lismore. Our major shopping and many doctor visits (including my weekly visit to #4) were also in Lismore. Between travel, and Saturdays trekking across the Northern Rivers for Kyle and Danny's soccer games, we had no time, let alone energy, to make the farm work.

I remember walking up to the house after filling the cows' water trough because the auto feed system had broken again. I stared at the house, realising I felt trapped. Trapped because it seemed there was no way out. How do you leave this? We had invested everything in this place, and it was falling down around us. But something had to be done. Tom had already checked out, so it was up to me.

In retrospect, I believe this is when my healing journey began. Maybe healing is the wrong word; perhaps it was more about control. In coming to terms with *The Girls*, and their daily influence on me, I had lost any vestige of control over my life. I had done so much work in therapy with #4 already, but what I needed to do was put this work, well, to *work*.

I walked into the house, sat at the kitchen table, putting my mental 'to do' list on paper, trying to wrap my head around the actual scope of the work that faced us. I sighed with each bullet point, knowing the effect this would have on Tom. He would withdraw more. I got lost in how we would never be able to find the money or time to get these things done. It was then that the solution became obvious – we needed to move. I needed to let go of this dream. But in order to move, the farm had to be fixed up to sell. This would be my pitch to Tom; the hard work would have a payoff.

The kids had gone to bed, and we were settling in to watch something on TV. I pulled out my list. 'I know you don't want to see this, but here is the list of the things we need to get done around the farm.'

Even before he looked at the list, I watched his shoulders droop. He took it, read it quietly and then looked at me. 'Yeah, okay. Just prioritise and I'll figure something out.'

'I have a different idea,' I said in a positive, *we-can-do-this* voice. 'I know you don't love the farm. What if, instead of doing this list of stuff which will, frankly, be never-ending, what if we do all this to sell the place.'

He stared at me, puzzled.

'Our lives are in Lismore, the kids could do more with friends. They are old enough to get work, I could get work.' I paused. 'Anyway, that's my idea. Fix up the farm to sell it.'

Tom was shocked. I could see it in his eyes.

'Okay. But I need to sit with it for a while, give me a few days.'

'Sure, not a problem.'

Conversation done, we went back to the TV.

It didn't take a few days. The next morning, I was out shifting hay bales and Tom walked up. 'Yeah, okay. I'm happy to see if we can make it work.'

It was June, 2018. The kids were excited about the idea of going back to town life. We told them, same school, same friends, just a different place to lay our heads each night. To curb their excitement, we said it was probably a year away, but everything we did on the farm would be to get it ready to sell, so we could move.

I contacted Anthony, a real estate agent we knew. When he came out, I saw the dubious look on his face. He told us the market was tight and the place would need to be uncluttered and in pristine condition to get even a nibble. I assured him we were well aware of the enormity of the work needed, and would be in touch when we were ready.

I put the wheels in motion. I told a few friends, hoping someone would take our animals – the cows at least. I loved these creatures who so generously gave me luscious milky goodness each day. I called my farmer friend Eloise to tell her we had decided to move, hoping she might know someone who would be interested. She and her husband Bob lived a self-sufficient life and as well as managing their bee colony, Bob did odd jobs in the area. Eloise rang me a few days later. She wanted to buy our cows but couldn't afford to pay market price and proposed that they give us a small injection of cash, but also offer eight days of Bob's time to do odd jobs around the farm. I knew the cows would be well cared for and was thrilled to have the help. It was the perfect solution.

Bob spent a day a week with us. I put him to work with a list of things to do, starting with fencing and pulling down the cow stall. He worked on the outside while I worked on the inside. I took to heart Anthony's decluttering advice. Unless I was absolutely sure I had to use something in the next year, it went in a box. The kids had to do the same thing. Their rooms had to be painted and we had minor internal repairs to do on the house.

Week by week, our 'to do' list shrank. The farm was getting cleaned up.

The house had one glaring deficiency: flooring. We bought the house with a cement slab, intending at some point to put in a wood floor. But finances never allowed it. Proper flooring would undoubtedly increase the selling price. Tom started looking at options. We didn't want to spend much; we simply didn't have the money. Tom found a bargain lot of carpet tiles left over from an office fit-out. Not glamorous, but it would do the job. It quickly became a family project. As each room was painted and finished, we would lay the carpet tiles. This small thing transformed the house.

I remember the last day Bob worked for us. We sold all our chickens, apart from the extra roosters and older birds which were not laying. They would be processed. Bob was adept at this, and between his processing and my cleaning, we got through a dozen birds in half a day. As I turned out yet more chicken mince sausages, I remember thinking how much I would miss this natural way of living, eating off the land, knowing what went into our animals and therefore what went into us. I was sad but knew without any doubt this move was the right thing for our family.

Tom and I began having conversations about where to live. I still wanted to find somewhere a bit rural, but Tom squashed this. We had poor internet on the farm, and Tom was embarrassed by this. He was an IT Manager, so anywhere we moved had to have good bandwidth. We ended up drawing a line roughly 20 minutes north, south and west of Lismore. This would be our search area. We would get an idea of the market, what we liked, and what we could afford.

 The look on the estate agent's face when he walked through the front door reassured me that all our hard work hadn't been for nothing. Anthony commended our efforts and indicated we should get a good selling price. I was proud. There were still a few details to wrestle with, but those were easy. A few drone shots of the property and various house pictures later and by mid-November, five months after we made the decision to sell, the farm was ready to go on the market.

We began looking at properties, but nothing struck us. The kids really wanted a pool, so that came into the mix. It was fun to look around Lismore and get a better understanding of the market. And farms don't usually sell quickly so we weren't in a rush.

When it comes to my faith, I don't believe in coincidences, and mind-blowing miracles are simply not the norm. (But yes, they do happen.) I do believe God guides our path if we choose to let Him. I believed He had guided us this far and knew the right home would be waiting for us at the right time. I even felt a small nugget of peace in my always anxious heart.

The farm went on the market in early December: one hundred acres in the middle of nowhere. Within days we had an offer so close to our asking price it wasn't worth negotiating. The next day we went to an open house for a property in the heart of Lismore. It was easy walking distance to amenities and many of the kids' friends. It had the requisite pool and a funky boho feel. I fell in love with it instantly. By mid-January 2019 we had moved in.

I miss the farm on a regular basis. The honk of horns and screech of tyres has replaced the moo of a cow or cock-a-doodle-do of a rooster. I feel hemmed in on all sides. But at the end of the day, I knew the move was the right thing. It took the pressure off Tom and gave the kids new social opportunities. And it was reassurance to me of the need to take control of my life and push toward something I knew would be good for our family.

NARRATIVE THERAPY

I began to come out of those dark, depressed days. They were still there, but with less intensity. The kids were doing fine, even accounting for some typical teenage angst. Tom and I had worked out that by keeping our relationship superficial we could drift along in an uncomfortable but manageable impasse. Our conversations were about the kids, scheduled activities and his work. But still, I needed to find an outlet. I needed something to replace the farm which would allow me to express myself.

 I started writing again. I say again because I knew it had been a huge part of Annie's life as she was growing up. I had postcard memories of her spending hours in the study at home, exploring new ideas and searching for the right rhythm for what she was trying to say through the written word. She felt whole when she wrote, and I wanted the same feeling.

 In the early days, my writing was more an extension of the journals I wrote for therapy. But I eventually turned to poetry (Annie did this too), and the words began to flow. Because I was writing about a childhood I had never actually experienced myself, I found this an instantly freeing experience. Pulling the pain out of my head, figuratively speaking, and capturing it in verse freed my mind from its inner turmoil. I would occasionally show my pieces to #4, an avid reader himself. Therapeutically he affirmed my expression of pain, but artistically, he also appreciated how I expressed the emotion of my life.

I became aware of an alter named *Writer*, the only one who seemed to have no gender. They were a grey fog, a force and determination. They had no trauma, instead their drive was simply to write. Their presence was a healing mechanism for the pain of *the system*. In many ways, *Writer* was my muse; the inspiration to create words on a page, communicating stories, a compulsion to facilitate writing about Annie's life, about *The Girls* lives, and now, apparently, my life as well. I was grateful there was no trauma or pain attached to this alter.

In this way, pouring out my soul on the page, I made writing central to my healing, with no thought of anything coming of it. It was an expression of how I processed whatever was going on in my life, Annie's life, or with *The Girls*.

There was a ritual I began shortly after I started seeing #4, something to keep me accountable to attend my weekly sessions, especially in those manic days when I wanted to run. I would go to my favourite café and get coffee for both of us. In my mind, having bought the coffee, I was then obligated to follow through on my dreaded appointment each week. Those chaotic days of finding a routine to get through the fear passed, but this coffee ritual remained a part of my therapeutic routine.

This particular week, as I put #4's long black and my jumbo latte in the drinks cradle of my car, I listened to an interview on local ABC radio. A well-known local author was promoting an eight-week course sponsored by Byron Writers Festival, exploring the idea of writing as therapy. She and another local author would walk participants through creative exercises as they wrote about suicide. Participants would be chosen through an application and interview process. I madly took down the details.

I applied and was delighted to be accepted into the group.

I was filled with cautious excitement. Excited to learn more about the writing process, cautious because I was afraid of telling anyone I was MPD. I decided I wouldn't share this information until I was comfortable with the group, which I doubted would ever happen. I would share instead how I was dissociative/PTSD, which was true. This was how I'd taken to describing myself if the situation required; it was an ingrained habit, a way to alleviate my fear of rejection if I told the whole truth.

But I did disclose my MPD in my interview with the group facilitator and support psychologist. Concerned that another alter might emerge in a writing session, the psychologist talked to #4 about my participation. #4 assured him that was not how my system functioned, and there would be very little chance of this happening. Rather, #4 told him, writing had become a powerful way for me – and my system – to process our history. He reassured the psychologist that he thought the group would be a positive therapeutic experience for me.

Story Circle was a group about suicidality. Nine wannabe writers, each with our own histories and beautiful flaws. We were a mixed bag, all different ages, backgrounds, ethnicities and genders. But we all had one thing in common – we had yearned for the peace of death and had chosen instead to live. We met each Wednesday afternoon for eight weeks, working with these two thoughtful and creative authors. We were a fragile bunch, and I was grateful that the facilitator made sure we each had safety rules in place while we built the foundation for our stories. My rule was simple. No hugs. That would equate to trust, and while I enjoyed these people, even liked them, I could not fathom trusting them.

I went each week keen to learn about the art of writing. *Writer* was close at hand as I soaked up all that these two authors had to share about free writing, story arc, character development, the hero's journey and so much more. We wrote a lot, sharing our writing with each other and learning to trust the truth of what we had written. I loved it. I was picking up finer details of the craft of writing from award winning authors who were also constantly honing their work.

Week after week we were challenged and nurtured. In a one-on-one reading, one of the authors gave me affirming feedback on a piece I had tweaked from a previous session. I sighed and said I thought I was done. She smiled and said, 'I think you have more to write. Try working on something new.' I was happy to be pushed, sure I had more to give.

Another week I was with the other half of this amazing duo. I had found my writing came out in fragments which I was never sure would accumulate to a meaningful narrative. She had loaned me a copy of Michael Ondaatje's *Running in the Family,* to see how another author had applied the same mosaic style to his writing, especially when writing about family. It was so useful, so informative

– and such a relief to be reassured that if I kept going, my little fragments might amount to something more.

These two authors believed in each of us, always asking for more detail, more story, more *picture* as we explored the truth of our lives with the artistic tools they were sharing with us each week. I thrived. And over and again I found the words and narrative voice to describe my life, allowing my heart to begin to heal. I credit this group and these wonderful authors for re-igniting my passion for writing. At the end of our workshop we published an anthology, *9 Ways Not to Die, Survivor Perspectives on Dealing with Suicide*. It can be found in doctors' rooms across NSW. We were giving something back to others who were in need. This did my heart good.

Barely a year later, life seemed to have come full circle. I was taking a course through Byron Writers Festival called *The Year of the Novel*. It spanned an entire year, structured to support writers working on longer projects, and it was taught by one of the authors from the Story Circle group. We were an eclectic, wildly creative group of writers. As well as meeting to improve our craft, we were creating amazing stories on topics ranging from Australian colonization to a teenage coming-of-age story, a tale of finding cultural roots, memoir, an insanely creative sci-fi story and everything in between. When the course finished, we knew we needed to keep the dynamic going and formed a writing group. We even managed to wrangle our mentor to keep meeting with us. We would connect via Zoom as often as our schedules allowed.

We talked about organising writing retreats, time when we could escape our daily lives and focus on our writing. And so it was, hidden away in the Byron hinterland, I discovered the joy and productivity of spending extended time with like-minded writers. Our first retreat was so successful, we organised more. On the first night of each retreat, we would gather around the table and the question would be asked, 'What's everyone's goals for the weekend?' The responses were as varied as the writers themselves.

'I haven't written in months. I just want to write again.'

'I've just done a major restructure, and want to start filling in the holes.'

'I need to get 10,000 words done for my mentor.'

'I have edits I need to get done before it goes off for another manuscript assessment.'

And of course, 'I just want to stop and relax and enjoy you folk.' To which there would be a hearty response, because in the end, our camaraderie was a big part of our inspiration.

The structure of our retreats would be to write for the bulk of the day and come together mid-afternoon when our mentor joined us and we would read to each other and receive feedback. After that, we would take turns cooking dinner, and never before had I tasted such rich, decadent healthy food. We brought wine, and our conversations over dinner were full of lively discussions about the latest books we were reading, what was going on in each other's lives.

I had started working on this memoir, and the group knew it was about abuse, but not about MPD. I would have to come clean. I was terrified, but told myself that if I couldn't share the truth of my MPD with these beautiful people, I'd never be able to.

I decided to read on the first day. Rip off the band-aid and get it over with. I would read what is now the opening of this book. (Although it was five, much rougher drafts ago).

I read from my laptop, *I was diagnosed over 30 years ago with a disorder identifying me with individual personalities living in my head. Today, professionally it is called Dissociative Identity Disorder, however, it is still commonly known as Multiple Personality Disorder.*

It felt like I read for an eternity. Even while I was speaking, I was wondering if everyone would think I was psychotic. I grounded myself by rubbing my clammy hands against my leg. I coughed once or twice and took a few deep breaths to slow myself down. Was I crazy for doing this? Exposing myself? Even as the words came out of my mouth, my internal dialogue was gurgling away doing its destructive job.

When I finished, there was silence, then a loud whoop as I was congratulated for my honesty. As always, this was followed by my colleagues' gentle and constructive feedback. Affirmed but not coddled, they gave me a frank perspective on the holes in my work, or where it seemed to sag – points where I could tighten it up for better impact. This process normalised not only my MPD, but treated me, well, like I was okay, which was astounding.

To this day, we continue to meet every six months. Each time I read, my truth becomes easier to own and to share. I can be honest about who I am, knowing I will be accepted and not judged. And merely talking about what I am writing is its own narrative therapy, continuing my healing process.

Writing Towards Truth

It starts with pen and paper.
Write the trigger, what is seen and felt,
    in the mind's eye.
Not to capture what it is, but to write what it is for.
Cathartic, exposing, healing.
There is an absurdity to this process.
Triggered, exposed to something that insights historical pain.

Write it out, what is remembered,
    held in memory.
First. Simply write.
    Write the ugly.
    Write the pain.
    Write the hurt.

It is in writing that healing begins.
Shadow truths that destroy souls.
Written into something lyrical, tangible,
held on the page, so we never forget.

Second. Editing begins.
Edit each phrase, subtle and nuanced.
Strip away the pain, no longer crippling.
Cut the self-loathing,
    the words spoken to a child who deserved more.
I don't understand, but somehow, this is healing,
how pain is processed.

SPLIT

Some draw or paint,
some run or garden,
finding that thing that nurtures their soul.
For me, it is the written word.
Tactile. Touchable.

Of course it's ugly. That's the point.
It is exposing darkness to light.
Framing it to capture and control.
    So write damn it.
    Write towards truth.
    Write towards healing.
    Write towards wholeness.

I CAN'T BREATHE

[*Trigger Warning. This chapter contains descriptions of sexually explicit violence.*]

This time, it started with a text message. Dread oozing out of the recesses of my brain. My personal cauldron of crap bubbling over, leaving me to wonder – would I be triggered?

It was a year into the pandemic when I received the reminder for my CT scan, a simple text stating appointment details, followed by, *Due to health restrictions, face masks are required.* Medical professionals walked a tightrope on the front line against Covid. Their workplaces needed to be places of safety. Accepting this didn't mitigate the anxiety rising in my bones at the thought of having my mouth covered, the restricted breathing, the fear of powerlessness. I was ashamed. Why was this my life?

I travelled up the elevator to the lab, feeling the walls closing in on me, my chest becoming tight, my breathing short and shallow. I clutched the railing. I hated not being able to control these reactions. People passed me in the corridor, faces masked. They stared at me, glancing down at the *I Am Exempt From Wearing a Mask* card on the lanyard around my neck. They veered to the far side of the corridor. Did they think I was deliberately trying to risk their health? Did they think I was making it up, that my fears weren't real? Hell, I didn't know if they were real. All I knew was the idea of putting on a mask made me panic. I had tried once, but ripped it straight off. There was no way I could wear it.

I walked into the lab, prepared to explain myself. I adjusted my lanyard so it was clearly visible to the receptionist. I handed her my paperwork, including my medical letter of exemption from Shrink #4, which I placed on top, unfolded, so she could see what it said – due to PTSD and anxiety I was exempt from wearing a mask. This was my armour, how I avoided conflict and found some calm in the midst of my fear. The receptionist read my letter and handed it back. I sat in the waiting room clenching my fists, trying to control my anxiety about whether or not my exemption would be accepted.

The technician called my name, and I followed her into the next room. She was lovely, with a perky brunette ponytail and eyes smiling above her mask. I donned my hospital gown and sat quietly as she put the cannula in my arm.

'You'll have to wear a mask for the CT,' she said casually.

'I have an exemption.' I flashed my badge at her. 'I can show you my letter too if you like, it's in my wallet.'

'Doesn't apply here. It's medical equipment, we have to ensure there is no opportunity for Covid to get on the machines.'

Of course, it made sense. In my mind I could see droplets being sneezed onto the large CT array, where they would wait to infect the next patient.

She taped down the tubes which would carry the dye into my body. 'All good here. Follow me this way.'

I wanted to run, not care about this scan. Instead, I followed obediently and sat down on the CT bed. She handed me a mask. I held it between my fingers, staring at it. 'I just don't think I can do this.' Did I see pity or irritation in her eyes?

'I tell you what, let's try a face shield. You'll have more space around your face. I'm sure it'll do the trick.'

I sighed. 'Okay.' Then lay down.

'I'll just get your arms above your head.' She reached for the face shield. 'See, you don't even have to put it on. I can just rest it on your forehead.' She didn't stop, she kept going. As if somehow she could make the next five agonising minutes vanish. What she didn't realise was that the shield was flat on my face. Instead of putting it on properly, it was touching my forehead and nose, obstructing my airflow even more.

I lay there, heart thumping, the motor whirring as I was cranked in and out of the big machine, the plastic shield rigid against my face. With every breath I took, it felt as if the air became thicker, denser, making it harder to breathe. I closed my eyes, desperate to fend off the panic that was consuming me. The engines of the scanner roared – I was trapped. I couldn't breathe. I told myself it would be over soon, but I still couldn't breathe. My voice was lost. I was crying.

Suddenly it was finished. The tray I had been lying on slid out of the machine, and the technician let me know she had taken the tubes out. I threw the shield off my face.

'Sit up carefully.' She reached for my arm to steady me.

Shaking, I couldn't feel my body. My mind was in a fog. I sat rigid on the side of the bed, unable to move as she asked, 'Are you okay?'

'PTSD,' I uttered.

'I'm sorry. Take your time.'

***

His hand casually flops on her face.
He braces himself, taking his pleasure.
Unaware, in his drunken stupor
He is covering a child's mouth and nose.
His weight on her feels like she is going to explode.
She cries out in her mind,
I can't breathe.
She gags, suffocating.
She does not feel the pain of his entry
Only trying to breathe exists.
A hand shifts. A breath taken. A gasp.
He is squeezing every breath out of her.
He finishes, shudders his release.
She is released.
Coughing as she gasps for air.

***

These postcard images of my childhood left me empty and exhausted. I walked out of the medical lab in a fog and sat in my car. I didn't cry. I had no obvious physical reaction. I was simply numb. This was how I coped with overwhelming situations I couldn't handle. Another memory, another girl existing somewhere in the recesses of my mind. They lived through the abuse and shame of a childhood I managed to suppress – most of the time.

LEARNING SELF CARE

Any event could be a trigger. Too often my life was defined by this. Unexpected things would throw me for a loop, even predictable situations when I knew what to expect. I spent an inordinate amount of time organising my routine so I could remain physically and emotionally safe. I was, of course, cognitively aware this happened because of *The Girls*. But this awareness rarely eased my hyper-vigilance, the fear that something *might* erupt.

When Annie and *The Girls* were growing up there was never a sense of safety at home, or anywhere for that matter. How could there be? Annie was a child at the whim of the adults around her. At any moment it may have been Mother emotionally berating her for not being beautiful enough, or Father who needed to control her through sex. Then there were Father's associates who would come and go, treating *The Girls* as sexual toys he made available to them. Were they really his friends or were they business partners? Sometimes I wonder if he was used as well, simply because he had a product they wanted to purchase.

All this meant that every day Annie and *The Girls* were on edge, wondering when and what might happen. They were not safe. Annie was not safe.

It made sense then, why I too would feel this need for security. Every day I made calculated choices to either listen to Annie or *The Girls'* needs or ignore them. Perhaps I was trying to play the role of parent to the system. Sometimes I had to proactively create a place of safety. I might sit with my back to a wall so I could see everyone coming into a café. Or at the movies, I would take the seat on the end of the aisle. I would go so far as to say my mind is often numb to these choices. These days, they are rarely conscious. Rather, I just know how to pre-empt a trigger. Sometimes I acquiesce to *The Girls'* fears, and this becomes a tolerable co-existence. It doesn't always work, but I give it my best go.

I have hoped that by living out healthy, positive interactions, the system would get the message that things can actually change for the better and that *The Girls* do not need to feel that they are trapped in their past.

There are unavoidable situations where I had to learn to fight through the fear. At the dentist, for instance. The vulnerability of lying prostrate in a chair, and worse, my mouth being covered, would make my blood run cold with fear. On one visit, I ran out screaming and crying. To manage this for the future, the dentist and I put together a plan. He would give me a detailed step-by-step breakdown of what he was going to do. The check-ups weren't too bad, but when he put the protective mouth cover on to replace an old filling it did me in, even though he would try to move the covering so I could breathe more freely. In these situations, I end up clenching my fists in my lap, legs crossed and pushed tightly together, giving me something to focus on. This helps alleviate my fear, but I still have laboured breathing and a loud anxiety in my head pleading for the dentist to stop. I am left feeling weak and worn out. After these procedures I often sit in my car, regaining the strength to get on with my day. I would remind myself that I had, at the very least, survived.

I have light bulb moments which become important reminders there is healing going on, even when circumstances blind me to it. I remembered *Runaway Girl* was forced to take drugs to make her compliant. During my early years with #4, when I was really overwhelmed, he encouraged me to use an anti-depressant to help me get out of that dark place. We talked about my fears and how it might trigger me. In the end I acquiesced in the hope I could overcome those fears. But I learned after a few pills that my mind was just too pliable – I became almost comatose, reminiscent, of course, of what *Runaway Girl* had lived through.

Recently, I was admitted to hospital with significant headaches after a bad fall. Medication was offered, and I took it without thinking. Yes, it did impair my cognitive functioning, but it also took care of the headaches and allowed my head to heal. What was the difference? I realised I had agency. Whether it was an alter who took drugs to be controlled, or me taking an anti-depressant because my therapist was concerned, I did what I was told. In the case of my hospital admission, I was never required to take drugs. They were offered, and I could take them as I needed. This simple act gave me a sense of control over my life which I didn't have before.

Maybe, I dared to hope, paying attention to triggers and mitigating them was part of my healing process? I would like to think so. Instead of the decades that I (and Annie) spent pushing the needs of *The Girls* aside, I had actually started listening to them. By being aware, I began to heal my own soul. Some days are better than others. I understand that unpredictable triggers are a part of my life, blindsiding me from time to time. But if I am willing to work at it, in partnership with Annie and *The Girls*, maybe we can all feel a bit safer each day.

PIVOT POINT

Tom and I went for marriage counselling, again. (Was this the third time?) We'd had a significant blow-up which I'm pretty sure would have ended in divorce had we not sought the help of an objective third party. We went through several weeks of trying to listen to each other, neither of us budging from behind our protective armour.

'What I hear you saying,' I would start, 'is you feel like I cut you off and don't give you time enough to think through your response.' But instead of then trying to build a bridge, I would continue, 'Have you ever thought maybe you need to learn to accept how I am? I do verbal diarrhoea from time to time. Why do I always have to be the one who is changing?'

In our next session, I suggested that we should name the elephant in the room, to acknowledge we had no emotional relationship, we were simply roommates with shared responsibility for our children. We talked around this, but he wasn't happy with the idea. I could see the hurt in his eyes. It was as if he had never considered that this was what our relationship had become.

'Maybe it's time to get a divorce then,' he said. 'If all we are is roommates, then maybe we're better off splitting up.'

I leaned back in my chair and exhaled. I had been waiting for years for him to say this, to acknowledge what I suspected – that he wanted out. I felt a rush of relief, then terror as I contemplated what this might mean. It was a poor, but convenient relationship – it was familiar and it paid the bills.

'Sure. If that's what you want.' I took a deep breath. 'But it's not what I'm looking for. All I'm asking is that you acknowledge what our relationship has become so we can find some sort of new normal – sharing responsibility for the kids while living our own lives.' Tom looked at me with bewilderment; he didn't get it.

But suddenly I understood. He was never going to change or adapt to include me in his life – and neither was I willing to change to accommodate him. We each had put up such high self-protective walls, we ended up with a relationship in which the only things we could talk about were the practicalities of raising our kids and soulless discussions about his work, politics, and the ills of the world. We were neither to blame, and both to blame. My life was focused on understanding who I was as someone with MPD and a history of abuse. Tom didn't get this. He was still trying to find himself, what he wanted, what his needs were and how he wanted his life to look.

This was my pivot point. I had to accept that by staying in this relationship I would be giving up on emotional intimacy.

It was easy for me to remember the things I found attractive about Tom in the first place. A gentle giant of a man who was kind, who enjoyed laughs and jokes. He even had a sense of adventure in the early days. He was romantic at heart and I knew beyond any doubt he loved his children. Ours was a complicated marriage, but I knew people who had it worse. Could I remember all this as I accepted how we had changed and could no longer meet each other's needs? From my perspective, I had changed much more than he had. (Let's face it, I wasn't the person he met, literally!)

Acceptance of my circumstances helped me to set the old aside and look at what the future with Tom and our family could be. Could I find some of the joy I had lost?

It begged the question: as a person living with MPD, was such a thing as joy even possible? And could I do it in a safe way? There was no getting around MPD as the central theme in my life. Both Annie and I had tried numerous times to ignore it, Annie by forgetting it all and living an anxiety-ridden life and me by simply trying to believe MPD was no longer an issue in the new life I was building. In both cases, our lives had imploded. Wouldn't I be better off trying to appreciate the diversity of perspectives which *The Girls*, and specifically Annie, could bring to my healing? Could I be thankful for this creative mind which had allowed me to survive the horrific circumstances of my childhood and the resilience it gave me?

BIG AND STRONG

Parenting with MPD presented me with more challenges than I cared to admit. I was afraid that Annie and *The Girls* presented an internal threat to my children. How could I be sure that the voices I heard in my head wouldn't allow some harm to come to them? I knew that Annie wasn't overly fond of my kids and often wondered – loudly – why I put up with them.

I realised, by accident, if I allowed *The Girls* – in safe ways – to engage with my children, it settled not just my anxiety, but their curiosity. *The Girls* wanted playmates, so what harm could it do for me to sit on the carpet and let them build Lego castles and spaceships with Danny and Kyle? Or paint flowers with Maria? Annie was never keen for this, becoming less so as the kids got older. I learned to use this to my benefit. I could rely on her to control *The Girls*, making sure they didn't actually incite me to flip, instead allowing them to be the carefree kids they never could in Annie's childhood. I just hoped that Annie could see how this would benefit all of us.

The kids grew, and life changed. For Annie, the kids fulfilled her lifelong dream to adopt from the Philippines. But when they started growing up, developing attitudes and challenging the status quo in our home, she was not happy. As usual, it was all my fault that these kids were no longer the soft cuddly babies she'd desired. She couldn't understand that kids grow up – that this is what kids are supposed to do – grow up. In retrospect, I can understand why this was challenging for her. She had a tribe to manage, and they remained, forever, the age they were created for. They didn't grow, they didn't change. My kids confounded her. And as I had come to learn with Annie, when things were difficult, this was her cue to leave and step back into the dark corners of my mind from where she would accost me with her trademark grumbling and complaining.

And, I realised, this made my life easier. Instead of wondering what influence *The Girls* might have on my kids, I could focus on being a real parent. Perhaps, I dared to hope, even a normal one.

I wanted my kids to grow up big and strong. By this, I mean they would be big in their willingness to embrace the challenges life would throw at them and strong in their knowledge of themselves and confident that they would always have the love of their family. Even with Annie and *The Girls* often playing havoc in my head, I knew this was the bedrock of my approach to parenting.

Talking to my children was the most important thing I could do. As small kids, those conversations were easy: respect others, dream big, be kind to everyone. As tweenies it was still generalities, but became about self-awareness. No meant No – for them and for other kids. If someone makes you uncomfortable, walk away. There was no reason to subject yourself to things that didn't feel right. All still safe and manageable.

We talked about adoption, although not as much as when they were younger. They knew their histories, and weren't afraid to discuss their birth mothers, details of their past and their lives at the orphanage. But as teenagers, it was easy to forget they were different. To me they were, well, just my kids.

Maria and the boys gave me two extremes to deal with. Maria, on the one hand, was determined to tell me everything. She and I would have late night conversations cocooned in the familiarity of her room. Sometimes, all she wanted was to have me close by to remind her that everything was right in her world. I knew the grief she felt over the loss of her birth mother and how it translated into her current relationships. It was important for me to be a rock so she could face the ever-flappable world she lived in.

The boys on the other hand simply didn't want to talk – at least not at first. It required persistence. As teenagers, the easiest place to have frank conversations was driving somewhere in the car. With no escape, I could start discussing difficult topics like safe sex and bullying. At times, this provoked an 'Oh gross!' while their hands covered their ears and they begged me to stop. But I persevered, trying the best I could to have conversations about life after school, relationships, anything I felt I could wrangle into their constantly developing minds.

There came a point in my writing journey when I realised I was going to have to tell the kids that I was MPD. I had already shared with them less confronting generalities about my history of abuse. But if my story ever actually made it into print, I didn't want them blindsided by the granular detail I'd kept from them. The boys were sixteen and eighteen. We'd talked about many difficult things, so I was pretty sure they could understand this. But then this was not about them understanding who they were, but them understanding who I was. And I've got to say, it terrified me. What would they think of me? I speculated the worst. Would they react like Tom and push me away? But then I reminded myself that in the end, this wasn't about me at all – it was about them, ensuring they weren't caught off guard if I did make my background public.

I decided to make a day of it. We went to a movie and then had fish and chips at a cafe on the beach. I intended to soften them up by talking about easier things, like school, life goals, girlfriends – before introducing the topic of MPD.

We sat at an old wooden table with boats bobbing at the nearby marina and seagulls milling around for some of our fish and chips. I let the boys get lost in their phones until the meal arrived, with the knowledge that then anything I said would be lost in the rush to ingest food, because as they told me, they were always hungry – always. When I did start talking, things cratered. My chit chat about school was met with grunts and a complete lack of interest. As they shovelled in chips, the boys' eyes didn't leave their phones. It didn't look like there was going to be an easy way to slide into a conversation about their mother's mental health.

So I took a deep breath and dived right in. I started by talking about the book, which I reminded them I had mentioned over dinner a while back. Then I told them that they would be able to read the book anytime they were ready. Still nothing. Kyle reached over and squeezed another slice of lemon on his fish before going back to his phone.

I took a wobbly, terrified breath.

'Have you heard of something called MPD?' I asked, fearful I would be overheard by prying ears at the next table, 'Multiple Personality Disorder? Have you heard of that?'

The boys put their phones down, their eyes wide, brows furrowed, but still feeding chips into their mouths.

Kyle spoke up, 'Yeah, I've heard of it.'

'So, I wanted to discuss this with you because, well – that's me – that's my life.'

I had their undivided attention now. I breathed out.

'It's how I managed to survive the abuse from my parents.'

They listened in silence as I described what it was like living with MPD. I shared how, in many ways, it was a creative way to protect my mind. I suspected I wouldn't be alive today if it hadn't been for the MPD. I also told them how just as there is a spectrum for people with autism, there was a spectrum for people with MPD. Some people had hundreds if not thousands of alters, or alter fragments, and could barely function. I was high functioning, with thirty or forty alters who instead of commandeering me like a puppet, would influence my behaviour. Then I jokingly said most of my alters had opinions about just about every aspect of my life.

Danny jumped in, 'What do they think of me?'

I smiled. 'Ah well, there is one in particular who doesn't like your sarcastic attitudes and thinks you're a bit of an asshole.'

'Well, I think they're an asshole too!'

We all laughed, beginning the delicate process of normalization.

But I needed to dig a bit deeper. I wanted them to be prepared, just in case.

'You know, I'm going public with this. I'm putting it on my website and in my social media. It's the heart of my book. Some of your mates follow me, they might read my posts and have questions. How do you think you'll go with that?'

'They won't care. They probably won't even notice.'

'Yeah, you might be right.' And they probably were, but I wasn't finished.

'What if, say, they read something I posted and told you that your mum's screwed in the head.'

Then, in absolute unison, they said, 'I'd tell them to fuck off.'

Kyle looked at me. 'You may be a pain in the neck, and you really do drive me crazy sometimes, but you're Mum. I know who you are.'

My heart started to return to its normal rhythm, my anxiety levels dropping.

On the way home, I was curious what they were thinking, I knew this would not be an easy conversation to continue at home so wanted to make sure all the bases were covered.

'You boys have any more questions? Or anything you want to talk about?'

'Nah, not really,' Danny said.

But from the back seat, after a bit of thoughtful contemplation, Kyle asked, 'So when you do things at home that don't make sense, can I ask you if it's an alter influencing you?'

'Sure, good idea.'

Whew, that was easy.

And then, 'So every time we argue, or you get all pissy at me, is it an alter?'

I laughed. 'No. Sometimes you really do just piss me off and drive me crazy.'

I could see the smirk on his face in the rear-view mirror.

I was so proud of my boys. Proud that they were willing to talk to me about difficult issues and proud that they knew they had a history with me which didn't put me in a box but instead helped them understand who I was.

And maybe, at the end of the day, I'd done a better job at this thing called parenting than I thought.

RU OK?

How do you end a story that isn't finished?

I'd love to say that endings are really new beginnings. Why? Because then this could be the end of *her and I*, of Annie and I fighting and being separate, and instead, it could be the beginning of *us*. Not integration, but in the hope of contentment rather than just survival, some sort of team effort. No doubt it would be a tentative agreement at best, but surely we must try. Sounds good, doesn't it?

The reality is that *we* are far from any sort of fairy tale ending. I suspect I will live for the rest of my life with overwhelming triggers and voices and attitudes I can't handle, and the perpetual fear of things spinning out of control. That's my reality. What if I could accept this as truth? That instead of wishing for some sort of unattainable, different life, I could welcome *The Girls* and even Annie (fractured relationship and all) as part of *this* life?

Would this be the next step in my healing process? Surely this is something more pragmatic and realistic to hope for?

But that's no way to end a story. Or is it?

Annie once said to me, and I think she is probably right, being MPD is a sign of a creative mind. An innate ability to carve out a place of safety deep in my psyche when my physical body was being tortured. My life has forced me to learn grit and resilience. When things have gotten hard, whether because my history was frying my brain or because I was being triggered, I have always survived. If I look at the life Annie lived, the rejection, anger and consequences of her childhood – the knowledge that I have inherited this history holds me in good stead. However uncomfortable, this is what has made me strong and helped me survive.

So, I think what I want to say is, I'm okay. Friends and faith have been the bedrock of my survival, with a fair bit of therapy thrown in along the way. My intimate friends know my heart and mind and have always been there to support me. Faith in a God who loves me reminds me of how deeply I am cared for, and how He carried me – and Annie – through those dark childhood days. And of course, there is writing. As #4 has often said, writing is my own version of narrative therapy. Recording my story in my own words means my circumstances don't have control over me. The written word gives me a voice, when as a child that voice was taken from me.

So, if you ask me, RU OK? I would say, Yeah I am ... most days. And thanks for asking.

The Girls on the Boat

I think about me, before I split,
Before everything changed,
Before one became many.

That little girl
standing on the deck of a cargo ship,
staring down waves as they
bashed against the boat.
Her face an expression of laughter and glee,
daring the gods of weather
to try and possess her.
I am in awe of her tenacity and fearlessness.
Her desire to face the world head on.

I could easily lose myself
in what happened to her, after.
When her world split apart.
Rather, I choose to think of her as she was in that moment.
A portrait of joy.
An ode to the strength and character
That was an innate part of her existence
If only for a short while.
That is me.

EPILOGUE

An Ordinary Life

The first draft of this book was an obscure jump into the world of MPD. I meant it to be that way. I was trying to show how my mind functioned with the voices of alters as my constant companions, how fragmented life was, for both Annie and I, as we strove to live each day as well as we could. I was seeking a way to make our complex intertwined existence fit into a neurotypical framework.

And that is exactly what my first draft was. I laid out my story in a mosaic of poetry and prose, allowing *The Girls* to speak non-stop through the entire process, thinking it would explain itself in an obvious way. This cathartic process consumed my existence. It became a kaleidoscopic head trip as I tried to tell my story by writing around my experiences rather than the detail of those experiences. This made complete sense to me, and friends who were my beta readers responded kindly. (I suspect this was because of the subject matter rather than how my first draft was written.) But what I was doing, I eventually realised, was *telling* my story, instead of *showing* through the lens of my day-to-day life, what the reality of living with MPD was like.

I would share some of the raw notes for my book with #4 at times, seeking affirmation of the truth of my story as I painted a picture of what my life was like. I knew that as a psychologist, he would find the information helpful.

'But would it make any sense to a reader?' I would say. 'My life is just so boring and ordinary.' I would hear myself blurt this out whenever we talked about my writing – which was often.

I am sure he found my self-doubt amusing, at the least. He would tilt his head slightly and say with a guarded smile, 'Your life is anything but ordinary. Trust me, people will find this book interesting.'

When I think back on it now, throughout my life I have wanted nothing more than to be ordinary. Being ordinary would mean no abuse, no MPD, a neurotypical happy and mentally healthy life. I wouldn't have to wrestle with the ramifications of my childhood, the hyper-vigilance and anxiety, obesity and resulting health consequences and the ever-present trust issues.

I was experiencing cognitive dissonance. I might have yearned for an 'ordinary' life, but I also knew that writing this story of my/our real life, would reveal it to be anything but 'ordinary'.

My first draft was my baby. Words I had coaxed into existence. And when I sent it off for its first formal professional edit, I was hoping it would be practically perfect in every way. I was sure my editor would be astounded at how fabulous my work was. (I suspect this is the naivete of many novice writers). My short, jarring fragments of truth would tell the story all on their own. Surely a philosophical treatise on the concept of trust or shame didn't require detail? Wasn't deep-thinking discussion enough? I couldn't have been more wrong. And as I requested, this editor carefully and thoughtfully ripped my manuscript to shreds. I would be less than truthful if I didn't confess to spending a few days on the couch, binge-watching *West Wing* until I was numb.

After meeting for coffee with a friend or two, some self-reflection and conversations with people I respected in the writing community, I went back to the editor's comments. I was determined to fight back, to be proud of this baby I had brought into the world. As I re-read her report, I realised she loved my writing style and willingness to deal with such difficult subject matter. She simply wanted more detail and a stronger narrative voice. It was a great first draft she said in her report, but it was a first draft, written to help me get all the information in my head out on the page. The next part of the process would be to mould this into something readers could engage with. I sighed and made a concerted effort to take on board and understand what she said. Right up front she had reiterated that this was my baby, and her job was only to give me feedback. It was then my job to take on board what I wanted. In hindsight, when I look at the comments from my first draft, she believed I had more to give because she believed in me.

We had a Zoom meeting about a week later, and discussed a lot of what she had written, and the challenge of putting more detail on the page, not only of my life, but of Annie's and any of *The Girls* who might want their story heard. She agreed it would be a challenge, but one I would have to navigate – and she believed I could. We talked about structure and how I could make it work, about how 'in my mind' some of the concepts were around shame, trust and suicide, reminding me I needed to ground these concepts in story, with examples of how I or Annie got through each day.

I sighed. 'But that's so boring, so ordinary! Would people want to read that?'

She smiled and said, 'Maggie, your life is anything but ordinary.'

Even through the computer screen, I could feel her warmth and reassurance – her genuine belief in me.

She might have started as my editor, but this wonderful woman soon became my mentor. With her encouragement and some grit, I embarked on my next draft (And another, and another, and so on). Each draft became a richer linear narrative, pulled forward by the experiences and detail in both Annie's and my life. This book started life as a grab-bag of dissociated (if poetic) ramblings of two very different minds; what it does now is simply attempt to tell our *story*.

I am pretty sure, while she won't admit it, Annie would agree that telling her story in a more linear fashion became a way to recreate the journals I had burned. And it allows her to process the life she lived from a different, and dare I hope, healthier place. I can see her in my mind as she sits in the window, still a sentry, still the guardian of *The Girls*. She has examined every page of this manuscript, unafraid to demand changes she felt important. I am unsure if she approves, but I am fairly sure she accepts this as *our* story.

And for me, this linear approach to our shared history has carried through to my life. It has helped me to own, rather than push away, the reality of my life as someone who lives with MPD.

I still wrestle, almost daily, with the feeling that my life is all very ordinary. And when I do, I think back on the comments made by these people I trust with my truth, and then set pen to paper again to speak about this life, *The Girls* and MPD, acknowledging perhaps, that mine is most likely not an ordinary life after all.

ACKNOWLEDGEMENTS

Words have come and gone and come again for me – in themselves, an ode to the way I have lived my life. As a teenager, Annie loved writing poetry – it was the way she found to express herself. But a shifting life, with an eye always on safety, meant that for a long while, the written word eluded both of us. I would stare at books in window displays, but never allow myself to get lost in those pages. It was only when I started seeing therapist #4 – and trusting him – that I returned to writing. First it was a purely cathartic outlet for my feelings, then a story began to form. I would, in the second half of my life, come to treasure and appreciate how the written word could change lives.

I credit the *Story Circle* group on suicidality for reigniting my love for the written word and instilling in me the belief that maybe I could write. Led by the wonderful Northern Rivers authors the late Jesse Blackadder (I miss you!) and Sarah Armstrong, it was all about using writing as a tool to process our pain – in this case, our experiences with suicidality. I am so grateful to every member of this group for the heart and soul that they brought to our sessions each week. And especially to Heather, who brought the entire project together.

In Australia, I first came out as being multiple to Simone. Her love of the written word and keen eye for grammar was the perfect place for me to start my journey of sharing who I really am. I gave her my first draft to read and edit and I will always appreciate the way she so graciously accepted me.

I would be nothing without my writing groups. To my Byron Writers Festival *Year of the Novel* Writing Group – Sue, Kath, Kumari, Belinda, Janet, Jeanne, Deb and Penny – our retreats are not only a creative environment for critique and encouragement, but I would go for your company alone. These weekends are filled with laughter and joy and each of you has nurtured me more than you can ever know. To my Varuna Writing Group – Belinda, Annie, Cynthia, Kathy, Dom and Rach – our monthly catch-up and your commitment to excellence is always inspiring. My Byron Writers Festival *Year of the Memoir* course classmates – Libby, Nel, Sarah, Abi, Belinda, Jeanne, Ana, Chelsea and Jen – it was a privilege to traverse the hills and valleys of writing memoir with you!

The writing community is an eclectic and supportive bunch. Up here in the Northern Rivers, I would like to acknowledge the singular role Byron Writers Festival plays in nurturing local writers. I have been a part of numerous BWF workshops and classes which have taught me much about the craft of writing.

And there are other authors across Australia who have encouraged me in my writing, and to write my truth. Ailsa Piper was the first person to challenge me to find my narrative voice – at a time when I wasn't even sure what that was! Sarah Armstrong, a nurturing and encouraging teacher, who gave so much to our writing group and whose ability to critique with a gentleness that always asked for more, is something I am eternally grateful for. Michelle Tom and Ashley Kalagian-Blunt encouraged me and my writing and provided invaluable insights into the publishing industry from an insider perspective. Anna Featherstone, I suspect that without your nurturing and encouragement, I would not have had the fortitude to dip my toes in this world of indie publishing. I am blessed and fortunate to have these people and so many more in my life.

Two authors somehow found their way into my life and deserve a special mention. Their friendship and mentorship has forever changed how I approach writing. To my mentor, Lee Kofman, if it wasn't for you I would not have had the fortitude to keep editing and keep searching for my inner truth. You have believed in me and challenged me at every turn to dig deeper, explain better and share more richly who I really am. Your belief in me made all the difference to actually getting my manuscript completed. Al Close, our intrepid leader for *The Year of the Memoir* course and his ongoing support, I am grateful for your perspectives and wisdom. Your laidback and insightful way of posing the necessary questions has always helped me think that little bit further. Al also took on the role of fearless editor for my final draft of SPLIT, a tough gig, ensuring that what I wanted to say was actually on the page. Thank you.

For my friends who know my heart and love me anyway – Corry, Katja and Rachelle – my love for you is boundless. I shared my journey, fears, and worries about this story, and you were there for me. You give me courage. Every. Day.

Therapist #4, for insisting, even when it was confusing, chaotic and frustrating, that writing was my own form of narrative therapy and therefore good for me. Thank you.

For Kate, my lifelong friend and sister, you are always in my heart. With you I have experienced so much joy and created such beautiful memories. There are no words. I love you.

To Annie and *The Girls*. Thank you for trusting me to share your story on our journey, this is as much your story as it is mine.

And, of course, my family. Where do I start? My husband Tom. Together we are raising this amazing threesome of kids. It goes without saying that these kids wouldn't have come into my life without you. I have never for one moment doubted your love for them and what you have brought to their lives as a devoted, funny and committed father.

My kids, Maria, Kyle, and Danny – you are, simply, the lights of my life. You give me reason to get up in the morning and your love of life keeps me going through even the hardest days. I have had the privilege to love you, nurture you and watch you grow into the awesome individuals you are. You piss me off sometimes (a job you take very seriously I might add!), but I wouldn't trade you for a hundred worlds. You have made me so proud, and I love you each so very much.

And lastly, because He is the most important, God. He made me who I am – MPD and all, and has walked with me through every part of my life, and walks with me still. I would be nothing without His love and grace.

RESOURCES

If you or a loved one are struggling, remember you are not alone.

In an immediate emergency call
    Lifeline 13 11 14
    Emergency 000

For all other circumstances
    Beyond Blue: beyondblue.org.au
    Black Dog Institute: blackdoginstitute.org
    Head Space Australia: headspace.org.au
    GROW: grow.org.au
    Blue Knot: blueknot.org.au (for those with complex trauma)
    Social Futures: socialfutures.org.au
    Sane Australia: sane.org
For those seeking a Christian perspective
    The Jericho Road: jerichoroad.org.au
    Christian Counseling & Education Foundation: www.ccef.org

For *The Girls*

We need to talk.
There are things to be said.

If I am honest, sometimes you frustrate me.
You get inside my head,
    speaking half-truths that protect you but hang me out to dry,
    controlling my moments and life,
    which makes me doubt my sanity.

So, because starting fresh is never a bad thing,
    I want to say thank you.

Thank you for quite literally saving my life.
You took on your fragile child-sized shoulders,
    experiences and pain meant to be mine.
Day after day, year after year,
    it was your hearts that were shattered,
    wrecked and ruined – for me.
You hid my soul away in regions unknown,
    protecting me in the shadows.

I want to believe that I am stronger today than yesterday.
Maybe not by much,
    these are not things that can be measured
        in quantifiable ways,
        but rather by a condition of the heart.

I want to assure you that this thing called healing can exist.
Not just for me, but for you as well.

I say with absolute confidence that you won't agree.
How could you, when you know that the predictability
    of status quo both works and keeps us safe?

But I will dare to say that I know things can be different.
I suppose at the end of it all
    and at the end of the day,
  I am asking, perhaps with your permission,
    to simply have hope.

ABOUT MAGGIE

Maggie lives in the Northern Rivers of NSW, where she spends her days developing her writing skills and raising three teenagers. After meeting her husband, she immigrated to Australia from the U.S., and spent the bulk of her career in various marketing roles before returning to her long-held love of the written word.

Expression through words has become a driving passion in her life, a tool for healing her own abusive past. Maggie is an active member of Byron Writers Festival and a member of several writing groups that meet regularly and continue to nurture her craft.

As a trauma survivor, she shares her courageous commitment to wholeness, while confronting stereotypes surrounding Multiple Personality Disorder/Dissociative Identity Disorder. She educates and encourages others to break down the barriers and stigma around mental health.

Want to learn
more about Maggie and
stay in contact?

www.maggie-walters.com

You can

- Sign up for her newsletter and get an inside scoop on an author's life!
- Find out where her speaking tour is taking her.
- Discover more about her next project!

She'd love to hear from you!

www.ingramcontent.com/pod-product-compliance
Lightning Source LLC
Chambersburg PA
CBHW022026290426
44109CB00014B/765